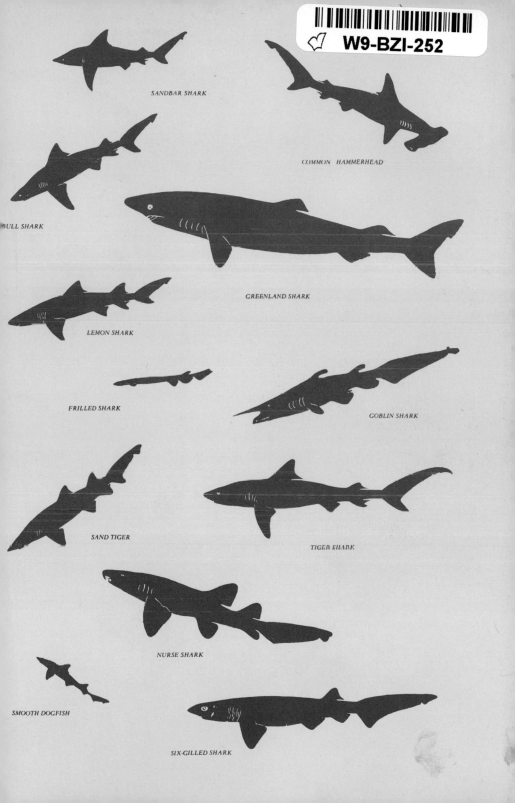

SANDBAR SHARK

COMMON HAMMERHEAD

BULL SHARK

GREENLAND SHARK

LEMON SHARK

FRILLED SHARK

GOBLIN SHARK

SAND TIGER

TIGER SHARK

NURSE SHARK

SMOOTH DOGFISH

SIX-GILLED SHARK

THE NATURAL HISTORY OF
SHARKS

The Natural History of

THOMAS H. LINEAWEAVER III

RICHARD H. BACKUS

J. B. LIPPINCOTT COMPANY

SHARKS

Foreword by N. B. MARSHALL

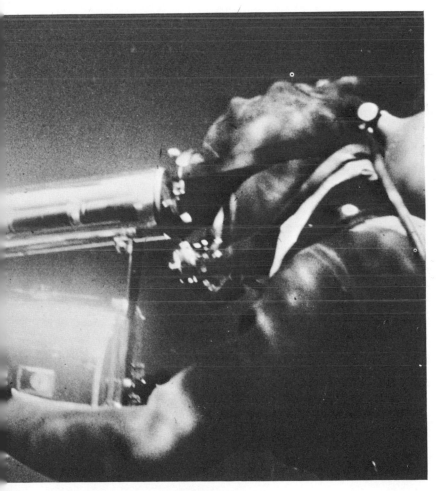

Philadelphia and New York

ISBN-0-397-00660-8

Seventh Printing

Printed in the United States of America

Library of Congress Catalog Card Number: 75-109174

Chapter 13, "Sharks and the Discouragement Thereof,"
has been published in *Sea Frontiers.*

Foreword

N. B. Marshall, MA, SCD

Man, who is 'fearfully and wonderfully made', is apt to think the same of sharks. Yet the largest species, the whale-shark and basking-shark, are inoffensive beasts, deriving most of their nourishment from small planktonic animals. On the other hand, the great white shark, which is the largest predatory form, is voracity incarnate and sometimes grievously dangerous to man. How much, then, do we know of the life of this fish? We are not even sure of its maximum size and weight. It is less surprising that little is known of its migrations and breeding patterns, for this shark ranges over the vastness of the tropical and temperate belts of the ocean. Still, we learned recently that the great white shark, like its relatives the mako and mackerel sharks, is warm-blooded. In this and other respects, particularly of dynamic form, these sharks have imitated the tunny-fishes (see page 208).

Sharks are elusive animals, coming and going as they seek their living in the oceanic wilderness. In more than their predatory ways, they remind us of cats. Their eyes, which gleam in the light and have mobile pupils, are designed to see in dim surroundings. And, as divers know very well, sharks can be very curious, and certain of the larger species, like the larger cats, may occasionally turn on man.

If we made more economic use of sharks, we should certainly know much more of their biology. As things are, a great stimulus to the considerable advances in our knowledge over the past twenty years or so, has been the need to learn more of shark ways, so that man, whether in peace or war, may be better protected against their attack. It is opportune, then, that here is a book that reviews this work in a just and lively fashion. But this is not another book about man and sharks. After all, we are also curious, and some of us, whether ichthyologists, physiologists, ethnologists, and so forth, are interested in sharks as marine organisms. Such aspects of shark study are treated in this book. It is right and proper too, that the first author happens to be closely associated with the Woods Hole Oceanographic Institution, Massachusetts, while the second is a senior member of the staff. To the late Henry Bigelow, the first director of this institution, and to his colleague, William Schroeder, also of W.H.O.I., much is owed. Their careful work on the systematics of sharks and rays has led to a renewal of interest in elasmobranch biology.

There are nearly two hundred and fifty kinds of living sharks, most of which live in the subtropical and tropical belts of the ocean. They range in size from the 60-foot whale-shark to *Squaliolus*, a deep-sea form that is mature at a span of six inches. In depth they extend from coastal waters to oceanic depths of 1,500 fathoms or more. Though sharks do not begin to approach the diversity and adaptability of the teleost bony fishes, they have kept their hold on the sea since Devonian times, over 350 million years ago. When a shipmate with one author, (R.H.B.) during an oceanographic cruise in the tropical Atlantic, I glimpsed something of shark persistence. More often than not, whenever we made a station one or more white-tipped sharks would appear, seemingly from nowhere, and cruise lazily around the ship. The whitetip seemed to own these parts of the ocean, and we were not misled by the fact that the individuals we caught appeared to be starving. Like other sharks, the whitetip has a very large liver, which is charged with food reserves whenever feeding is good, and so serves as a store during lean times. The charging process starts, of course, with the jaws, and they are not awkwardly placed. When a whitetip—and most other kinds of shark—bites, the underslung jaws emerge from the head and the shearing, cutting teeth begin their work.

The whitetip belongs to the most diverse family of living sharks (Carcharhinidae), sometimes called the grey sharks. But the authors range over all the main groups of strong predators. We also learn of those that depend largely on invertebrate life. Besides the whale-shark and basking-shark, there are such groups as the carpet-sharks, cat-sharks and smooth dogfishes.

Consideration of shark groups and their food brings us to an apparent enigma of shark life. Unlike most teleost fishes, sharks, whether live-bearers or egg-layers, maintain their place in the ocean through the production of a few, but well advanced, young. Now, concerning the larger predatory forms, at least, the greatest enemy of one shark is a larger one. How then, do these species manage to survive? We are learning that restraints have been evolved. For instance, there is a distinct tendency for such sharks to be segregated according to size and sex. Moreover, when the sexes come together the males stop feeding, as do the gravid females when on the nursery grounds, which may be outside the normal range of sexually mature males. As the authors imply in their penultimate chapter, these are crucial aspects of shark biology.

Here, then, as I have been concerned to show, we have an absorbing book, and it is time to introduce the authors. Unlike his co-author, Richard Backus, Thomas Lineaweaver is not a professional biologist. But both are alike in certain essential ways: they have an abiding interest in sharks, so naturally they have studied them at sea. Lastly, it is the constant endeavour of both to use the English language effectively. The result is a concise book that can be thoroughly recommended to all manner of curious readers.

Authors' Preface

The authors have little to say about this book. It derives, simply, from many years of professional and personal interest in what we consider to be a most absorbing creature.

Beyond that, we would like to emphasize that the citations of books and journals in the text are there not to illustrate relentless library research, but to obviate the necessity for a cumbersome bibliography and still point the way for the reader who wishes to pursue a particular matter.

Lastly, we wish to thank all who gave of time and material to this effort. There were many and they contributed much. To name them is impossible, but there were those so closely associated that they surely deserve mention. Our special thanks, then, to Mary Ridolfi Blanchard and Diane Sears who shared the typing of manuscript. To Elaine Kelley Wetzell who spent long hours in the library searching out references. To Anne T. Lineaweaver for her work on the *Glossary*. To Ann V. Ramsey for her assistance with the *Index*. To Dr John Musick who contributed the *Key to the Families of Sharks*. To Dr Richard Haedrich for his guidance on the *Bibliography*. To Miss Frances Williams who prepared the endpapers. And, to Jane Fessenden, Librarian of the Marine Biological Laboratory, Woods Hole, where this book was for the most part researched and written, and, of course, to her accommodating staff.

Thomas H. Lineaweaver III, *Marine Biological Laboratory, Woods Hole*
Richard H. Backus, *Woods Hole Oceanographic Institution*

Contents

List of Illustrations

A Sampling
of the
Written Word...

...ABOUT SHARKS, SOME OF WHICH IS FANCIFUL
AND SOME OF WHICH IS NOT.

And they raved for food with increasing frenzy, being always
anhungered and never abating the gluttony of their terrible maw:
for what food shall be sufficient to fill the void of their belly or
enough to satisfy and give respite to their insatiable jaws?

Oppian Fishing **second century A.D.**

Queequeg no care what god made him shark . . . wedder Fejee god
or Nantucket god, but de god wat make shark must be one dam
Ingin.

Herman Melville Moby Dick **1851**

You may rest assured that the British Government is entirely
opposed to sharks.

**Winston Churchill, in reply to a question about shark
repellant, House of Commons, February 20, 1945**

The old Hawaiian Kings preferred to use human bait for sharks.
It was cheaper than pigs and just as acceptable for the sharks.

J. L. Baughman Sharks, Sawfishes and Rays: Their Folklore
1948

15

Who can open the jaws of his face? His teeth are terrible round
about.

Job 41:14

That I may win praise this day
I shall rescue the dear one this day
This is thy charm Lord Awao
This is thy charm Awao-throwing-gall-on-sharks.

Incantation to protect a man in a canoe, W. G. Ivens
Mellanesians of the South-East Solomon Islands **1927**

If you were asked to hunt the lion in the plains of Atlas, or the
tiger in the Indian jungles, what would you say? Ha! Ha! it seems
we are going to hunt the tiger or the lion. But when you are invited
to hunt the shark in its natural element, you would perhaps reflect
before accepting the invitation.

Jules Verne *20,000 Leagues under the Sea* **1870**

I have no doubt that one shark in a dozen years is enough to keep
up the reputation of a beach a hundred miles long.

Henry David Thoreau *Cape Cod* **1865**

'You see,' he went on after a pause, 'it's well to be provided for
everything. That's the reason the horse has all those anklets round
his feet.' 'But what are they for?' Alice asked in a tone of great
curiosity. 'To guard against the bites of sharks,' the Knight replied.
'It's an invention of my own.'

Lewis Carroll *Through the Looking-Glass* **1871**

There was a young lady from Guam
Who said, 'The Pacific's so calm
I'll swim for a lark.'
She met a large shark . . .
Let us all sing the 93rd Psalm.

Anon.

I'm what the sailors call a shark, that is I'm a lawyer.

Frederick Marryat *Poor Jack* **1840**

Vast numbers of sharks infest the sea in the vicinity of the sponges, to the great peril of those who dive for them.

Pliny the Elder *Natural History* **circa A.D. 77**

Those who wear pearls do not know how often the shark bites the diver.

Abyssinian proverb

. . . young Fortinbras . . . Hath in the skirts of Norway here and there, Shark'd up a list of lawless resolutes . . .

Hamlet, **Act I, Scene I**

despite the sleek shark's far flung grin
and his pretty dorsal fin
his heart is hard and black within
even within a dentist's chair
he still preserves a sinister air
a prudent dentist always fills
himself with gas before he drills

Don Marquis *archy and mehitabel* **1927**

The natural conclusion is that the shark offers no unusual hazards to a swimming or drifting man . . .

U.S. Navy manual *Shark Sense* **1944 edition**

All you have to do is look at the record. Never count on a shark not attacking you. He may do it.

U.S. Navy manual *Shark Sense* **1959 edition**

Swimmers very often perish by them; sometimes they lose an arm or a leg, and sometimes are bit quite asunder, serving but for two morsels, for this ravenous animal.

Thomas Pennant on the white shark *British Zoology* **1769**

CHAPTER 1 | # Derivations and Differences

In the mind's eye of many people there is a generalized or model shark. It is, say, ten feet long and sombre in colour. It weighs several hundred pounds and its mouth is a forest of sharp teeth. It is streamlined and strong and with its dorsal fin cutting the surface of some warm sea it is always on the hunt. It is a picture of grim efficiency, an eater of men.

There are sharks like that, lots of them. But there are lots of other sorts too. There are sharks barely a foot long at most and there are sharks that grow to 40 feet and more. There are tropical sharks, temperate sharks and sharks as arctic as walruses. There are inshore sharks and offshore sharks. There are sharks that frequent rivers. There are surface sharks and sharks in the great deeps. There are drably-coloured sharks, brightly-coloured sharks, piebald sharks and sharks patterned like oriental rugs. There are flat sharks, rotund sharks, fast sharks, slow sharks, shy sharks and bold sharks.

Sharks, then, are diverse, but their species are relatively few in number. Of the 20-odd thousand species of fish now living, only about 300 are sharks. The reasons are evolutionary. Sharks emerged in Devonian times more than 300 million years ago and by the close of the Cretaccous period, some 63 million years ago, their evolution was essentially complete. For a host of creatures, however, the Cretaceous spelled disaster. The German geologist Johannes Walther called it 'the time of the great dying' and when it ended dinosaurs were gone from the land and ichthyosaurs from the ocean and pterosaurs from the sky. Their world had changed and they could not change to survive in it. Sharks survived and, furthermore, they did not have to change very much to do it. From their beginnings they have been fit to weather great change without greatly changing and that accounts for the small number of shark species. Most fishes, on the other hand, had to be more responsive to environmental change and from much trial and error in form and function many species developed. Fishes, in fact, comprise the largest group of vertebrate creatures with three times the species of the next largest, the birds.

In the zoological hierarchy where scientists group all creatures according to their natural and evolutionary relationship, sharks share the phylum Vertebrata with all vertebrates; the superclass Pisces with all fishes; the class Chondrichthyes with skates, rays and chimaeras or ratfishes; the subclass Elasmobranchii with skates and rays; the order Selachii—from the classical Greek *selachos* meaning *shark*—they have to themselves.

But, while sharks are fish, they are markedly different from those in the superorder Teleostei which houses most of the existing fish species. 'Tiburon or Sharke be all one . . . That creature hath no bone in his back, as vast as his strength is . . . His back-bone is all gristly . . . The Seamen usually cut them into Walking-staves.'

That seventeenth-century passage refers correctly if not completely to one of the major differences between the teleosts, or bony fishes, and sharks. Sharks have no bone in their back nor anywhere else. Their skeleton is entirely cartilage—the class name Chondrichthyes means cartilaginous fishes—a hard and gristly material formed from certain proteins and toughened by fibres. It is much more stretchable than bone and, by the same token, much more compressible. However, at points of stress in shark skeletons it is reinforced by small interlocking plates of apatite, a mineral substance composed of calcium phosphates and carbonates. Such calcification is generally limited to surface areas of the cartilage, but shark vertebrae which must bear the considerable stresses associated with swimming movements, are often braced with radial apatite wedges.

Although the lack of true bone works no hardship on sharks, it does complicate the precise tracing of shark evolutionary development. Cartilage, unfortunately, does not lend itself to detailed fossilization. Bygone shark species more often than not mouldered away in their graves and a discovery like *Cladoselache*, the name means branch-toothed shark, is therefore a rare surprise.

The fossils of this Devonian hunter are the earliest shark remains now known and they were collected in the 1880's by Dr William Kepler, an American prelate and amateur paleontologist. Kepler found them in the Black Cleveland Shales which lie bare along the banks of the Rocky River a few miles south-west of the city of Cleveland. They were encased in enormous, petrified mud pies or concretions and by some quirk in the geological process certain specimens were detailed indeed. Preserved were calcified skeletal cartilages, impressions of the skin and body shape and details as fine as muscle fibre.

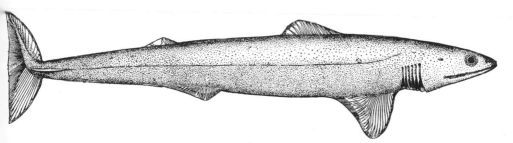

A reconstruction of the fossil shark *Cladoselache*. Some specimens, however, had a pronounced spine before the first dorsal. *Cladoselache* is the earliest shark thus far known to science. It ranged the seas in Devonian times more than 350 million years ago.

At the very least, *Cladoselache* underscores the fact that sharks have not much changed. The creature was four to five feet long and so essentially shark-like that if an angler were to hook and haul up one today he would recognize it as a shark and probably not as a very ancient shark at that.

Shark teeth with their jacket of enamel are very hard. Conse-quently, the fossil record is as rich in shark teeth as it is poor in shark skeletons and this had led some paleontologists—a particularly distinguished one being Harvard's Alfred Sherwood Romer—to challenge the long-standing assumption that sharks are among the most ancient of living fish groups. 'In past times,' writes Romer in the 1966 edition of his *Vertebrate Paleontology*, 'it was generally assumed that the absence of bone in the Chondrichthyes was a primitive condition and that the sharks represented an evolutionary stage antecedent to that of the bony fishes. This assumption appears, at the present day, to be a highly improbable one. Bone . . . appears in groups much lower down the evolutionary scale . . . Nor are the sharks, as one might expect according to earlier beliefs, an early group geologically. They are in fact, the last of the major fish groups to appear in the fossil record. No member of the class is known before the latter half of the Devonian. . . .'

Bony fishes, Romer points out, were present well before that and he then counters speculation that perhaps sharks were too. 'It might be argued that absence of an earlier record is due to the fact that the ancestral sharks were soft-bodied and not preserved. But the first sharks were far advanced in the evolution of jaws; and it is difficult to believe that the teeth of these supposed earlier forms should have escaped our attention.'

Romer draws the conclusion that: 'The record . . . fits in better with the opposite assumption: that the sharks are degenerate rather than primitive in their skeletal characters; that their evolution has paralleled that of various other fish types in a trend toward bone reduction; and that their ancestry is to be sought among primitive bony, jaw-bearing fishes. . . .' Sharks, moreover, are of the sea. Most species evolved there. Bony fishes evolved in fresh water and only later emigrated to the sea.

Shark ancestry for the moment aside, the differences between present-day sharks and bony fishes is not confined to the stuff of skeletons. Reproduction also figures prominently. Most female bony fishes spawn an immense number of eggs which male bony fishes afterwards fertilize with milt. A female cod may cast as many as nine million eggs, a haddock three million, a hake one million and a mackerel five hundred thousand. In any case, prospects for the eggs are bleak. Many are destroyed by bacterial or fungal

22

diseases or by inhospitable water conditions or by tiny planktonic predators. Hatchlings are only a bit less vulnerable. A newly hatched mackerel, for instance, is about $\frac{1}{8}$ inch long. If it survives for 26 days it will reach $\frac{1}{2}$ inch. If it survives 40 more days it will reach two inches and take on its adult form. By then it is also apt to be the one survivor of one million mackerel eggs originally spawned. Yet, pitiful as that rate of survival may seem, it is sufficient to maintain the species.

Sharks take the opposite tack. Males are equipped with a pair of penis-like organs, inappropriately called claspers, so males copulate with females—more of which later—to fertilize the eggs internally. Furthermore, most shark pups are hatched internally and delivered into the water fully formed, little replicas of the adult and quite able to fend for themselves. An eight-foot shark, after all, can give birth to 18-inch young.

Shark litters are therefore small. They rarely exceed 60 pups and some count just two. Large litters simply are not necessary. Few sharks are born because many survive. Many bony fishes are born; but few survive. The means are very different. The ends, survival of enough to perpetuate the kind, are identical.

In the matter of staying afloat, bony fishes have an easier time of it than sharks do. They possess a gas-filled vessel or swim-bladder which is related to the lungs of more advanced animals and it allows them to adjust their buoyancy and, if need be, hover weightless in the water. No shark has one. Shark buoyancy is somewhat enhanced by a large and oily liver, but all sharks are still a trifle heavier than water and either sharks swim or sharks sink and even swimming has its problems.

Shark tails are asymmetrical. The upper fork is invariably longer than the lower and as a shark swims, the side-to-side sweeps of this sort of tail tend to tilt the creature head-down. What saves it from swimming into the bottom are its pectoral fins. These look like the wings of an aircraft and perform a similar function. They—and to some extent the underside of the snout—give the shark lift at the bow to compensate for lift at the stern. But a price is paid in that shark fins are quite rigidly fixed. To keep sharks afloat and on an even keel they must be. So the price paid is in agility. Sharks cannot, for one thing, use their pectorals as brakes to make an abrupt stop. Faced with an obstacle they can only swerve on by. Bony fishes are more versatile. With swimbladders and symmetrical tails they do not need rigid fins to correct for negative buoyancy or pitch. Their fins are consequently very manoeuvrable and they can deploy them for use as brakes, as paddles to move forward or back, as pivots to turn around upon, and more. This is not to say that sharks are a clumsy lot. On the contrary, whatever niceties of movement they concede to bony fishes, many shark species swim with great elegance.

Even at first glance it is apparent that sharks and bony fishes vary in the arrangement of gills. Both have several gill arches, but among sharks these open to the outside through from five to seven vertical gill slits—usually five—situated on either side of the throat. Among bony fishes all the gills on a side rest within a single aperture which is shielded by a gill cover or opercle. Less apparent at first glance is the extraordinary nature of shark skin.

Most bony fishes are covered shingle-fashion with thin, more or less round scales. Sharks are covered with a latticework of teeth, so-called dermal denticles or skin teeth, each consisting of a firmly anchored and calcified base from which an enamel-capped spine sprouts point towards tail through the skin. Shark skin, in short, is something to be reckoned with. It can dull a knife and, if brushed against the grain, scrape a person raw and the ichthyologist who has sawed mightily to open the belly of a dead shark on deck suspects that the swipe-of-a-knife disembowelling of a live shark in the water is an art peculiar to and jealously guarded by film folk.

In days gone by, shark skin was put to a number of uses and a case can be made that one use involved surviving a whack at the head. The case rests on the fact that a Roman soldier's helmet was called a *galea* and that *galea* may be more closely related to the Greek word *galeos* meaning shark than to the Greek word *galei* meaning weasel. A Roman emperor, logic would seem to dictate, might drape his empress with ermine, but the heads of his men he would shield with shark. Regardless, until the turn of the century if not later, cabinetmakers knew shark skin as *shagreen* and used it to sand and polish and, because the pattern of the tiny denticles

was so attractive, other craftsmen used it to dress a variety of artifacts. 'At the Paris Exhibition, 1878,' notes P. L. Simmonds in *The
Commercial Products of the Sea; or, Marine Contributions to Food,
Industry, and Art* in 1879, 'were exhibited two cases with numerous
illustrations of the ornamental applications of the prepared skin in
large office-table inkstands, candlesticks, boxes and caskets, paper
knives, reticules, card-cases, frames for photographs, bracelets,
scent-bottles, etc.'

Tanned and with the denticles removed shark skin makes an
excellent, multi-layered and very tough leather. Quality varies from
shark species to shark species, but the better grades have twice the
tensile strength of cowhide and a considerable amount today goes
into the manufacture of fashionable shoes, belts, handbags,
tobacco pouches and so on. *Shagreen*, sad to say, except perhaps in
out-of-the-way places, seems to be a decorative thing of the past.

It is impossible to divorce the teeth in shark skins from the teeth
in shark mouths. The latter are simply large modifications of the
former and their supply is constant. Shark teeth are not, as are
the teeth of bony fishes, set securely in the jaws. They are set in the
gums and often are lost in the violence of feeding or the natural
process of ageing. But they are only briefly missed. Layered rows
of replacement teeth lie behind both jaws and as functional teeth
are knocked out or fall away the rear ones move to the fore and
fill the gaps. And the turnover in shark teeth may be much more
rapid than heretofore suspected. In 1966 an American scientist
discovered that in the young of one common species the teeth in the
upper jaw were replaced every 7·2 days and the teeth in the lower
jaw every 8·2 days.

Shark teeth give pause to gloomy thoughts, thoughts as various
as the teeth themselves. Some shark species have single rows of
teeth ready to bite. Some have two or more rows set at different
angles and they bring to mind the tilted white tombstones in a
country graveyard. Some have rows that form flat, crushing surfaces
known as pavement teeth. Many have teeth that are protusible. As
the jaws open, the teeth tip forward. As the jaws close, the teeth tip
back. It is an arrangement that allows a large bite at the bite's
beginning and a firm one at the bite's taking hold.

A section of the upper jaw of a 265-pound white shark, *Carcharodon carcharias*. The soft tissue has been removed to show the rows of replacement teeth behind the erect functional row.

In general, shark teeth are shaped to grasp or cut or do both. But here again there is variation. Some species have cutting teeth in the upper jaw and grasping ones in the lower jaw. The cutting ones are broadly triangular with serrated edges. The grasping ones are narrow and smooth. Some have cutting teeth that are not presented point first. Instead, because the teeth are asymmetrical in shape, they are presented edge-on. Nor do all sharks bite alike. Certain species, when attacking an animal too large to swallow whole, accentuate the cutting action of the upper teeth and slice away chunks of flesh with quick and eerie tremors of the entire forebody. Other species accomplish a like end with rolls and twists. Whichever it may be, tremors or rolls or twists, they do help to answer Ishmael's puzzlement in *Moby Dick*. '. . . they scooped out huge globular pieces of the whale of the bigness of a human head. This particular feat of the shark seems all but miraculous. How at such an apparently unassailable surface, they contrive to gouge out such symmetrical mouthfuls, remains a part of the universal problem of all things. The mark they thus leave on the whale, may best be likened to the hollow made by a carpenter in countersinking for a screw.'

Though shark teeth can shred any animate thing, science concedes them a saving grace. Such is their variation in size, shape, number and arrangement that an ichthyologist can often identify a species with nothing more than a single tooth to go on.

Shark senses, needless to say, lead shark teeth to shark prey and while sensory mechanisms will be explored in later pages, it should be emphasized here that sharks have a full and effective complement. Sight, sound, taste, touch and smell, and more figure together in a ceaseless hunt for food and smell is uncannily acute. Sharks can get wind of something as faint and dilute as one part scent to millions, possibly over a billion, parts water.

The foregoing, then, are some of the ways in which sharks differ from bony fishes. They invest sharks with a quality of gothicness and sharks in their turn invite comparisons. 'There is,' wrote Jonathan Couch a century ago in *A History of the Fishes of the British Islands*, 'no reason why the lion should occupy the elevated place he does in popular estimation as the king of beasts, except with reference to his power over the weaker inhabitants of the wilderness. It is his united strength and courage which establish his rank. . . . We grant indeed, that in the opinion of the moralist and philosopher, the possession of mere strength and commanding— perhaps ferocious—powers and dispositions, should not be estimated as the sufficient mark to which supreme rank ought to be assigned. But the human mind has shewn a disposition to regard these qualities as such a mark; and as a beginning even in this kind of superiority must be somewhere, and the consent of the ages has ascribed it among beasts to the lion, and with the same conviction of feeling, among the birds to the eagle; we are only proceeding in the same direction when we view the Sharks as holding the same relative rank among the families of the ocean.'

1

A blue shark, or bluedog, *Prionace glauca,* attacks a dead porpoise making the remarkably symmetrical bites which so puzzled Ishmael in *Moby Dick.* Actually such bites result from the head and body motions of the shark.

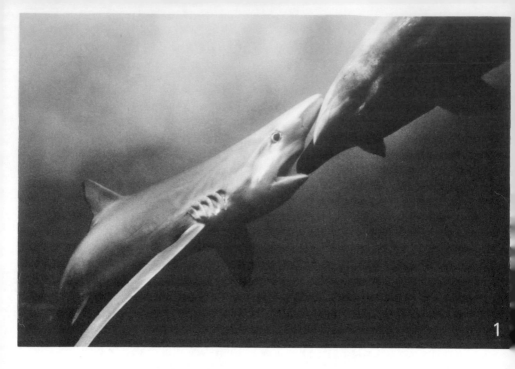

2

CHAPTER 2 | *Facts and Fancies*

The following, culled at random from the scientific record, is by no means an exhaustive inventory of what has been found in shark stomachs.

In a shark caught in Australia was found a goat, a turtle, a large tomcat, three birds, four fish heads and numerous fish including a shark six feet long.

In a shark caught in the Adriatic was found a raincoat, three overcoats and a car licence plate.

In a shark caught in the Florida Keys was found grass, several tin cans, a dozen cow vertebrae and the cow's dehorned head.

In a shark caught in the Philippine Islands was found seven leggings, 47 buttons, three leather belts and nine shoes.

In other sharks caught at other times and places were found six hens and a rooster; 25 quart bottles of Vichy Water bound together with a wire hoop; a nearly whole reindeer; a ship's scraper; six horseshoe crabs; three bottles of beer; a blue penguin; a piece of bark from an oak tree; parts of porpoises; a 100-pound loggerhead turtle; a handbag containing three shillings, a powderpuff and a wristwatch; sting rays; a full grown spaniel; seaweed; a Galapagos seal pup; orange peel; squids; a 25-pound lump of whale blubber and seven strands of whalebone; paper cups; a yellow-billed cuckoo.

Lastly, there is this citation in Jerome Smith's 1833 *Natural History of the Fishes of Massachusetts*. 'In the records of Aix, a seaport in France, in the Mediterranean Sea, is the account of a shark, taken by the fishermen, twenty-two feet long, in whose

Winslow Homer's famous canvas *The Gulf Stream*. Contemporary criticism of the picture was unduly harsh, so Homer wrote the following to a dealer: 'The criticism of *The Gulf Stream* by old women and others are noted. You may inform these people that the Negro did not starve to death. He was not eaten by the sharks. The waterspout did not hit him. And he was rescued by a passing ship which is not shown in the picture.'

stomach, among other undigested remains, was the headless body of a man, encased in complete armor.'

Quite obviously, sharks scavenge. But the common notion that they are nothing more than scavengers is a too simple one. Given the choice, field tests have shown that sharks prefer fresh meat. Given no choice, or not enough, sharks take whatever they chance upon. Omnivorous, then, is the word that best describes many shark species. As Gilbert P. Whitley phrased it in *The Fishes of Australia*, 1940: 'All is grist to their mill.'

More than 2,000 years ago Aristotle reflected on the mouths of fishes. 'For in some,' he wrote, 'this is placed in front, at the very extremity of the body, while in others, as . . . the Selachia, it is placed on the under surface; so that these fishes turn on the back in order to take their food. The purpose of Nature in this was apparently not merely to provide a means of salvation for other animals, by allowing them opportunity of escape during the time lost in the act of turning—for all the fishes with this kind of mouth prey on living animals—but also to prevent these fishes from giving way too much to their gluttonous ravening after food. For had they been able to seize their prey more easily than they do, they would soon have perished from over-repletion. An additional reason is that the projecting extremity of the head in these fishes is round and small, and therefore, cannot admit of a wide opening.'

It is still commonly thought that sharks must turn belly up to bite. But Aristotle's reasonings—they can be found in his *De Partibus Animalium* which is the earliest known treatise on the function of animal organs—are faulty on all counts. Most shark jaws are hinged in such a way that they can be opened to a nearly vertical gape and sharks can and do bite right side up. How the misconception arose is a matter of conjecture. Probably, the rolls and twists of feeding sharks had something to do with it. Aristotle, however, who was more often right than wrong, gave it to literature and like other misconceptions about sharks it has proved durable.

Although almost anything may be found inside sharks, sharks are not often found inside anything except other sharks. Shark cannibalism, of the same or a different species, is at the least routine but the incidents on record occasionally offer small surprises. 'About this time,' one account reads, 'a shark, larger than any of those taken, swam up to the one hanging from the boom, and raising its head partly out of the water, seized the dead shark by the throat. As it did so, the captain of the *Fish Hawk* began shooting at it, with a 32-caliber revolver, as rapidly as he could take aim. The shots seemed only to infuriate the shark, and it shook the dead one so viciously as to make it seem doubtful whether the boom would withstand its onslaught. Finally it tore a very large section of the

Sharks will scavenge if they must, but fresh food is preferred. This giant bluefin tuna, the species *Thunnus thynnus,* was attacked after being hooked.

unfortunate's belly, tearing out and devouring the whole liver, leaving a gaping hole across the entire width of the body large enough to permit a small child to easily enter the body cavity. At this instant one of the bullets struck a vital spot, and after a lively struggle on the part of the launch's crew, a rope was secured around its tail. The four specimens, all females, were brought to the laboratory for examination. The last shark was 365·8 cm (12 feet) in length, and the liver of the smaller one was still in its stomach, the estimated weight of which was 40 pounds. At the time of capture one of the sharks regurgitated a rat. . . .'

At São Miguel in the Azores in 1964 one of the authors was present when an eight-foot shark was found in the stomach of a 52-foot sperm whale. The sperm whale, *Physeter catodon*, has large teeth and the undeniable capacity to eat large sharks but in the normal course of events, apparently, it does not. 'So far as I could understand . . .,' he later reported in *The Journal of Mammalogy*, 'the occurrence of such a shark in Azores sperm whale stomachs was very rare, if not unique. . . .'

The same can be said about other sectors of the sperm whale fishery. 'While the taking of small elasmobranchs for food,' the report concluded, 'should probably be regarded as a not too frequent but normal happening, the taking of large pelagic ones should probably be likened to the taking of glass floats and coconuts such as have been reported from the stomachs of Bering Sea sperm whales by Nemoto and Nasu. . . . These authors reasonably suggest that it is curiosity about such objects that causes them to be swallowed.'

Whether it is because they are relatively indigestible or generally formidable, the fact is that sharks have virtually no natural enemies. Again, other sharks are excepted. Porpoises, contrary to enduring nautical lore, are not.

Sharks and porpoises have been seen to feed together in the wild and as a rule they leave one another alone in captivity. Nonetheless, sharks can and do eat porpoises. According to Stewart Springer, for many years with the United States Fish and Wildlife Service and an old shark hand, sharks '. . . have been found with parts of sea turtles and porpoises in their stomachs so often that

Sharks and porpoises generally coexist in aquariums. But in the wild, the relationship is uneasy, with porpoises getting the worst of it.

these must be considered among the normal foods of the larger individuals'.

Porpoises cannot eat sharks. Their jaws and teeth are not up to the task. But neither are porpoises helpless. They can fend off sharks by charging them and, on the basis of one incident observed in an oceanarium, perhaps kill sharks by butting them about. Unfortunately, so far as we have been able to gather, the scientific record contains no observation of either creature killing the other in the wild. There is, though, this from Springer: 'We were loafing along at three or four knots, washing down the deck after a frustrating early morning purse seine net that caught little except jelly fish, when about 50 porpoises came and manoeuvered close against the ship's side. This was unusual because we were moving too slowly to give them any sport. They were an unusual kind for the mid-Gulf of Mexico, *Delphinus*, and their behavior was startling. It was obvious that these porpoises were dead tired and some were injured. By looking closely, we began to see the dim shapes of sharks staying perhaps 30 yards away from our boat and the porpoises. There were six or eight quite young porpoises, not more than three feet long, and these were herded in close to the boat while some of the large ones patrolled the fringe of the porpoise school that now had our vessel to protect one flank.

'The porpoises trusted us with their young and our 250 ton tub of a fishing vessel responded as well as it could. We tried stopping but this seemed to bring the sharks in and to disturb the porpoises so we went ahead as slowly as possible, slower than big diesel engines like to go. Someone thawed some frozen fish and tried to feed the porpoises but they appeared to be too exhausted to be interested. Now and then a shark would come closer and one or more of the patrol porpoises would burst into a series of dashes. We could not see whether any contact was made between the porpoises and sharks. The sharks always retreated but did not go away. Some of the patrol porpoises had been injured. Several were scarred and one had a badly shredded tail fin.

'It was easy to see that the porpoises were co-operating and that they were not only protecting their young, but also were protecting each other. One shark would not have given the porpoises much trouble but a large group of sharks working with the same objectives, had seriously endangered the entire school of porpoises and possibly had already decimated it. There was no real evidence that the sharks were co-operating. Given a little intelligence or some pattern of co-operative attack, there seems little doubt that the sharks could have finished the action in short order and, at least, could have eaten the young porpoises as well as any last ditch defenders.

'We felt badly because we could not do anything about the sharks and we didn't feel like abandoning the porpoises. Our dilemma was resolved in about an hour by a small but violent rain squall. When we came out of it the porpoises and sharks were gone. Perhaps, the short rest and the surface disturbance caused by the squall, allowed the porpoises to escape with their young.'

Sparse as the evidence may be, there is enough to draw logical conclusions. Since porpoises do not eat sharks, they have no reason to attack sharks unless sharks attack them. Since sharks do eat porpoises, they have a natural reason to attack.

Orcinus orca, the killer whale, deserves some mention. It is not really a whale. It is the largest of porpoises. Males grow to about 30 feet and females to about 20. They have large conical teeth in both jaws and are every bit as voracious, though not as indiscriminate, as the most voracious of sharks. They hunt in packs and will attack even the largest of baleen whales. But, like smaller porpoises, they prefer animals that can be swallowed whole. So they often swallow smaller porpoises whole and the belly of one beached orca once delivered up the remains of 13 porpoises and 14 seals.

Seals seem to afford the orca both food and fun. 'I saw,' one California boatman recounted, 'some ten to fifteen sea lions heading toward shore as fast as I have ever seen sea lions move. . . . Herding them were several (five to seven) killer whales, apparently enjoying themselves. . . . Occasionally a killer whale would dive under the sea lions and come up under one. When this happened the sea lion was either bumped or thrown several feet into the air. It did not seem, however, that the killer whale was attacking the sea lion . . . it appeared . . . a game . . . until the sea lions were about a city block offshore. At that time the entire group of killer whales attacked and for a few minutes not much could be seen but flying spray and large heaving bodies. The water over several hundred feet was churned into a bloody froth, and there were no more sea lions visible.'

The killer whale is the only cetacean, whales and porpoises are cetaceans, to prey upon other cetaceans (though the creature is not known to be cannibalistic in the species-eat-species sense) and upon other marine mammals like seals and walruses as well as upon marine birds like penguins. That they may now and then prey also upon sharks is possible. In 1958 in another California incident, onlookers watched three orca in ten minutes devour a large electric ray and rays are closely related to sharks.

Finally, in still another 1958 incident in California, the late Conrad Limbaugh reported this: 'Dr. Gifford Ewing, Dr. Wheeler North, and I saw a large California bull sea lion eating a $3\frac{1}{2}$-to-4-foot shark at the surface in the entrance to Magdalena Bay. When first observed, the sea lion was shaking the shark in the air and was surrounded by sea gulls. The shark was repeatedly jerked from the water, thrown, and then recovered by the sea lion. The body cavity was ripped open, and the sea lion ate what appeared to be the entrails. The sea gulls joined in the feast. During the incident we circled the sea lion in an airplane at close range. The presence of the plane probably caused him to abandon the shark, which was last seen swimming at the surface with its head at a high unnatural angle.'

Stories about the tenacity with which sharks hold to life and about their seeming insensitivity to pain may strain the imagination. For example, in their *Field Book of Giant Fishes*, 1949 edition, J. R. Norman and F. C. Fraser, both of the British Museum, tell of a shark that had been gutted, thrown back over the side and caught again on a hook baited with its own intestines.

We do not think the story an exaggeration. One August night a few years ago the small research vessel *Bear* was hove to on the old Hatteras whaling grounds south and east of Virginia. The sea was gentle and we sat on the after rail and watched the sharks gather. They swam out of the dark into the light cast by the ship and there they circled with an economy of motion and a patience that can be more than faintly unsettling to the watchers.

The crew put over hooks and the sharks quickened the tempo of their swimming. They hurried to the bait, passed it by, turned and passed it by again. The turns tightened and then a shark mouthed a bait. Sailors hauled back on the rope and the shark, beneath the surface, danced and spun on its tail like a kite flying in an uncertain breeze. They dragged it aboard and lashed it down head to winch and tail to sampson-post. They sawed away its jaws for keepsake teeth and slit its belly to see what might be inside.

We slopped about and slipped in blood and when the crew was done with a shark we measured it, determined its sex, if female noted the condition of ovaries and oviducts and examined stomach contents which this night were the undigested beaks of previously eaten squids.

By the time the fishing subsided there were a dozen or more sharks on deck. Some had been lying there for half an hour. Yet when they were thrown over the side most of these ruined creatures tried to swim and one, innards trailing, wobbled 100 feet from stern to bow, made a feeble pass at a bait and then settled away toward the bottom 1,500 fathoms below.

Scientific purpose aside, it had been a saddening spectacle. There had been beauty and grace to the sharks and it was not enough consolation that to catch and mutilate them was a ritual old to seafaring. Jan de Hartog, a sailor's sailor and the sailor's modern Boswell, knows of this and he explained it in *A Sailor's Life*. 'The focs'le fantasies about whales, however extravagant they may be, are always friendly. . . . The shark, on the contrary, embodies all that is evil . . . when a shark is caught and hoisted on board ship, as occasionally happens on long voyages, the aft-deck turns into a slaughter-house. The men go berserk in a prehistoric orgy of fury and blood . . . at those moments, the jolly old tars are not lovable. When the orgy is over, there is a bewildered sense of shame and they will pretend that the slaughter had a purpose . . . I have seen a grim, fat bosun struggle for weeks with a bit of corrugated iron skin, trying to make a handbag.'

CHAPTER 3 | ***Consorts***

It seems strange that two small bony fishes should have forged an intimate relationship with such uncompanionable creatures as pelagic sharks. Yet in the course of evolution, the pilot fish and the remoras have done so and they have tickled mankind's fancy too.

Naucrates ductor, the pilot fish, is a species of the family Carangidae which includes, among others, the jacks and pompanos. It is blue in colour and banded with stripes of a darker blue. It grows to a length of about two feet, frequents temperate seas and a hint to the habits of the creature can be found in its scientific name. *Naucrates* is a classical Greek word meaning ruler of ships, *ductor* a Latin one meaning a leader. Parenthetically, the scientific and colloquial names of a living thing often refer to some aspect of its form or function—real or legendary—and rummaging through dictionaries old and new can be an intriguing preoccupation.

As to pilot fish, they may keep company with a slow boat for days on end. But they also travel with sharks—and with large rays and schools of tuna—and when Herman Melville composed his rather poor poem *The Maldive Shark* he managed to incorporate much of the fanciful that still surrounds the relationship between pilot fish and sharks. To wit:

About the Shark, phlegmatical one,
Pale sot of the Maldive sea,
The sleek little pilot-fish, azure and slim,
How alert in attendance be.
From his saw-pit of mouth, from his charnel of maw,

They have nothing of harm to dread,
But liquidly glide on his ghostly flank
Or before his Gorgonian head;
Or lurk in the port of serrated teeth
In white triple tiers of glittering gates,
And there find a haven when peril's abroad,
An asylum in jaws of the Fates.
They are friends: and friendly they guide him to prey,
Yet never partake of the treat—
Eyes and brains to the dotard lethargic and dull,
Pale ravener of horrible meat.

Melville, possibly, had poetic tongue in cheek and possibly he did not. Pilot fish, however, do not find a haven in shark mouths. They intuitively avoid shark mouths. They do not lead sharks to prey. Sharks have eyes and brains enough to capture prey on their own and with great capability. But pilot fish do partake of the treat and that is a fundamental of the pilot fish–shark relationship. It is known as *commensalism* and can be described as the relationship between two sorts of organisms in which one gets something beneficial from the other and the other is neither benefited nor harmed in the process.

In the pilot fish–shark relationship the pilot fish are the beneficiaries. They feed mostly on shark leavings—the noun *commensal* means, literally, *one who eats at the same table as others*—and they may profit in two additional ways. They may derive a measure of protection from sharks, inasmuch as proximity to sharks could well discourage other predators. And they may help themselves along by riding the pressure or bow wave which a swimming shark generates. Pilot fish, then, do nothing for sharks. In fact, they will abandon a shark that is not feeding for one that is.

Remoras are members of the family Echeneidae and very different from pilot fish. There are about a dozen species of them and they range in length from a few inches to over three feet. Some are reddish brown, some are grey, some are green and the sides of at least one species are marked from snout to tail with a broad, dark, white-edged stripe. Like pilot fish they are common to temperate seas, but remoras are much more specialized. Adaptation has modified their first dorsal fin into a suction disc that sits well forward on the head and with which they can fasten to and be carried about by whales, sailfishes, marlins, turtles, sharks and sometimes boats. Their association with sharks, however, is particularly complex, but before delving into it we will dispose of some remora fact and fancy.

The mechanics of the remora suction disc are not completely known and neither is it known just how much suction the disc can create. Some years ago a curious American scientist yanked a 27-inch remora by the tail—the remora was stuck to the wet deck of a boat—and later wrote: '. . . I pulled on this fish so hard that I feared that I would tear it in two, but it resisted all efforts to pull it off backwards—a pull of possibly 50 pounds. On pulling upwards on it, it held fast until the disc began to tear loose from the head.' And, in 1961 in the British journal *Nature*, B. Bonnell described the disc as '. . . a mechanism precisely built and as efficient as any that human ingenuity can invent, in which case the sucking power must be 15 lb./sq. in. As some of the suckers cover an area of more than 8 sq. in., the fish, theoretically at least, must be able to suck with a power exceeding 100 lb.'

Nevertheless there is no doubt, though it has been doubted, that remoras can stick fast enough to be employed in the catching of fish and turtles and the first to take note of the practice was Christopher Columbus in May 1494 at Jardines de la Reina, an island chain off the south coast of Cuba. Columbus's own account is missing. But of the several based upon it, that by his close friend Andres Bernandez is believed to be among the more faithful. 'On the day following, the Admiral being very desirous to fall in with some natives with whom he might parley, there came a canoe to hunt for fish, for they call it hunting, and they hunt for one fish with others of a particular kind. They have certain fishes which they hold by a line fastened to their tails. . . . They are very fierce, like our ferrets, and when they are thrown into the water they fly to fasten themselves upon whatsoever fish they may espy, and sooner die than let go their hold till they are drawn out of the water. The hunting fish is very light, and as soon as he has taken hold, the

A sand shark, *Odontaspis taurus*, with a remora on its belly. The shark-remora relationship is a complex one, but remoras are not, as is widely believed, parasites.

Indians draw him by the long cord attached to his body, and in this manner they take a fish each time on drawing both to the surface of the water. . . . As the boats came up to them, these hunters called out to the men in mildest manner . . . to hold off, because one of the fishes had fastened upon the under side of a large turtle and they must wait till they got it into the canoe. . . .'

Almost 450 years later, in 1932, C. Ralph DeSola reported on a Cuban turtling expedition in *Copeia*, the quarterly journal published by the American Society of Ichthyologists and Herpetologists. 'We set out from the *marina* at daybreak and motorboated from Matanzas Bay to a village between that point and Cardenas. Here we got into several small carvel type row boats and went out off the sandy beaches with native crews. Along the lower side of the craft a pair of *pega-pegas* or *pegadores* (as sucking-fish are called in Cuba, meaning stickers) were firmly attached by their discs to the planking. A thin lanyard of *majaqua* bark made them secure to the boat. . . . Once clear of the sandy shoal water we sighted a sea turtle basking on the surface. Our boatman immediately headed in its direction and gave us instructions to fasten the *majaqua* lanyards that held the remoras to a coil of rope that was faked down in the bow. At this moment the turtle may have sensed our presence and began to make off leisurely. The fisherman seized the sucking-fish by their heads, [remoras can be unstuck by moving them forward or sideways but, however the disc functions, a backward pull only tightens their hold] loosening their grasp from the boat; tossed them in the direction of the sea turtle which was about two points on our starboard bow and they swam rapidly in its direction. The lines ran out of the bow quickly and, using our hands as a check, we soon felt the lines go taut and the vibrations that came back indicated that our living fish-hooks were fast to their quarry. The fisherman implored us to hold tight and by no means to let the lines slacken as the tighter we held them the better the hold of the remora. We rowed up to the turtle, pulling in our lines and found it to be a hawk's-bill. The fisherman made a noose fast to its neck and front flippers and with some effort we got him amidships in the boat. Once out of the water, the remoras relaxed their hold on the plastron of the turtle, the native boatman all the while indulging in much gentle talk concerning his friendship for the *pega-pegas* and reassuring them that they would be well fed and cared for on their return home.'

Time, clearly, hasn't much altered the practice and neither has place. In his book *The Green Turtle and Man*, 1962, James J. Parsons asserts that remoras still serve to catch turtle in Cuba and the Caribbean, northern Australia, the South China Sea and, most extensively, along the east coast of Africa but not, so far as is now known, anywhere in between. Yet, remora turtling techniques are strikingly similar from one of these widely separated areas to another. And Parsons comments on an additional similarity. 'It is noteworthy that wherever it is so employed for taking turtle the suckerfish is reported to be treated with extreme respect by the native fishermen. The relationship is apparently somewhat similar to that between a hunter and his retriever dog. It is stroked, spoken, to with soft words of encouragement or thanks, and fed special food. When it fails to perform, it is verbally scolded, given the lash, or even bitten . . . the natives seem to believe that this remarkable fish will understand human speech.'

The similarities are a problem in ethnology. They result, perhaps, from some long ago transoceanic cultural contact. It is more likely, though, that turtling with remoras is an example of convergent cultural evolution which is to say that it developed independently from area to area. After all, given remoras and turtles, there are only so many ways of using the one to catch the other. But, Parsons concludes: 'We will probably never have sufficient information to completely resolve this enigma, which is but part of the larger question of pre-Colombian culture transfers between the Old World and the New World.'

The family name of the remoras, Echeneidae means *those that hold back ships*. Remora means *a holding back* and among the common names of the creature itself, along with suckerfish and shark sucker, is ship-holder.

The origins of the idea that remoras could hold back ships are lost. However, Pliny the Elder made the first literary reference to it in his *Historia Naturalis* of A.D. 77 or thereabouts. 'Winds may blow and storms may rage, and yet the echeneis controls their fury, restrains their mighty force, and bids ships stand still in career; a result which no cables, no anchors, from their ponderousness quite incapable of being weighed, could ever have produced! A fish bridles the impetuous violence of the deep, and subdues the frantic rage of the universe—and all this by no effort of its own, no act of resistance on its part, no act at all, in fact, but that of adhering to the bark! Trifling as this object would appear, it suffices to counteract all these forces combined, and to forbid the ship to pass onward in its way! Fleets armed for war, pile up towers and bulwarks on their decks, in order that, upon the deep even, men may fight from behind ramparts as it were. But alas for human vanity!—when their prows, beaked as they are with brass and iron, and armed for the onset, can thus be arrested and rivetted to the spot by a little fish, no more than some half foot in length!'

That myth, too, proved its durability. It persisted in some degree into the nineteenth century and the noun *remora* and the adjective *remorid* are still at times used to describe that which holds back or delays.

Remoras and sharks, like pilot fish and sharks, are messmates. When a shark finds food, its one or two or more remoras detach themselves to pick up the scraps. Also like pilot fish they feed on their own if prey is conveniently close. But remoras utilize a third food source. They feed in part on shark ectoparasites—mainly specialized copepods which are small crustaceans—and the remora–shark relationship is therefore a case of *symbiosis* which differs from *commensalism* in that each creature, rather than one alone, realizes benefit from the other. In this instance the remoras are transported about and provided with food while the shark is relieved of parasites.

Remoras tend to be host specific and the species most usually fastened to sharks is *Remora remora* which reaches a length of more than two feet. Large individuals of the species, if the large sharks they prefer are unavailable, can revert to the free-swimming existence of their younger days when the urge to attach was not yet obligatory. On the other hand, small *Remora remora* may need sharks for more than food and transportation. There is evidence that they need relatively fast-moving water to convey dissolved oxygen to their gills and that unattached and bereft of moving sharks to satisfy this need they experience severe and possibly fatal respiratory troubles. The evidence is not conclusive, but those echeneids, large or small, that fasten to sharks will have a somewhat chancy time of it anyway. Sharks are imperfect symbionts. Occasionally, they eat remoras.

| # Man and the Maneater

At St Thomas in the Caribbean's Virgin Islands, Magens Bay is a pleasant place to swim. Sheltered from the boisterous easterly trade winds, it is usually calm and clean and such were conditions on April 20, 1963, the day that John Gibson, a young naval officer, decided to swim the seven-tenths of a mile across the bay. His companion, Donna Waugh, elected to walk around to meet him.

Gibson started swimming from the beach on the south-west side of the bay toward the rocky shoreline on the north-east side. Miss Waugh walked along the beach and paused to talk with someone. It was about one-thirty in the afternoon and she may have heard a scream. She looked out at Gibson. She noticed only that he had switched from a crawl to what seemed a sidestroke. She walked on. By the time Miss Waugh reached the far side of the bay it became evident that Gibson was in distress. He rolled in the water and she saw that one of his hands was gone. She swam out to help him. He told her to go back. He was, he said, being attacked by a shark. She continued to help him.

Even in the shallows the shark kept at Gibson, but bystanders and Miss Waugh ultimately got him into a skiff. He was then dead or nearly so. His right hand had been severed. Massive bites had been taken out of his left shoulder, right thigh and hip. His left foot also had been bitten, though no flesh removed.

It is likely that Gibson was first struck in the foot and lost the hand trying to fend off the shark. The bite in the thigh cut the femoral artery and after that he could not have lived much more than 15 seconds.

Lines were set in Magens Bay the next morning. Late in the afternoon a shark was caught. It was ten feet long and in its stomach were Gibson's hand and pieces of his body. A curious footnote: the shark was a Galapagos shark, a species never before reported from the Atlantic.

The details of shark attacks may vary, but not so much the results. The victim is either killed or he is not. If it is not, he is at worst maimed, at best scarred. A discussion of shark attacks, nonetheless, has its virtues. To know what is known about shark attacks could lessen the chances of figuring as a principal in one. Furthermore, the subject begs for perspective.

From 1962 through 1966, sharks, worldwide and without evident provocation, attacked 30 small boats and 161 inshore swimmers, divers, waders, surfers and waterskiers. They also attacked 26 other people who prodded or speared or in some way provoked them. And offshore, in the aftermath of air crashes and ship sinkings, they attacked 476 people.

Of the 30 small-boat attacks and the 26 provoked attacks none was fatal. Of the 161 inshore attacks 70 were fatal. Of the 476 offshore attacks 350 are listed as fatal, but the number of people still alive when attacked can never be known.

Thirty-two of the 161 inshore attacks occurred in the United States, 22 in Australia and 16 in South Africa. But there were also attacks in such places as the Bahamas, Bermuda, Mexico, Hawaii, the Philippines and Fiji Islands, Japan, Taiwan, New Zealand, India, Italy and Greece. In modern times, as far as we can gather, no unprovoked attack on a swimmer has been reported from northern European or British home waters even though the requisite sharks are there. However, in July 1960, a provoked but non-fatal attack was reported from Wick, Scotland and on August 4, 1960, there was a second from the coast of Devon. Back in 1937, two attacks on boats were reported from Scotland; the details of one are scant; during the other, at Carradale Bay, the shark capsized a sailing boat and the three occupants drowned.

The foregoing information was provided by *The Shark Research Panel* of the American Institute of Biological Sciences. The panel— and there are similar panels in South Africa and Australia—

arranges conferences about sharks and shark attack. It encourages and co-ordinates basic and applied research into sharks. It evaluates proposed methods, chemical or mechanical, for preventing attack. And under Leonard P. Schultz at the Smithsonian Institution in Washington, it maintains a record of attacks. Whenever an attack is reported from anywhere in the world—used, among other sources, are five press cutting services—a marine scientist or physician in the vicinity is asked to document it in the greatest possible detail. The hope is that factors common to attack may emerge and suggest ways of avoiding or forestalling it. So far, nothing very suggestive has emerged. To the student of sharks, what has emerged seems logical. To the layman, however, the logical may be disturbing.

In *Chesapeake Science* in March 1967, Schultz analyzed 1,406 attacks dating from the middle of the last century to the present. He found that sharks attacked on sunny days, on stormy days, in clear water, in murky water, in daylight, in darkness, in estuaries, in bays, in rivers, in lakes with an outlet to the sea, in the sea itself and at all times of the year; that sharks attacked at water temperatures as low as 53°F., but that the great majority attacked at water temperatures above 68°F.; that 50·1 per cent of unprovoked attacks occurred within 200 feet of shore and some within five feet; that 69·8 per cent of those people attacked without provocation were at the surface of the water and 17·6 per cent were standing or wading in water from knee-deep to chin-deep; that the attacking sharks were from two to 25 feet long, but that most ranged from four to 15 feet; and that 45·8 per cent of the people attacked without provocation were killed.

The lesson is a plain and simple one. Attack can occur almost any time and anywhere. But it occurs most often, as one would expect, when and where the most sharks and the most people occur. That means in the summer season in temperate regions and all year around in tropical ones. Most attacks in United States waters occur in Florida, but there have been incidents all along the coast from Swampscott, Massachusetts, to Trinidad Bay in northern California. Most attacks in South African waters occur on the east coast in the province of Natal. Most attacks in Australian waters also occur on the east coast and mostly in Queensland and New South Wales. Most attacks in European waters occur in the Mediterranean.

Schultz's analysis, the chances are, fairly reflects some of the fundamentals of shark attack. But no one knows and no one claims to know the frequency of attack. The number of unprovoked attacks reported to *The Shark Research Panel* averages about 50 a year and the number is really meaningless. Many attacks, particularly those in remote areas, are not reported. Some are not witnessed except by the victim who shortly thereafter may be quite beyond testimony.

It should be some comfort that, whatever the actual frequency, shark attack is still a rarity among the misfortunes which every day befall mankind. Rarity, though, does not seem to damp his fear of sharks and perhaps that is as it should be. The shark, ever the opportunist, is in its element. The swimmer, the diver, the castaway is not and what does it matter that the probability of a shark attack is very distant. An attack is still and always a possibility and a singularly frightful one to contemplate. Even so, there was a time when innocence overcame reason and men of science ridiculed sharks.

William Beebe, the American naturalist, in *The Arcturus Adventure*, 1926: 'The ability of the human imagination to see what it thinks it ought to see is astonishing. As long as my book-and-legend-induced fear of sharks dominated, I saw them as sinuous, crafty, sinister, cruel-mouthed, sneering. When I came at last to know them for harmless scavengers, all these characteristics slipped away, and I saw them as they really are—indolent, awkward, chinless cowards . . . a ladyfish has a thousand times less weight and double their courage.'

Frederick A. Lucas, Director of the American Museum of Natural History in New York, in the *Brooklyn Museum Science Bulletin*, April 1916: 'One of the commonest statements is that "the shark bit off the man's leg as though it were a carrot", an assertion that shows the maker or writer of it had little idea of the strength of the apparatus needed to perform such an amputation. . . . The next time the reader carves a leg of lamb, let him speculate on the power required to sever this at one stroke—and the bones of a sheep are much lighter than those of a man. Moreover, a shark, popular belief to the contrary notwithstanding, is not particularly strong in the jaws. . . . I remember my own disappointment at witnessing the efforts of a twelve-foot shark to cut a chunk out of a sea lion. The sea lion had been dead a week and was supposedly tender, but the shark tugged and thrashed and made a great to-do over each mouthful.'

J. R. Norman again, of the British Museum, in *A History of Fishes*, 1931: 'The common statement that a man's leg was bitten off by a shark "as though it were a carrot", betrays a complete ignorance of the strength of the apparatus required to perform such an amputation. As Dr. Lucas remarks: "The next time the reader carves a leg of lamb . . .".'

Recently, Perry W. Gilbert of Cornell University, using an instrument called the *Snodgrass Gnathodynamometer*, measured the force exerted by the jaws of a typical eight-foot shark. It was an extraordinary three metric tons—6,613·8 pounds—per square centimetre. But scientists concerned with the problem of attack, Gilbert among them, did not in one sense need the measurement. They have seen all too many photographs of bodies with this or that limb lost to sharks.

E. W. Gudger, a naturalist and bibliographer at the American Museum, also depreciated sharks. 'The ordinary shark is usually an arrant coward,' he wrote in his 1918 monograph *Sphyraena Barracuda: Its Morphology, Habits, and History*, 'If a shark is "hanging around" a boat or wharf, and a man falls overboard or any large object is thrown overboard, generally that shark will depart in a panic. . . . But it is not thus with the big barracuda. He is inquisitive, utterly fearless, and seemingly of implacable temper.'

The many shark incidents of World War II discouraged absurdities, though not entirely. In a popularly written book in 1951—it was still in print in 1969—one of North America's foremost zoologists did not quote Gudger, but he must have had Gudger in hand or mind. 'Barracudas,' the passage reads, 'rarely grow longer than six feet, but even a three-foot barracuda is more to be feared by fish or man than any shark. Most sharks are scavengers, many are cowards. . . . As a rule when an uninjured man falls overboard any nearby shark departs in a panic. But a barracuda, large or small, is inquisitive, utterly fearless and of implacable temper. . . . Barracudas are probably responsible for most shark horror-stories.'

The notion that barracuda are as dangerous as sharks, or more so, is and always has been rooted in hearsay and folklore. But the record was not put straight until 1963 when Donald P. de Sylva published *Systematics and Life History of the Great Barracuda, Sphyraena barracuda (Walbaum)*. De Sylva, an ichthyologist at the Institute of Marine Science of the University of Miami in Florida, states after ten years of research: 'Attacks have been authenticated by the unmistakable tooth marks of a barracuda . . . its cleaver-like bite can be distinguished from that of a shark in that it consists of two, nearly parallel rows of tooth marks, whereas that of a shark leaves a parabolic wound with jagged tooth marks. The shark also tends to clamp its prey and tear off flesh with a sawing motion. My research and observations indicate that the barracuda depends almost entirely upon sight and usually makes a single attack which may be severe but is seldom fatal. In general, a shark is further stimulated by the presence of blood drawn so that repeated attacks occur which often result in fatalities.'

De Sylva discusses the evidence and then summarizes. 'From the literature and newspaper accounts I have listed 29 separate attacks attributed to barracuda upon humans; 19 are documented, two are probable, and the remaining eight are possibly due to barracuda.'

The earliest barracuda attack acceptable to de Sylva occurred in 1873 or 90 years before the publication of his monograph. It has been said here that *The Shark Research Panel* documents, on the average, 50 unprovoked shark attacks a year and that the figure must be taken as a minimum because many attacks for one reason or another are not reported. So, in the 90 years for which de Sylva was able to document 19 barracuda attacks, there had to occur at least 450 shark attacks. In the tropics, certainly, barracuda bear watching. However, even if a generous allowance is made for unreported attacks by the creatures, the case that they are as dangerous as sharks, if not more dangerous, would seem to be much overstated.

Incidentally, the current world angling record great barracuda

This fragment of a tooth, 17·2 mm long, of a white shark, *Carcharodon carcharias*, was extracted from the thigh of a diver attacked off northern California in 1964. Though severely injured, the diver did recover and the finding of the fragment represents the rare instance when the offending shark can be positively identified.

weighed 103 pounds, four ounces; it measured five feet, six inches in length and was caught in the Bahamas in 1932. The current world record shark weighed 2,664 pounds; it measured 16 feet, ten inches in length and was caught in Australia in 1959.

To any question about the number of dangerous shark species there is no even faintly precise answer. By dint of size, disposition or environment, some species are more dangerous than others. But post-attack identification of the offending species is invariably difficult. Positive identity, in fact, is established at a ratio of one in 25 attacks. After all, the shark that attacks ordinarily escapes and, ordinarily, observers no more than glimpsed a grey or brown shape and for no more than a few confused seconds. Unless, therefore, the shark leaves distinctive teeth in the victim or unless the shark is caught and evidence of the attack found inside it—and both eventualities are infrequent—the identity of the species can only be guessed.

Common sense would have it that sharks in general be treated with respect. A minority of species may be involved in unprovoked attacks, but under proper circumstances the majority can do injury. For anyone inclined to annoy a shark there is this aphorism from an anonymous source in *La Ménagerie*, 1868, by Théodore P.K.: *Cet animal est très méchant. Quand on l'attaque il se défend.* 'This creature is very naughty. He defends himself when attacked.'

What may impel sharks to attack and what may be done to prevent or ward off attack will occupy later chapters. The six following chapters concern species, not only species implicated in attack but also species with other or coincidental claims to attention. In the preoccupation with attack, it is often forgotten that sharks are many-sided creatures.

Typical Ones

Among the several unknowns about sharks is the total number of living shark species. The 300 mentioned earlier are only those with which science is acquainted and today or tomorrow an ichthyologist exploring some strange corner of the sea will maybe find and describe a new species. The chances are that it will be caught at great depth for the deeps have been little explored. But the shallow ocean still yields its share of the new. In 1950 a large and abundant shark was first scientifically described and named from fairly shoal water, 50 to 100 fathoms, off the Florida Keys in the United States and the ichthyologist who did it, Stewart Springer, said: '*Eulamia* [now *Carcharhinus*] *altima* appears to be the most common large shark of the edges of the continental shelf in the West Indian region.' Yet, despite its tardy scientific recognition, this species had long been familiar to the shark fishermen of south Florida. They called it Knopp's shark and it made up a substantial part of the catch when their lines were set on the bottom at more than 50 fathoms.

There are other examples from other oceans, but a catch of some years ago illustrates the difficulty confronting scientists who would sort out shark species. In 1906 Samuel Garman, the late Harvard ichthyologist, described a new shark species, *Paragaleus pectoralis*, from a single specimen which popped up in a display of living sea creatures called Aquarial Gardens. Exhibits for the display were collected off Massachusetts and Rhode Island and the ocean fauna of these states has been pretty thoroughly scrutinized and catalogued. Yet not one specimen of *pectoralis* has been seen since and one might suspect that Garman had described a freak. In 1935, however, a very similar species, *Paragaleus gruveli*, was described from numerous specimens collected off West Africa. Thus, *pectoralis* may be a valid species but the question is where on the heavily fished New England coast it hides itself.

When a marine biologist believes he has a new species in hand he must do certain things. He must determine if his specimen is in some significant way or ways structurally different from all other species. If it is he must next publish a paper describing and naming the new species. Also, he must preserve at least one specimen which is know as the *type specimen*. The locality where the specimen was collected is known as the *type locality*.

Whatever the scientist may name the species, he must conform to the binomial system devised by the Swedish botanist Linnaeus in 1735 and now regulated by the International Commission on Zoological Nomenclature.

The first name of the new species will be *generic*—similar species comprise a genus, similar genera comprise a family and so forth— but its second name will be *trivial*. The two names together form the *specific* name and no other animal or plant, living or fossil, can have that same name. The names, furthermore, will usually be taken from latinized classical Greek or from Latin itself or from another latinized tongue since Latin is by tradition the language of scholarship.

Lastly, the name of the new species will always appear the same way in scientific literature. The generic name invariably commences with a capital letter. The trivial name never does, not even if the species is named for a person. If the person's name is Smith, the species' trivial name is *smithi*. It is not mandatory, but a species' scientific name is often followed by the last name of the scientist who first described it and the year he did so.

Common or vernacular names are virtually useless to scientists. To begin with, two or more species may share the same vernacular name. Imagine, for one example, an ichthyologist who writes to another ichthyologist for information about a shark he knows only as the mackerel shark. The return information could well concern the wrong shark. Several species of sharks are in the vernacular called mackerel sharks. Then too, a single species may from place to place be known by several different vernacular names. Imagine again, for a second example, an ichthyological correspondence in which one correspondent asks for information about a shark he knows only as the white shark. The other correspondent might recognize the species and he might not. In the English speaking world alone the vernacular names of the white shark include maneater, blue pointer, white pointer, great white, death shark, Tommy, uptail, cowshark, mudshark, and probably more. The use of scientific names is therefore a necessity because they usually resolve any doubt about the species in question. The scientific name of the white shark is *Carcharodon carcharias* and is known to ichthyologists everywhere as such.

The system does have its imperfections. In one instance, an ichthyologist in Great Britain might describe and name the new species *greyi* and later it develops that *greyi* is the same species known elsewhere as *greeni*. The reason could be that the ichthyologist could not assemble enough domestic and foreign specimens to make a thorough comparison. In another instance, a species known as *kelleyi* in both the Atlantic and Pacific oceans might, after careful study and comparison, prove to be a separate species. So the classification of sharks is being continually revised and if scientific names lead at times to small bits of confusion the binomial system is still essential, essential not only to the orderly classification of life but also to the exchange of reliable scientific information. It sets a universal standard that is universally understood. Without it there would be chaos.

Probably any new shark species will fit into one of the 19 families that now include all sharks. Just five families, though, contain about 75 per cent of known species. And, one family, the Carcharhinidae, now contains almost the remaining 25 per cent. However, the family is being revised by J. A. F. Garrick of New Zealand's Victoria University College at Wellington and many species currently considered separate are expected to prove the same.

The Carcharhinidae, or carcharhinids, if the word is anglicized, are, at the moment, represented by upwards of 100 nominal or named species. They are sometimes called the typical sharks. They are large, strong swimmers, sharp-toothed and always moving. They frequent shoal water and the surface over the deeps and they bear their young alive. They prey on the fishes and squids of the world's warm seas. They lack distinctive features, resemble one another closely and are difficult even for the trained biologist to identify. These are the sharks of song and story and of the species implicated in unprovoked attack on man, most are carcharhinids. But the life history of very few is known at all well. Their geographic distribution, their seasonal comings and goings, their food and breeding habits, their behaviour etc. are subjects about which science has much to learn. Nor will the learning be quick or easy. Observations made from a research vessel are prone to be fleeting and observations made from beneath the surface entail a measure of depressing uncertainty. Of course, captive sharks can be studied and many worthwhile physiological and behavioural things learned. But not all sharks take to captivity and those that do, do not migrate, rarely breed and probably do not feed or behave as they do in the wild. Rather a lot, nonetheless, has over the years been learned about sharks, and curiosity, which is the heart of research, will lead to the learning of more.

The whitetip shark, *Carcharhinus longimanus*, is called so because its fins are tipped with white. But some fins are also distinctive in shape. The first dorsal is smoothly rounded, the pectorals very long and rounded at their tips. The teeth in the upper jaw of the whitetip are broadly triangular and serrate. Those in the lower are broad at the base, but their centres are long, narrow and also serrate. Overall, the whitetip is olive drab above and white below and with the white fin tips there is no mistaking the species.

The whitetip is a creature of the high seas' very surface and will be found wherever the water is warmer than 70°F. and deeper than 100 fathoms. It is extraordinarily abundant, possibly the most abundant large animal, large being over 100 pounds, on the face of the earth. Reportedly, the whitetip grows to 13 feet. However, an eight-foot one is considered to be large and most are smaller.

After a gestation period of a year the whitetip bears about six pups 25 to 30 inches long. The season for giving birth is early summer and the nursery grounds are in the lower latitudes. The young grow rapidly and may reach sexual maturity before the age of two. In summer, as the water of the higher latitudes warms, whitetip males and young, non-breeding females migrate from the tropics.

Swimming at the surface the whitetip seems lackadaisical, but it is singularly stubborn. Once, while bailing bloody water from a dory, we time after time hit an attracted whitetip on the head with an oar. This backed it off a few feet, but it would soon again swim up to the dory and get another drubbing. As Springer has remarked: 'I do not know of anything except a beaker of formalin poured down the gullet that elicits a very strong reaction. They continue a slow and persistent attack in spite of non-mortal bullet holes.'

In the light of the whitetip's lethargy, it is difficult to believe that the creature could catch one of the fastest of ocean fishes. But,

A group of whitetip sharks, the species *Carcharhinus longimanus.* **Whitetips are found at the surface of the open ocean and, while lethargic, are persistent and resourceful hunters.**

according to Harvey R. Bullis, Jr., of the U.S. Fish and Wildlife Service, it contrives to and in a thoroughly remarkable way. 'Of particular interest . . . ,' Bullis reported in the journal *Ecology* in January 1961, 'was the presence of small tunas (weighing approximately 5 to 15 lb) in the stomachs of some of the captured white-tips. . . . There were no indications that these fish had been taken from hooks or had suffered any crippling injuries which would have enabled the sharks to "run them down" . . . an explanation of at least one method of capture of such active swimmers was apparent after observations from the *Oregon* on Cruise 62, north of the Virgin Islands in September 1959. Late one afternoon, about 2 miles off the 100 fathom curve, a strong tide-rip paralleled the shelf contour for several miles, and along the rip were continuous schools of tuna feeding on numerous but scattered small Spanish sardines *Sardinella anchovia*. . . . The tuna schools were very dense and the feeding behavior of the tuna was typical—fast darting rushes at the surface with frequent leaps clear of the water. It is difficult to describe the frenzied cut and slash of small schooling tuna working bait fish.'

Bullis continues: 'Mixed with the tuna were many white-tip sharks, ranging from about 3 to 6 feet in length. Each shark was swimming slowly in a rather erratic, sinuous course with its snout protruding from the water, its mouth wide open at just about the surface level. At one point, the sharks were so numerous that they were spaced not over 10 feet apart in an area some 50 feet wide by 300 feet long. No attempt was made by the sharks to chase after or snap at the hundreds of tuna in the same area. It was an inescapable conclusion, however, that the white-tips were merely waiting and ready for those moments when tunas would accidentally swim or leap right into their mouths.

'The identical behavior of so many sharks,' Bullis concludes, 'observed over a 30 minute interval, would indicate this to be a well-established pattern. Only with the first hand observations, at close quarters, can one give complete credence to the likelihood that oceanic sharks obtain a segment of their food in the manner described.'

In the same paper, Bullis reported on another startling bit of whitetip feeding behaviour, this time off Honduras in the Caribbean in August 1957. 'Late in the afternoon a flock of about 20 red-footed boobies and white-bellied boobies were observed diving. We approached the area and saw that they were working on a tight, dense ball of threadfins, *Polydactylus* sp. The ball was about 6 feet in diameter and, when first sighted, was within a foot of the surface. A few of the boobies were sitting on the water and reaching down to take big gulps of the threadfins. Lying alongside the school was a large white-tip (estimated 7 to 8 feet in length), which was biting off mouthfuls of fish, much in the manner of a person eating an apple. Apparently the school of threadfins was completely indifferent to the predation in progress and displayed no evasive action whatever. We attempted to drift the *Oregon* up to the school to dip-net a sample, but . . . caused the school to sink down beyond the reach of the dip net. By this time the boobies had left, but we watched the white-tip continue to gnaw away at the school for several more minutes.'

The whitetip has not been known to attack man, but there is every reason to believe that it will and there have been suggestive incidents one of which involved John E. Randall, a marine biologist then at the University of Puerto Rico.

Randall was diving off the outer reef of a Pacific atoll and shortly after he had speared and wounded a fish an eight-foot whitetip appeared. 'It swam in a leisurely manner,' Randall relates, 'and as it came in close I hastily offered it a small speared fish, which it declined. After the shark had circled once, I made an aggressive swimming movement toward it. Unlike the common whitetip reef shark of the Pacific (*Triaenodon obesus*) and the small blacktip shark of the Pacific (*Carcharhinus melanopterus*), which invariably swim away when overt movements are made toward them, this shark did not respond at all. While it was circling again, I was able to reach the safety of a nearby outrigger canoe.'

The blue shark, the great blue, the bluedog and the blue whaler are one and all *Prionace glauca*—some carcharhinids do not have the generic name *Carcharhinus*—and in range and abundance it may be second only to the whitetip. Where the water is temperate there are blue sharks and off New England in the summer months they can be so thickly packed as to defy counting. Were they then cobblestones, one could almost walk the Continental Shelf on their backs. They also defy prediction. Hook one today and its school-mates will pay it no heed. Hook one tomorrow and they will destroy it in seconds.

The blue shark is the shark of a particular legend which Oppian set to verse in a 3,500-line poem about fishing, *Halieutica*, in the second century A.D.

> Others, when aught disturbs the ravaged seas,
> And trembling young their conscious fears express,
> Extend their jaws, and show the safer way:
> The frighted stragglers soon the call obey,
> Within the concave roof uninjured rest,
> Safe as the chirper in his mossy nest.
> Thus the Blue Sharks, secure from chasing foes,
> Within their widen'd mouths their young enclose.
> Beneath the circling arch they fearless hide,
> The bulky forms drive on the rising tide.
> Of all oviparous kinds that throng the seas,
> The fond Blue Sharks in tender care surpass.
> They near their fondlings, like some careful nurse,
> Observe their motions and restrain their course,
> Eye every wave, and show the doubtful way.
> Teach where to hunt, and where to find their prey.
> When big with secret guilt the waters heave,
> They in their mouths their shelter'd young receive,
> But when the waves at their own leisure roll,
> And no fierce robber drives the scatter'd shoal,
> Again the parent's pointed jaws compress'd
> By force expel them from their pleasing rest.

Denys W. Tucker, then of the British Museum, traced the perpetuation of the legend in *The Annals & Magazine of Natural History* in September 1957: 'There was, however, a significant legend of the Blue Shark as the ideal parent, first put about by Aelian (*ca.* A.D. 140–220) and by Oppian (*ca.* A.D. 172–210) and subsequently copied by Rondelet (1554); Gesner (1551–87); Aldrovandi (1613) and so into the British literature by Pennant (1769), followed with slowly diminishing credulity by Yarrell (1859), Hamilton (1876), Couch (1877) and eventually even by Day (1880–84). . . . John Ray deserves mention here for his avoidance of the legend. Ray (1673) was the first author to mention the "blewe sharke" as a British species in a catalogue of "Fishes taken about Penzance and St. Ives, given us by one of the ancientist and most experienced fishermen, the most whereof we saw during our stay there." In 1686 he provided a full description and figure. . . .'

The legend was, no doubt, compounded of faulty observation and the fertility of imagination—blue shark pups are seen swimming around parental heads or almost full term pups are found in the womb by people who confuse womb with stomach and do not understand viviparity in fishes, and there you have it—but the tale will still on occasion be told and not only about the blue shark. The tale, though was not of prime interest to Tucker. In his paper just quoted, and in another in the same journal in May 1958, he concentrates upon the probability that the blue sharks in British waters pup there. Previously, they had not been thought to.

•The blue shark is a dark indigo blue on the back shading to bright blue on the sides and to pure white below. The pectorals are long and sickle-shaped. The snout is very long and pointed. The first dorsal is placed well back.

The upper jaw of the blue shark is so filled with teeth that their bases overlap. They are triangular, serrate and set obliquely. Their outer edges are deeply concave, inner ones convex. Their tips are cocked to the right or left. Teeth of the lower jaw are more erect, more slender, more finely serrate.

The blue shark is slimly built. One of seven feet will weigh about 70 pounds, one of eight feet about 100, one of nine feet about 150. However, the current world angling record measured 11 feet 6 inches and weighed 410 pounds. It was caught off Rockport, Massachusetts on September 1, 1960. Sea lore has it that the blue shark often reaches 15 feet and sometimes 20, but 12 feet 7 inches is the longest on scientific record and, unfortunately, the record does not include the weight.

The portrait of a blue shark, *Prionace glauca*, in the wild.
It is an abundant species and a popular one with anglers.

Catch-as-catch-can is descriptive of blue shark feeding. The creature can be lively when inspired and squids, mackerel, herring and other small fishes are its usual fare. It will not ordinarily attack large living animals, but its enthusiastic attendance at the cutting in of whales accounts for *blue whaler* as a common name. 'During the execution of this process,' one narrative about the blue shark reads, 'when the water for an acre around the ship was stained a ghastly yellow from outpouring blood, the scrambling sharks would make the sea a living mass as each fish tried to bury its teeth in the exposed surfaces of dark red muscle. Now and then a shark would flounder right out on top of the whale, and cling there until a descending "blubber spade" had put an end to all its ambitions.'

Knowledge of blue shark reproduction is meagre. The northward movement of the species in summertime may have something to do with breeding, but gravid females are present in all seas in all months and breeding may be an all year activity. Litters are, for shark litters, large and a female may give birth to as many as 70 pups 18 inches long after a gestation period of perhaps a year. Some scientific speculation is that the pups reach three feet in their first year and become sexually mature at seven to eight feet in their third or fourth year. Tucker suggests that blue shark pupping in

British waters takes place before the end of June and 40 to 50 miles off the Cornish coast.

The International Game Fish Association, or I.G.F.A., recognizes the blue shark as a sportive sort of fish and members of the Shark Angling Club of Great Britain at Looe in Cornwall catch thousands between June and October. The current British record blue shark stands at 9 feet and 235 pounds—very large blue sharks do not seem to frequent British waters—and was caught on July 5, 1964. The I.G.F.A. all-tackle record is the aforementioned 410-pound catch made off Rockport, Massachusetts. The offices of the I.G.F.A., incidentally, are in Miami, Florida and the organization every year publishes a chart of current records. Interestingly, the current record blue shark to be taken on a 12-pound test line, the lightest of several I.G.F.A. tackle categories, weighed 312 pounds.

The blue shark does not often stray close inshore and has not as yet made a verifiable attack on man. But, when and if it does, no scientific eyebrows will be raised. Scientists think it has already made unverifiable ones. It is considered dangerous in Australia and one American ichthyologist recently had this to say: 'On several occasions, skindivers have had to drive them away with spears. Recently a specimen 8 feet long approached two of our divers who were diving in a school of porpoises. On another occasion, Mr Earl Murray of Scripps Institution of Oceanography [in La Jolla, California] had to fight off a blue shark with a spear. They will often strike back if struck with an oar.'

On October 27, 1937, Jack Brinkley and Norman Girvan were attacked by a shark while surfing off Kirra Beach at Coolangatta in New South Wales, Australia. Brinkley was rescued, but soon afterwards died in Coolangatta Hospital. Parts of Girvan's body later washed ashore. The next day an 11 foot 9 inch shark was caught nearby. In its stomach were pieces of arms and legs among which was Girvan's scarred right hand. This shark was a tiger shark, *Galeocerdo cuvieri*.

On July 27, 1966, Douglas Lawton, aged 8½, and his brother, 12, were swimming in the vicinity of Sarasota on the west coast of Florida when a shark seized Douglas by the left leg and pulled him down. The brother kept Douglas's head above water and both boys tried to beat off the shark. The parents and an aunt and uncle who had been sitting on the beach rushed to help. The uncle held Douglas by the shoulders while the father pulled the shark by the tail. The shark ultimately broke off its attack and swam away. It, the shark, was judged to have been about five feet long. It had attacked in three feet of water less than ten feet from shore. It had mangled the boy's leg so badly that the limb was amputated well above the knee.

Eugenie Clark, an ichthyologist at Mote Marine Laboratory near Sarasota, studied young Lawton's leg and found that the tooth marks could be duplicated by making bites in clay with the preserved jaws of tiger sharks. Other preserved jaws of other shark species did not duplicate the marks whatever angle of bite was tried.

Beyond question, the tiger shark is one of the most vicious of sharks. On the word of the late Sir Victor M. Coppleson it is probably responsible for most attacks off Australian beaches. Coppleson, a Sydney surgeon who studied shark attack and wrote prolifically about it from 1919 to 1965, also maintained that the species probably responsible for most attacks in Australian harbours and lagoons is the common or black whaler, *Carcharhinus macrurus.*

This one of several so-called whaler sharks reaches a length of 12 feet and a weight of perhaps 1,000 pounds. In colour it is sandy to dark grey above and off-white below. There may be a dark smudge along each side and the fin tips are often blackish. The teeth in the upper jaw are triangular and notched on the outer edge. Those in the lower jaw are similar though smaller and more erect. In both jaws the teeth are serrate. Litters may number 40 pups. About 12 pups, however, seems to be the average and they are large. One 768-pound female caught off Sydney was carrying ten almost full term pups that weighed from 16 to 19 pounds and measured up to 40 inches in length.

The tiger shark was named not for its temperament but for the vertical brown bars that mark the otherwise grey flanks of individuals five to six feet long. The bars fade as the shark grows and may eventually disappear. There is little doubt that the tiger shark

The tiger shark, *Galeocerdo cuvieri*, grows to 18 feet and the weight of a ton and is exceptionally vicious.

grows to 18 feet and over 2,000 pounds, but ten feet and 400 to 500 pounds is an ordinary size.

The range of the tiger shark is the world over in warm coastal water, warm being 70°F. and above, and the creature is most frequently encountered inshore of five fathoms and not infrequently in water so shallow that it can barely swim.

No shark, possibly no animal the goat included, is more notorious for its indiscriminate feeding habits than is the tiger shark. And again one draws on Stewart Springer's seemingly limitless fund of shark lore. 'The tiger shark,' he wrote in 1963, 'is completely omnivorous. It swallows individual large conchs, such as *Fulgur* or even the giant horse conch, whole, and those of moderate 6-to-8-

inch length by the dozen. In some undetermined way the shells are removed in the shark's digestive tract. . . . I have also found large tiger-shark stomachs full of horseshoe crabs, *Limulus*, as well as pieces of large sea turtles, porpoise heads or pieces of porpoise, sea birds, and pieces of large fish. Garbage and artifacts are commonly present. Apparently anything small enough to be swallowed by the shark may be eaten. I once found, in a tiger shark, an unopened can of salmon (the salmon was judged in excellent condition by organoleptic test); at other times I found a good leather wallet with no money in it, a 2 pound coil of copper wire, various articles of clothing, assorted nuts and bolts, and other articles in the stomachs of various tiger sharks. They seem to eat small fish only rarely, and . . . little evidence was found from the examination of stomachs to indicate that tiger sharks are often successful in capturing unhampered and free-swimming small sharks.'

Springer also made some further observations. 'Tiger sharks are not often seen in daylight, but they readily attack surface baits at night. Young tiger sharks are more often seen near the surface and give the impression of being less timid in light than the large ones. Aerial observations of daylight chumming [attracting fish with food] tests once revealed a group of tiger sharks at the bottom in about 40 feet of water beneath a pack of blacktips, *Carcharhinus limbatus*. But the tiger sharks could not be induced to approach the surface, and verification of the identification was made only by lowering a baited hook to the bottom and hauling in a sample.'

The snout of the tiger shark is very short and bluntly round. The tail is sharp-pointed. The teeth in both jaws are the same and unmistakable. They are broad with the tip bent obliquely outward. The serrations are coarse at the base, but become progressively finer toward the tip. The very tip, in fact, may be worn smooth. The inner edge is convex, the outer deeply notched.

The tiger shark is prolific and may throw a litter of as many as 80 pups 20 to 30 inches long. They are, it is thought, the product of springtime mating and beyond that nothing is known of the tiger shark's reproductive practices.

The English naturalist, explorer and buccaneer William Dampier on August 7, 1699 sailed into and named Shark Bay in Western

Australia. And later, in *Voyage to New Holland*, published in 1703, he told of catching sharks there. 'Of the Sharks we caught a great many, which our Men eat very savourily. Among them we caught one which was 11 Foot long. The Space between its 2 Eyes was 20 Inches, and 18 Inches from one Corner of his Mouth to the other. Its Maw was like a Leather Sack, very thick, and so tough that a sharp Knife could scarce cut it: In which we found the Head and Bones of a Hippopotamus . . .'

The hippopotamus was in reality a dugong—*Dugong dugong*, a species of sea-cow—and that should startle no one since hippopotami have never graced Australia. But, Dampier's description of the shark was the first description of an Australian shark and Whitley has surmised that it was a tiger shark.

The current, I.G.F.A. all-tackle record tiger shark weighed 1,780 pounds, measured 13 feet 10½ inches and was caught June 14, 1964, at Cherry Grove, South Carolina, U.S.A. For the angler it must have been an exhilarating if exhausting experience. Nothing, though, quite like the experience that Sir Arthur Grimble had some years ago in the Gilbert Islands of the south Pacific.

At Tarawa the tiger shark was and perhaps still is caught from canoes and in Grimble's early days as a British Colonial Officer on the island he was anxious to catch one. 'I could not,' he related in his *A Pattern of Islands*, 1952, 'get the brutes to take any kind of trolled bait or cast lure, so I had to fall back on the villagers' technique with a one-man canoe, a twelve-inch ironwood hook bought as a curio, and a lovely loaded club.'

When Grimble announced his plans the servants were no end amused, but they would not say why and the next day on arriving at the beach he found the entire village there. As he put it: 'The beach was crawling with sightseers. They were all immensely courteous, but the shining of their beautiful eyes gave them away. I was wafted on to the canoe and pushed off in a silence that throbbed with joyous expectation.'

Grimble paddled about 80 yards offshore, dropped over the baited hook and made the line fast. The rest is best left to him. 'I had certainly hoped for a quick bite, if only to save my face, but I was altogether unready for the fulminating success that fell upon me. I was not yet settled back in my seat when the canoe took a shuddering leap backwards and my nose hit the foredeck. A roar went up from the crowd as I was drawn whizzing away from it on my face. I picked myself up with much care . . . the shark reversed direction. The back of my head cracked down on the deck behind me; my legs flew up; my high-riding bottom was presented to the sightseers shooting at incredible speed toward them.

'In the next fifteen minutes, without one generous pause, that shark contrived to jerk, twist or bounce from my body for public exhibition every ignoble attitude of which a gangling frame, lost to all self-respect in a wild scrabble for handholds, is capable. The climax of its malice was in its last act. It floated belly up and allowed itself to be hauled alongside as if quite dead. I piloted it so into the shallows. There I tottered to my feet to deliver the *coup-de-grace*. But it flipped as the club swung down; I missed, hit the sea, somersaulted over its body, and stood on my head under water with legs impotently flapping in the air.

'This filled the cup of the villagers. As I waded ashore there was not a soul on his feet. The beach was a sea of rolling brown bodies racked on the extremity of joy, incapable of any sound but a deep and tortured groaning. I crept silently from their presence to the seclusion of my home. When my cook-boy was able to stand, he staggered back and told me the point of it. A Gilbertese youth is trained to sit a bucking canoe about as carefully as we are taught to ride. It takes him a year or so to master the technique. That was why the villagers had turned up . . . and gone away fulfilled. But they despatched the shark before leaving. . . . A few days later, the jaws, beautifully dried and cleaned, were sent to me, the champion of the wooden hook, as a consolation prize.'

The tope, *Galeorhinus galeus*, does not equal the sundry exertions of the tiger shark, but it figures prominently in the British sport fishery and allied or synonymous species, just which has yet to be determined, are or were commercially important elsewhere. Also, *G. galeus* presents an interesting problem in distribution.

Otherwise known in Britain as the toper, penny dog, miller's dog (after the light coloured young) and rig (after what we can not say), the tope is a smallish shark. Females reach about $6\frac{1}{2}$ feet and 100 pounds, males about 6 feet and 60 pounds with the average 65 and 45 pounds respectively.

The slender-bodied tope is dark grey, blue or brown above, light below. Its teeth, similar in both jaws, are notched on the outer margin and the lower part of the notch is divided into two to five cusps or points. Its diet is in the main small bottom fishes such as flounder and small pelagic fishes such as mackerel. Its migrations are made along the shore as well as from inshore to off and back again. Probably, the species is sexually mature at 5 feet and litters number some 30 pups 11 to 14 inches long.

The performance of the tope on rod and reel is, it would seem, variable. 'A good one,' notes a British angling author, 'will curvet and bore, leap and thresh, using every ounce of strength in its body. Others come sullenly to gaff with only the merest swirl of protest.'

None the less, the creature is hard sought by sporting Britons and the current rod and reel record weighed 74 pounds 11 ounces and was caught in 1964 at Caldy Island, Wales. The I.G.F.A. has not ordained *G. galeus* a game fish.

In Australia the genus is represented by *Galeorhinus australis*, the so-called school shark, which is commercially exploited as a food fish (more about that in another chapter) and which is regarded as no boon to anglers. 'Harmless to swimmers,' Whitley says in *The Fishes of Australia*, 'but mischievous to man indirectly, since this shark delights to bite the bodies and tails off snapper and other fish as the anglers are hauling them in. Thus the fishermens' only reward is a series of fish heads and the doubtful satisfaction of knowing that they have afforded the sharks a pleasant afternoon's amusement.'

In North America, the representative of the genus is *Galeorhinus zyopterus* which is known as the soupfin shark, because its fins make for a fine soup, or as the oil shark, because its liver is exceptionally rich in oil. Whichever, the creature ranges from British Columbia to southern California.

It is in North America, however, that we encounter the problem of distribution. For, while the tope is otherwise a coastal cosmopolitan, it simply does not exist on the North American east coast and ichthyologists are at a loss to explain why.

A Matter of Controversy

Lake Nicaragua, in the Central American country of Nicaragua, is about 110 miles long, 45 miles wide at the widest and with a surface area of 2,972 square miles, is the largest body of fresh water between the United States and Peru. To the north it is connected to the smaller Lake Managua by the Río Tipitapa. To the south it is drained by the broad Río San Juan which flows some 100 miles down to the Caribbean Sea. But the provocative thing about Lake Nicaragua—also known as Mar Dulce or the Sweet Sea—is that it has in it four species of marine fishes. It has the tarpon, *Tarpon atlanticus*. It has two species of sawfish of the genus *Pristis* which is related to sharks. And it has, the specifics of which later, sharks themselves. Moreover, they are dangerous sharks.

First literary mention of the lake and its marine fauna was made by the Spanish historian Oviedo y Valdez in 1526, only six years after the discovery of Nicaragua, in his *De la Natural Hystoria de las Indias*. Centuries afterwards, in 1852, Ephraim G. Squier—a journalist, archaeologist and for a short time the United States *chargé d'affaires* in Central America—characterized Oviedo as 'usually very accurate in matters of this kind' and went on to say: '. . . sharks abound in the lake. They are called "tigrones" from their rapacity. Instances are known of their having attacked and killed bathers within a stone's throw of the beach at Granada, and I have myself repeatedly seen them from the walls of the old castle, dashing about, with their fins projecting above the water.'

Then, in 1948, the American ichthyologists Henry B. Bigelow and William C. Schroeder, both associated with the Museum of

Carcharhinus leucas, **the bull shark, the subject of controversy, confusion and universal respect.**

Comparative Zoology at Harvard and the Woods Hole Oceanographic Institution on Cape Cod, published the still definitive work on sharks of the western North Atlantic. Its somewhat ponderous title is in the bibliography at the back of this book, but the authors comment thus on the nature of the Lake Nicaragua shark: 'It is reputedly a danger to bathers, as well as to any dog that may venture into the lake. And published accounts of its ferocity appear to be well founded, for a correspondent in whom we have full confidence reports that he has not only seen an attack on a youth swimming at San Carlos but has heard of actual fatalities at other localities around the lake. Very recently the press has reported attacks on bathers and fishermen at Granada, where one of the victims lost an arm, while another lost his right leg and had his left leg injured.'

There is, obviously, no question about the proclivities of the Lake Nicaragua shark. The question is, and has been for almost a century, how the shark got into the lake and whether it was land-locked there. To Oviedo, who continued to write about the region until 1557, the answer was clear. 'There are in this lake (or these lakes, if you think there are several) many and good fish. But I believe it to be one single lake, and there is a good reason for it, which is that it contains very large sea fish, and from the sea they come into it, such as sharks. . . . And what confirms and affirms my belief that it is only one lake and in communication with the sea, is that in the year 1529 I found on the coast of this lake . . . a dead fish that the waters must have thrown out, and which no man ever saw or caught but in the sea; it is called the sword fish, the one that carries a high snout at the extremity of the upper jaw; that ferocious sword full of sharp-edged teeth (on both edges) closely spaced. And this one I found dead, out of the lake, must have come into it by said outlet . . . .'

Oviedo's 'sword fish' was a sawfish and he was satisfied that it had traversed the Río San Juan from the sea into Lake Nicaragua. The fact is, and ichthyologists have long known it, that the kinds of marine fish found in Lake Nicaragua commonly do traverse rivers. The American scientists Theodore Gill and J. F. Bransford knew it in 1877 when they became the first to describe and name the Lake Nicaragua shark. They called the creature *Eulamia nicaraguensis*, since changed to *Carcharhinus nicaraguensis*, and expressed the opinion that it was most closely related to the sandbar shark *Carcharhinus milberti*, a species of wide inshore distribution including the Caribbean Sea. But, while Gill and Bransford granted that there were sharks throughout the length of the Río San Juan, they condescendingly rejected Oviedo. 'The worthy chronicler,' they wrote, 'must not be judged too harshly for his assumptions respecting the communicability between the sea and lake, because of the presence of sawfish and other marine types. In our days naturalists have based hypotheses and classifications upon even less data and in spite of known facts . . . the numerous rapids of the river discharging from the lake discourage, however, the idea that the species enumerated [tarpon, sawfish and the shark] have voluntarily ascended that river and entered the lake.'

Gill and Bransford theorized that Lake Nicaragua was once an inlet of the Pacific; that in distant times an uplift of land sealed off the inlet and trapped the tarpon, sawfish and sharks. Lake Nicaragua's marine species were, in short, of Pacific origin.

Over the years the geological aspect of the theory became entrenched. The faunal aspect, however, became increasingly disturbing to ichthyologists. The tarpon, *Tarpon atlanticus*, was not known to exist in the Pacific, but was abundant in the Caribbean. One species of the lake sawfish, *Pristis perotteti*, was seemingly the same as the species in the Caribbean. And the shark, apparently, was *Carcharhinus leucas*—the bull, cub, or ground shark—or a close relative; and *C. leucas* was and is notorious for penetrating up rivers for a great distance. *C. milberti*, the sandbar shark to which Gill and Bransford likened the lake shark, frequents the mouths of rivers, but does not make long upstream excursions.

The theory needed revision and, in 1953 in his book, *High Jungles and Low*, the respected American naturalist and author Archie Carr revised it. Carr did not challenge Gill and Bransford on the formation of Lake Nicaragua. It remained a child of the Pacific. But its marine fishes did not remain children of the Pacific. According to Carr they derived from the Caribbean and freely travelled the Río San Juan until a series of earthquakes between 1630 and 1663, well after Oviedo's day, raised the rapids and landlocked tarpon, sawfish and sharks in Lake Nicaragua. Carr noted that the lake shark averages six feet in length and 150 pounds in weight and added this comment: 'Nicaraguans are immensely proud of their fresh-water shark . . . even the fact that it chews them up from time to time has engendered admiration for the spirit of the animal more than resentment. The fishermen of Lake Nicaragua look down on those of Lake Managua because they have no shark in their lake, and the Managua fishermen are quite sensitive about it.'

That Lake Managua should be barren of sharks is a bit puzzling. True, the Río Tipitapa, 15 miles long, usually has dry patches of bed in it, but periodically it does flood full and sharks or tarpon or sawfish should be able to navigate it then. In any event, Carr's theoretical revision pardoned Oviedo and made him a tacit apology on behalf of the departed Gill and Bransford. But it did not appease everybody. There were those who still refused to believe that the sharks in Lake Nicaragua were landlocked.

In 1948 Bigelow and Schroeder had presumed *C. nicaraguensis* to be landlocked and separated it from *C. leucas*, with some misgivings, on the basis of a few minor physical characteristics. In 1961 they decided that the separation was invalid. They placed *C. nicaraguensis* in the synonymy of *C. leucas* which means that the bull shark of the sea and the shark of the lake are one and the same species whether the latter is or is not landlocked. That issue, in 1961, Bigelow and Schroeder did not touch upon.

The odd part of the entire controversy over the Lake Nicaragua shark is that not until 1963 did a scientist undertake to thoroughly test, in the field and laboratory, all theories and convictions subject to testing. That year, though, Thomas B. Thorson, a zoologist at the University of Nebraska, began to, and in September 1966 in *Copeia* he and his co-workers, Donald E. Watson and C. Michael Cowan, set forth the results in a paper to which we are considerably indebted for both material and references.

Thorson points out that Gill and Bransford had in 1877 described and named their *Eulamia nicaraguensis* from a single specimen caught no one knows where in the lake or river. For their major work in 1948 Bigelow and Schroeder had only four specimens—the only ones in the United States—all caught at San Carlos where the Río San Juan leaves Lake Nicaragua. Lastly, when, in 1961, Bigelow and Schroeder declared *C. nicaraguensis* to be identical to *C. leucas*, they did so from just one specimen caught about 30 miles from the river mouth and well below the first of the rapids. 'Those taken at San Carlos,' Thorson states, 'could properly be considered a part of the lake population, but those taken in at least the lower third of the river might, if the lake sharks are landlocked, represent marine *C. leucas* wandering up the river.'

To settle the matter of species, Thorson and his party in 1963 and 1964 caught a total of 19 sharks at four separate localities from the lake's far end to the mouth of the river some 220 miles away. They made measurements, counted and compared teeth, counted vertebrae and so forth of each set of specimens. Next, they compared the sets of data. 'We can,' writes Thorson, 'only conclude that there is no substantial difference between sharks taken at different locations and that on the basis of work done so far, only one species is represented in all parts of the lake and the Río San Juan.'

The scientists placed their data against published data concerning 38 marine specimens of *C. leucas* and found 'no discernible differences'. They placed their data against the published data concerning three shark specimens from the fresh water Lake Jamoer in New Guinea and entertained 'no doubt that the Lake Jamoer population has been properly assigned to *C. leucas*'.

They placed their data against Bigelow and Schroeder's and declared themselves 'in full agreement with Bigelow and Schroeder . . . fully convinced that they were correct in placing *C. nicaraguensis* in the synonymy of *C. leucas*'.

But the lake shark could still be landlocked. And it could be landlocked even though there have been recent changes in geologically inclined thinking. Some geologists now think that the area taken up by Lake Nicaragua and Lake Managua once opened to the Caribbean rather than the Pacific. Some others think that the area never was occupied by the sea, that it was a subsidence which filled from surface drainage and spilled over and to seaward by way of what is today the Río San Juan. Nevertheless, if Carr proved to be right about the Río San Juan, the Lake Nicaragua shark would prove to be landlocked.

Thorson, in *Copeia*, traces the history of European navigation on the river and grants that in the 1600's seagoing ships virtually ceased to use it because, possibly, its navigability had been reduced by earthquakes or other geological events or by normal channel erosion. But he conjectures that changes in the riverbed would hamper large ships much more than sharks and he makes the telling point that smaller vessels have not to this day stopped using the river as a freight route.

That, however, is by no means the whole of Thorson's case. In June 1963 when the Río San Juan was lower than usual, Thorson and his associates went down it from source to mouth in an outboard-powered dugout. In June 1965 when the river was even lower, they went both down and back. At no time did the eight named rapids offer more than minor difficulty and the party watched several loaded barges making their way upstream below, in and above the rapids. The barges, 30 to 50 feet long, drew from one to three feet of water and were driven by tugs. Thorson was told that they regularly trafficked up and down the river, periods of very low water excepted, and that there were channels through all of the rapids where the barges could pass at small risk if the pilot knew the way. To Thorson, if barges of that size could navigate the Río San Juan, 'it seems completely indefensible to assume that the rapids present a barrier to the movements of such strong swimmers as sharks, or for that matter to the more sluggish sawfish.'

But Thorson still does not rest his argument. In 1965 he and the others saw sharks in the vicinity of Rápides del Toro at least three of which were right in the rapids and swimming upstream. At Rápides del Castillo, the second worst of the eight rapids, they saw sharks just above and below the rapids and two directly in the uppermost part of the main rapids. At Rápides de Machuca, the worst of the eight, they saw sharks some of which were thrashing around in the shallows and some of which were swimming freely, most often upstream.

Thorson now sums up: 'It appears to us that . . . since the sharks occur the full length of the river . . . are of the same species throughout the river and in the Caribbean Sea . . . since the rapids almost certainly do not form a barrier to the movement of sharks, there is no real basis for the belief that the shark population in the lake is landlocked. Furthermore, in view of the statements and descriptions of the river from earlier times, there is no reason to believe that there has been any change in the river bed extensive enough to affect the status of the shark. We believe it unlikely that the sharks (or the sawfish, tarpon, or any marine species that may inhabit the lake), have been barred from passage from the sea to the lake at any time since Europeans arrived in the New World, and probably not

A co-worker of zoologist Thomas Thorson tags a bull shark in the San Juan River which flows out of Lake Nicaragua. If and when it is caught again, something may be learned of the species' migratory ways.

since the river assumed its present course and elevation gradient.

'Although circumstantial evidence is now strong in support of the free communication between the Caribbean Sea and Lake Nicaragua, there is as yet no definitive proof that the sharks actually pass between them.'

While this last may seem excessively cautious, Thorson, according to the dictates of science, is quite right. Sharks of the same species were seen throughout the river and lake system, but no sharks were seen to travel from sea to lake or lake to sea because such observations just are not within the present realm of possibility. Thus, Thorson's definitive proof can only result from a tagging

A Nicaraguan holds a tagged bull shark. The tag is the disc in the dorsal fin.

programme and he has started one. Suffice to say here that tagging fish is the equivalent of ringing, or banding, birds and that Thorson's programme will probably confirm what is already highly probable. *Carcharhinus leucas*, the bull shark, does trade between the Caribbean Sea and Lake Nicaragua. And events and observations reported by the explorer–journalist Kurt Severin in 1953 may enhance that probability. Well up the Río San Juan, Severin caught one shark with a nearly dead remora still attached and another with a sea animal in its stomach. Furthermore, he found that Nicaraguans who lived by the lake made a distinction about its sharks. There were those they called *visitantes* or visitors, and those they called *tintoreros* or, literally, dyers. The first had white undersides, normal for sharks in or not a long way from the sea.

The second had brownish undersides, normal perhaps for sharks in the lake for a time under conditions of light and bottom colour that differ from the sea. Finally, Severin caught mostly *tintoreros* in the lake. Down the river he caught only *visitantes*.

Carcharhinus zambezensis and *Carcharhinus gangeticus* are without much, if any, doubt also *Carcharhinus leucas*. The former was described and named in the middle 1800's by the German ichthyologist Wilhelm Peters who gave the type locality as 120 miles from the sea in the Zambezi River in south-east Africa. About the same time two other German ichthyologists, Johannes Müller and Jacob Henle, described and named *C. gangeticus*, but a century later their handling of the type locality provoked the French ichthyologist Paul Budker to some caustic questioning. They had stated it as 'sixty hours from the sea' in the Hooghly River, a ramification of India's Ganges. 'But,' asks Budker in 1947 in his book *La Vie Des Requins*, 'what distance was covered during these sixty hours, and by what means? By canoe? By sailing vessel (with or against the wind)? On foot? On horseback? By swimming? . . . one can only suppose that these sixty hours on the way, by going upstream in the Houghly [sic], places our shark in a region where the water is perfectly fresh.'

Budker's pique aside, one's first swim in the Zambezi or the Ganges could be, as it could in Lake Nicaragua or the Río San Juan, one's last. Bearing in mind, however, that *C. zambezensis* and *C. gangeticus* are in all likelihood *C. leucas*, the same can be and has been said of the east coast of Africa. In 1962 in the *Journal of the Royal Naval Medical Service* the late David H. Davies, South Africa's authority on shark attack, and G. D. Campbell, a physician, reported that: 'In a detailed examination of eleven cases of shark attack with specific reference to the species of shark involved it has been possible to make one certain identification . . . by examination of tooth fragments . . . extracted from the femur of the victim . . . and ten probable identifications from wound characteristics. In these eleven attacks it appears that only two species of shark were involved and that out of the eleven . . . ten attacks were almost certainly made by the Zambezi River Shark, *Carcharhinus zambezensis* Peters, known locally as the Shovel-nosed grey or Slipway Grey. . . . The evidence in favour of *C. zambezensis* being the most dangerous species . . . in the Natal area is considerable. . . . It is always inclined to be offensive . . . a particularly ferocious species which will attack large fish without apparent provocation and not for food.'

The attack in the aftermath of which Davies was able to positively identify *C. zambezensis* as the malefactor occurred on Christmas Eve 1960 at Margate, a resort town on the east coast of Natal. At 4:30 in the afternoon Petrus Sithole, a young man of 25, was swimming just outside the shark barrier which protects the beach. He was heard to scream and with arms flailing the upper half of his body rose vertically out of the water. Then he stopped screaming and fell forward. Two nearby swimmers made no effort to help him. Waves washed him toward the shore and a man standing on the beach waded out to meet him. He was dead. The shark had taken off both legs, the left one at the hip, the right at the knee.

In the preface to *The Fishes of India*, 1878, we find Francis Day's estimation of his labours. 'The work I now present to the notice of the reader is, I believe, the only attempt which has yet been made to publish a fairly complete account of the Ichthyology of our Indian Empire.' Some 710 pages further on we find his somewhat contradictory estimation of sharks, *C. gangeticus* included. 'Sharks are found all along the coasts of India, but their carrying off human prey is not a common occurrence. The most savage species appear to be the ground sharks of the rivers, as *Carcharias Gangeticus*, [an early synonym], which seldom loses an opportunity of attacking the bather. The *Galeocerdo Rayneri* [tiger shark], is likewise dreaded along the coast or in the harbours. Though stationed several years at Cachin, I could only ascertain a single instance of a living human being having been carried off by these fishes.'

But on page 715 Day again gauges *C. gangeticus*: 'This is one of the most ferocious of Indian sharks, and frequently attacks bathers even in the Hooghly at Calcutta, where it is so dreaded that a reward is offered for each that is captured.'

Day offers no figures to justify his use of the word frequently, but for 1880 in the Hooghly, it was noted in the *Indian Medical Gazette:* 'At Pannihattu, Barrackpore, Dackhineshwar, Barahonagore, Kashipur and Chitpur down to Baug Bazar Ghats more than 20 persons have been severely bitten by sharks this year. Almost all were fatal.'

We think that to be unexceptional even though reports from India are at best spotty. However, from July to September of 1959 at Machgaon near the mouth of the Devi River, also in north-east India, sharks killed five people and injured 30 more.

To Africa and India can be added Iran. In the Karun River between 1941 and 1951, a decade during which allied military authorities kept the record, there were 27 shark attacks near Ahwaz 90 miles from the Persian Gulf. Fourteen of the attacks were fatal and all were made in very shallow water. In one instance, a British soldier had driven an ambulance into the river to wash it. A shark took hold of his ankle and pulled him down. He managed to fight it off, but almost lost his right leg and had both arms badly lacerated and in water little more than a foot deep. The Karun, incidentally, is a tributary of the Tigris and Euphrates and sharks have attacked in that river system too.

The fact is that sharks are now known to frequent fresh waters and waterways the warm world over. They have not, except in South Africa and Lake Jamoer in New Guinea, been accorded quite the scientific attention as have those in Lake Nicaragua, but their presence has been noted none the less and in many localities above and beyond the ones already mentioned. In North America sharks are found, though irregularly, in the Atchafalaya River in Louisiana and the Pascagoula River in Mississippi. In Central America they are found in the Patuca River in Honduras and the Lake Izabal-Río Dulce system of Guatemala, the latter being the object of another investigation by Thorson. In South America sharks are found in Lake Maracaibo in Venezuela and in a plenitude of east coast rivers from the Magdalena in Colombia to the Río de la Plata in southern Uruguay. In Africa they are found on the west coast in the Senegal River in Senegal and the Gambia River in Gambia; on the east coast they are found in any number of rivers from the Ogooué in Gabon to the St. Lucia Lake system of South Africa. In Asia they are found in the Perak River in Malaya, the Saigon River in Vietnam, the Rewa River of the island of Viti

Levu in the Fijis and in Laguna de Bay (a lake), Lake Naujon, the Agusan and Saug rivers in the Philippines. In Australia they are found in the Liverpool and Victoria Rivers in the Northern Territory and in the Swan River in Western Australia; in eastern Queensland and New South Wales they are found in the rivers Ross, Burnett, Brisbane, Macleay, Parramatta and Georges and in Lake Macquarie.

The foregoing should not be taken as an all-inclusive directory to the peregrinations of sharks in rivers and ·lakes. Nor should the sharks be taken as all *C. leucas*. In the brackish lower reaches of sea-connected rivers, and some lakes, other species too may congregate. But sharks found in truly fresh water—and they have been so found in nearly all of the places just listed—are probably *C. leucas* and it follows that sharks which attack in truly fresh water—be it in Central America or Australia or elsewhere—are probably the same species, *C. leucas*, a species known to also attack in bays, harbours, estuaries and the coastal sea itself.

The bull shark, the vernacular name we will use, is white below, pale grey above when living over pale bottom and dark grey when living over dark bottom. The species is distinguished from possibly all other carcharhinids except the lemon shark, *Negaprion brevirostris*, and the whitetip, *Carcharhinus longimanus*, by its very short, very broadly rounded snout and by the absence from its back of a low ridge between the two dorsal fins. But, it is in turn distinguished from the lemon shark by its teeth which are serrate from base to tip. And it is distinguished from the whitetip most obviously by the shorter, broader and unmarked pectorals.

The teeth in the upper jaw of the bull shark are triangular and their serrations are moderately coarse. The two middle teeth are nearly symmetrical with slightly concave edges. Toward the corners of the mouth, though, the inner edges remain faintly concave or almost straight while the outer edges become more and more concave until the last three or four teeth are decidedly notched. In the lower jaw the teeth are also triangular, but much narrower, more finely serrate and they are set on wide bases.

Bull sharks are stocky and adult females usually weigh more than males. In a recently published study of the sharks in Florida waters, 11 male bull sharks weighed from 174 to 253 pounds and averaged 209; 11 females of the same length weighed from 197 to 339 pounds and averaged 284. Also females may be more often longer. Of the 129 bull sharks caught during the Florida project, from January 1955 to December, 1963, 14 females as against two males were 8 feet long. Bull sharks do reach 10 feet but specimens of that length are few and far between and 8 feet is longer than the mean.

In the western Atlantic the bull shark is resident from southern Florida south through the West Indies to southern Brazil. Summer finds migrants on the northern coast of the Gulf of Mexico and on the Atlantic coast north to North Carolina. Occasionally, a stray strays on to New York shores. Within its normal western Atlantic range—whether it ranges the eastern Atlantic is not yet clear—the bull shark is perhaps the most abundant of large inshore shark species and with its penchant for harbours and estuaries is the large shark most frequently caught from docks, bridges and piers.

Indications are that western Atlantic bull sharks mate in early summer and litters averaging five to six pups 30 inches long are born in estuaries about a year later. Bull sharks in South Africa, where ichthyologists at the Oceanographic Research Institute in Durban have been and are investigating the species, seem to follow the same seasonal breeding pattern and their seasonal abundance in South Africa corresponds closely in time to their seasonal abundance in the United States. Bull shark habits in other parts of the world may also closely correspond but the present lack of data makes comparison impossible.

Though at distinct odds with knowledge of the animal's propensities, the bull shark in the United States was long treated as an inoffensive dolt and Stewart Springer gave the only explanation we are aware of in 1963 in *Sharks and Survival*, a book of many authors and the outgrowth of an AIBS symposium. 'Before I really accepted the possibility that bull sharks could be dangerous,' Springer wrote, 'I encountered some while I was wading in waist-deep water at Cat Island in Mississippi Sound, and I found them so docile that I was able to give a couple of them a shove. Now that I have had more experience with the power of these sharks, I realize that I was lucky not to get my ribs cracked or at least a severe abrasion from the meeting. Actually, these bull sharks were probably females that had entered the shallows to give birth to their young and were, at that time, inhibited from feeding. In view of the abundance of bull sharks on summer days near beaches of the northern Gulf of Mexico, it is remarkable that this is not an area of frequent attack on bathers. I attribute the lack of attacks, by the bull shark at least, to the feeding inhibition of females in nursing areas.' A few years later, Springer made somewhat more succinct comment about the same incident. 'In defense of my own sanity,' he reflected, 'I did this [shoved the sharks] long ago when I did not believe that sharks attack man.'

Springer does not discuss male bull sharks because none are there. Except in the mating season, the males and females of an undetermined number of shark species shun one another. The phenomenon is called sexual segregation—another subject we will later enlarge upon—and it explains why presumably uninhibited bull shark males do not visit nursery grounds and attack nearby bathers. But where such special circumstances do not prevail, the bull shark is probably answerable for more attacks in the southern United States than once suspected. After all, the food preferences of the creature make it about as fussy as the tiger shark. Possibly, though, the bull shark is notable among all sharks for its inclination to feed on young sharks of other species and particularly on the young of its near relative *Carcharhinus milberti*, the sandbar shark.

Although the pieces of the bull shark's life history are falling into place, there are pieces enough yet to fall. Some would tell whether the creature enters fresh water randomly or purposively. Some would tell how long it stays in fresh water and whether it also breeds there. Some would tell how it makes the physiological adjustment to fresh water and this involves another fundamental difference between sharks and bony fishes.

The process called osmosis dictates that if a membrane more permeable to water than salts separates two solutions containing unequal quantities of salts, the water will pass from the weaker solution to the stronger one until the strength of the two is equal. In fishes, such permeable membranes include the delicate layers of skin that cover the gill filaments and the mucous membranes in the mouth and throat. Now, without exception, the body fluids of marine teleosts are less salty than sea water. These creatures, therefore, are ever losing water to the sea and to preserve their vital internal fluid balance, they must literally drink sea water and then dispose of excess salts.

Sharks take an opposite avenue. They retain in their blood an amount of urea that would poison any other vertebrate animal. They also retain a small amount of trimethylamine oxide and, thanks to these two waste products, the body fluids of sharks are a bit more salty than sea water. So there is no need for sharks to drink. The water they require enters through their permeable membranes. That being the case, however, bull sharks which invade such a weak solution as fresh water ought to become decidedly and perhaps even fatally water-logged. But they do not. The fluid volumes of bull sharks in fresh water and bull sharks in salt water are remarkably similar. Why, is thus far inexplicable.

CHAPTER 7 | # To See One
is
To Know One

Samuel Latham Mitchill in *The Fishes of New York*, 1815, tells us that September 1805 saw Joshua Turry of Riverhead, Long Island net three hammerhead sharks. 'The largest,' Mitchill reports, 'was eleven feet long. On opening him, many detached parts of a man were found in his belly; these were collected and buried; there was also found a striped cotton shirt, patched on the sides and sleeves with bright-colored pieces.'

The hammerheads, the sharks of the family Sphyrnidae, are related to the carcharhinids and could be taken for such were it not for their heads. But to see a hammerhead is to know one. The head is flat and extended laterally to look, in some species, like the bar of a T. In other species the head is less extended and more rounded to look like a bonnet. In all species the eyes are at the tips of the head and in all species save one the nostrils are at the outer forecorners.

According to a revision of the sphyrnids in 1967 by Carter R. Gilbert of the University of Florida, there are nine known species one of which is divisible into two subspecies. For the moment, however, we will confine ourselves to the three species that are large and ubiquitous.

Sphyrna mokarran (until revision *S. tudes*), the great hammerhead, reaches 15 feet and there is record of one that measured 18 feet 4 inches. *S. zygaena*, the common hammerhead, reaches at least 12 feet as does *S. lewini* (until revision *S. diplana*) which seems to have no generally accepted vernacular name other than, simply, the hammerhead. A fourth sizeable species, *S. couardi*, seems to have no vernacular name, seems to be restricted in range to West Africa and, seemingly, that is the present state of knowledge. The remaining three are vigorous sharks of the sea's surface layers. They are more abundant inshore than off and are often found in brackish water. *S. mokarran* and *S. lewini* inhabit the tropics, *S. zygaena* the fringes of the tropics and warm temperate zones. All are seasonal rovers moving in the summertime, as the hemispheric case may be, to the north or to the south. *S. zygaena*, though, the common hammerhead, moves much the farthest into cool provinces and does so in schools such as the one encountered by the *Santa Catalina* just north of Cape Hatteras on July 21, 1955. As later described by L. W. Bryant, a ship's officer who watched the school for some five hours, 'there were never less than 12 sharks visible to the naked eye at any time and at times as many as 20. Many more were seen with the aid of binoculars. Estimates of the total number ran as high as 1,200 . . . from 6 to 12 feet in length. They were heading in a generally NE'ly direction. . . .'

On the North American east coast, then, *S. zygaena* regularly makes its summer way as far north as southern New England— and occasionally as far north as Nova Scotia and the Grand Banks of Newfoundland—and remains until the autumn water temperature lowers to about 67°F. Seldom will *S. mokarran* or *S. lewini* be seen where the water is more than a degree or two below 75°F. or, on the North American east coast again, seldom north of the Carolinas. Elsewhere in the world ocean, similar water temperatures probably set similar migratory limits.

While one or another of the four large hammerhead species occupies either the eastern Atlantic or the Mediterranean or both, a hammerhead rarely happens into British waters. Francis Day, in *The Fishes of Great Britain and Ireland*, 1880–1884, could cite just five, all presumed to be *S. zygaena*, but among the five is the largest on British record. 'July 31, 1865, one, 13 ft. 7 in. long, was perceived floundering among the rocks at Ilfracombe; it was secured by ropes and towed inland . . . two thornbacks and a bass were found inside it. . . .'

The size is a bit unusual for *S. zygaena* anywhere. The presence of the thornbacks, *Raja radiata*, which is a species of skate, is not.

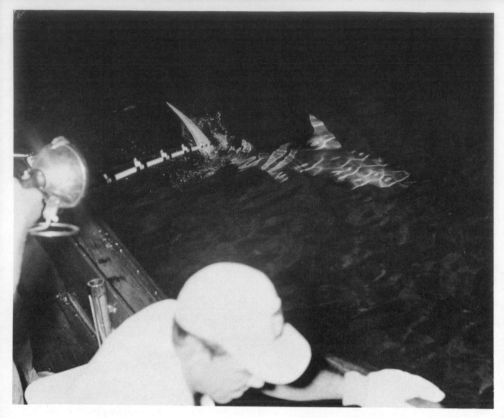

Anglers fight a hammerhead shark at night in the Bahamas.

Hammerheads show a marked liking for skates and rays despite the fact that many ray species, the so-called stingrays or whiprays, have on the tail one or more barbed and venomous spines. Circe, says Oppian, knew about stingrays and gave her son a spear tipped with a spine from one. Straight away, the lad tried it out on his father's goats and:

> 'Around the Plain contagious slaughter made,
> and in rank Heaps the bearded Victims laid.'

When the father protested he went the way of the goats.

In natural circumstances the venom of some stingray species can indeed be sometimes fatal to man or beast. Still it is manifestly no

At daylight, the catch is brought aboard. Science, incidentally, cannot yet explain the function of the strangely shaped head.

bother to the large hammerheads. One, for example, 12 feet 6 inches long and taken in North Carolina, had in its throat, mouth and jaws 54 spines, some freshly embedded. 'But for all these accumulated stings,' its captor reported, 'this shark was a living dynamo of energy when harpooned.'

Hammerheads also feed on hammerheads and in the May issue of *Copeia* in 1919 there is a report by Russell J. Coles, then active in the commercial fishery, in which he describes the enterprise of a female *S. zygaena* nearly 14 feet long. 'At the time of her capture,' Coles writes, 'she had just eaten four of her species from my net, two of which had been swallowed whole, except the head of 5 ft. examples, and there were four cleanly-cut pieces which represented entire bodies, except heads, of two more 6 ft. hammerhead sharks; then the stomach contained more than a peck of vertebrae of sharks. . . .'

The disjointed somebody mentioned by Mitchill in 1815 may well have been dead before his rendezvous with the hammerhead. But it is a certainty nonetheless that hammerheads constitute a menace. They have, in recent years and twice with fatal result, attacked swimmers or boats in Australia, British Guiana, the United States and Mexico where, at Mazatlan on the west coast, five species are harvested for table food. 'Of the five,' writes Anatalio Hernandez Carvallo in *Sharks, Skates and Rays*, 1967, the product of another AIBS symposium, '*S. zygaena* is the most familiar and probably the most dangerous when attacked by harpoon or fish spear, often charging the boat head-on and capsizing it.'

For a while, roughly from the late 1930's and throughout the 1940's, large hammerheads were valuable merchandise in Mexico and the United States too. Vitamin A was in demand and hammerhead livers were a rich source of it. One Florida catch, for instance, yielded an extraordinary 357,000 units of Vitamin A per gram of liver oil and priced the shark at $500. But even a much less extraordinary 55,000 units per gram brought $150 and it was a grey day for shark fishermen when Vitamin A was synthesized and the hammerhead remanded to economic modesty.

The sphyrnid species thus far discussed can be identified with comparative ease from heads, fins or teeth. All have T-bar heads but the head of *S. zygaena*, if one looks down upon it, has a nearly unbroken front edge. The heads of *S. mokarran* and *S. lewini* have front edges broken in the middle by a scallop-shaped dent. However, *S. mokarran* is the only sphyrnid with deeply falcate pectoral fins and pronouncedly serrate teeth. The teeth of *S. zygaena* are smooth to finely serrate, the latter in large individuals, while those of *S. lewini* are smooth always. *S. couardi*, it is reported, has white-tipped pectorals.

The five other species of hammerhead are small—four to five feet long at the longest—and geographically localized. *S. tudes* (until revision *S. mokarran*) ranges from the Gulf of Mexico south to Uruguay and is found elsewhere only in the western Mediterranean, a pattern of distribution that is unusual and to date inexplicable. *S. media* ranges from Baja California to Panama in the eastern Pacific and from Panama to Brazil in the western Atlantic. *S. corona* ranges only the eastern Pacific and there only from southern Mexico to Colombia and that makes it the most parochial of hammerheads.

S. tiburo, in its turn, has the roundest of hammerhead heads—therefore the vernacular names bonnethead, shovelhead or shovelnose shark—and is divided into a pair of subspecies. *S. tiburo tiburo* is found in coastal shallows from New England to southern Brazil. *S. tiburo vespertina* is found in like waters from southern California to Ecuador. It has a slightly broader and more pointed head than its Atlantic counterpart but, the overall difference between the two is not enough to allow a clean split into species.

On the night of November 22, 1962 L. A. Stanley, a commercial fisherman, saw an enormous school of fish churning the surface within 200 yards of shore at Sarasota, Florida. Convinced that the fish were Spanish mackerel, Stanley and his helper set a gill net. An hour later they hauled it back brimming full of gilled bonnetheads, well over 700 of them, two to three feet long. It took the men six hours to clear the net of this unwelcome, rough-hided bounty and their hands were left raw.

What impels these dense gatherings is open to question. They are not often observed and they do not seem to have a seasonal correlation. Among the sphyrnids, though, *S. tiburo* is the one species now known to so gather.

S. blochii, the last in this summary of the Sphyrnidae, ranges the Indo-Pacific from northern Australia to the southern Philippines. It is the hammerhead in which the nostrils, instead of being at the outer forecorners of the head, are more than half the distance from eyes to midline. The head itself is from side to side the widest and from front to back the narrowest of the hammerhead lot. In length it measures up to 50 per cent of total body length and from above the lobes look much like the moderately swept back wings of an aircraft.

In the matter of reproduction, the number of young in a hammerhead litter appears to be directly proportional to the size of the female and the maximum size of the species. The smallest brood on record, eight pups about nine inches long, was found in *S. tiburo*, the bonnethead; the largest, 38 pups about 22 inches long, in *S. mokarran*, the great hammerhead.

Finally, it would be interesting to know why the sphyrnids, otherwise typical sharks, developed such atypical heads. One theory, often stated as fact, is that they act as bow rudders and enhance manoeuverability; a second is that they compensate for the presumably poor forward lift of the small hammerhead pectoral fins; a third is that the distribution of sensory pores on wide heads affords some advantage in finding food. Now, there may be virtue in these theories, but they are still theories. None yet has been tested.

The Carcharhinidae and their specialized kinsmen the Sphyrnidae are successful and dominating sharks. But in fleetness and streamlined brawn they must give way to the mackerel sharks of the family Isuridae.

The Isuridae, at a time known as the Lamnidae, are a small family of three genera and perhaps just four species with, physically, much in common. The isurid head is conical, the chest deep. The tail is lunate and almost symmetrical and on either side of its stem are longitudinal keels, the seeming function of which is to stiffen the tail assembly and reduce turbulence. The gill openings are very large and probably answer to isurid energy and the consequent large demand for oxygen. The teeth are very alike in both jaws but differ from species to species.

Lamna nasus is an isurid with a place in the ecclesiastical, sporting and natural history of Great Britain. According to Day, *L. nasus* was first described by 'Dr. Caius, from a specimen stranded in Suffolk, between Lowestoft and Pakefield, February, 1570.' No other author seems to have so credited Joannes Caius, but he is remembered nonetheless. A naturalist, he studied divinity, successfully turned to medicine and letters and, in 1557, endowed Gonville and Caius College, Cambridge.

The most commonly used common name of *L. nasus*, porbeagle, the fitting amalgam of porpoise and beagle, first appeared on the printed page in 1758 in *The Natural History of Cornwall* by the Reverend William Borlase and therein also was the first illustration of the beast, executed early in the century, by the Reverend Georges Jago, '*Curé de Cornuailles*', of Looe, Cornwall. Another common name, the Beaumaris shark, first emerged in the 1776 edition of *British Zoology* by Thomas Pennant who acknowledged that a specimen had been observed at Beaumaris, Wales by his friend the Reverend Hugh Davies. Pennant, though, treated the porbeagle and the Beaumaris shark as distinct species and for 65 years British naturalists generally followed suit.

'According to Risso,' wrote Couch of the porbeagle in 1868, 'it is an article of food in the Mediterranean, and he goes so far as to say that as such it is much esteemed. This is a piece of luxury to which our [British] fishermen and the public have not yet attained; and consequently with us it is only employed as manure'.

Shark meat spoils rapidly and as it does ammonia is all too detectably released. Fresh or properly processed, however, the meat of many shark species compares well with that of edible teleosts. Still, while sharks are harvested on oceanic perimeters for local consumption, few species are important as food fish on a large commercial scale and one reason of consequence is that to much of mankind the shark is not just a fish let alone an admirably able fish. Rather, as phrased by the American naturalist and sportsman Charles Frederick Holder in 1913: 'If I had not known it was a shark, I would have been satisfied, but the taint of vermin was there.'

It happens that the porbeagle is a commercially important shark. In the middle 1960's Norway's yearly catch of the species was close to 9 million pounds—in rounded figures then worth $2,700,000— and virtually all of it was being exported to Italy where, in this day as in Couch's, porbeagle is made a meal of. But also in the middle 1960's it became evident that the porbeagle was being too hard pressed by the fisherman. Norway had to limit her North Atlantic catch and if minds boggle at the very idea of conserving sharks it still stands that sharks are not an inexhaustible resource. Some species, in fact, since they grow slowly or bear few young or both, are particularly vulnerable to over-exploitation and the porbeagle, although its growth rate is not known, seems to be among them. Porbeagle pups are large, up to 24 inches in length and 20 pounds in weight, but there are only one to four in a litter.

Couch's comment on the British palate for porbeagle also pertains today. In 1966 British commercial fishermen landed 12,000 pounds of the species and pocketed $1,800. However, British sport fishermen, who value the spirit of the animal, now land not several thousand pounds of porbeagle but several thousand porbeagles every summer season, and appropriately, most are landed at Looe in Cornwall where the Reverend Jago first sketched *L. nasus* in the cause of science.

L. ditropis of the North American west coast and Japan, *L. philippii* of Chile and *L. whitleyi* of Australia and New Zealand are, it seems probable, none other than *L. nasus* and we will risk terming the species pantemperate. In European waters the porbeagle is common from the Mediterranean to southern Scandinavia and no rarity off northern Norway and Iceland. In the waters of North America, a very few strays excepted, the porbeagle is common only from southern New England to Nova Scotia and from northern California to southern Alaska. Nowhere is the species thought to be migratory in the sense that it travels along the coast. Instead, it moves onshore with the warm months and off with the cold ones to stay the winter beneath the surface.

The porbeagle's other vernacular names—herring shark,

mackerel shark, salmon shark—are not all-inclusive. The creature also forages on flatfishes, cod, whiting, squids and whatnot and to the commercial fisherman not commercially interested in the porbeagle it is an outrage which thieves from his lines and nets and makes a costly mess of them. The porbeagle's generic name *Lamna*, so say Norman and Fraser, 'is derived from a Greek word for a horrible monster of man-eating tendencies, a creature used by the ancient Greeks to terrify naughty children.'

At a maximum size of 10 to 12 feet and over 500 pounds, and even at an average size of 5 to 6 feet and under 300 pounds, the porbeagle is potentially dangerous. But it does not often poke about the shallows, few swimmers share its choice of water 65°F. or cooler and for perhaps these reasons it has not been linked to an attack on man.

Two characteristics differentiate *L. nasus* from the other Isuridae. It is the only isurid with a small secondary caudal keel just below and a bit abaft the primary keel and it is the only one with teeth that are flanked at the base by a small point. The points are called basal cusps and they lend a porbeagle tooth the look of a tall and narrow spire rising between two lesser ones.

On August 25, 1955 a shark was caught off Looe that measured 8 feet 7 inches, weighed 352 pounds and was claimed as a porbeagle of angling record dimensions. Then somebody took a careful look at it. It had primary caudal keels, but no secondary ones. It had slender, smooth-edged teeth, but no basal cusps. It was, therefore, not a porbeagle. It was another isurid, a mako, the species *Isurus oxyrinchus*, and the mako was not known to be a part of Britain's shark repertoire. Now it is and there is excellent testimony that, although somehow unrecognized, it has been all along. The teeth depicted and described as porbeagle teeth by Couch in 1868, on page 41 of a *History of the Fishes of the British Islands*, are obviously mako teeth.

I. oxyrinchus is an oceanic cosmopolite. It is found everywhere and its seasonal range in temperate regions approximates that of the porbeagle. It grows to 12 feet and 1,000 pounds and probably larger, but in the middle sizes of 5 to 7 feet is more slimly built than

The jaws of a mako shark, *Isurus oxyrinchus.*

A rare and ghost-like view of a mako shark, *Isurus oxyrinchus*, in its own element.

the porbeagle. It is also more the surface shark and a lovely one at that. Its back is the deep blue of the surrounding sea, its belly a glittering white. Details of its reproductive ways are scant, but mako young are understood to be large, over 20 inches long, and there may be ten, give or take a few, to a brood.

Run-of-the-mill makos feed on much the same fish as porbeagles. Large makos may turn to more commanding prey such as the swordfish, or broadbill, *Xiphias gladius*, which, in good health, is no easy mark. It equals the mako in size and quickness and its upper jaw juts forward to form a sharp-edged, pointed, laterally flattened sword—a third as long as the fish itself—for the skewering or clubbing of whatever takes its fancy.

In 1823 the whale ship *Fortune* out of Plymouth, Massachusetts 'was struck near the floor timbers about midships by a swordfish whose sword went through the copper and thence through a $\frac{3}{4}$ inch white oak plank, a 9-inch white oak timber, and a $2\frac{1}{2}$ inch white oak ceiling, into the hold; then it passed through a white oak

1-inch stave into an oil cask, leaving the point the distance of an inch and a half in the oil. The sword broke off 2 or 3 inches from the outside of the ship and remained about 10 months when it was discovered at Talcahuano [Chile] harbor. During this time she leaked in moderate weather 250 strokes and sailing quick 130 strokes per hour. . . .'

The Norfolk, Virginia *Landmark* in February of 1876 reported that when the leaking brig *P. M. Tinker* was hauled 'it was discovered that the leak was caused by a sword-fish, the sword being broken off forward the bands, about sixteen feet abaft the forefoot. The fish, in striking the vessel, must have come with great force, as the sword penetrated the copper sheathing, a four-inch birch plank, and through the timbers about six inches . . . in all about ten inches. . . . The men were kept steady at the pumps until her arrival. . . .'

The American ichthyologist George Brown Goode remarked in 1883: 'Such instances could be found by the score, if one had the time and patience to search. The thing happens many times, and nearly as often affords a text for some paragrapher or local editor.'

Pieces of snapped off swords have also been found in whales but, while eccentricity cannot be altogether discounted, most rammed ships or whales are the probable result of swordfish chasing one object and colliding with another. Hooked or harpooned swordfish are a different matter. They have the motivation to charge a fishing boat and now and again they do. Further, in the New England commercial fishery where harpooned swordfish are fought or 'tended' from a cockleshell dory, men have been injured and even killed by swordfish that, in the local idiom, 'punched'.

Though swordfish with their small and toothless mouths are patently unable to feed upon sharks, they would seem to have, in their swords, the equipage to defend against sharks that might feed upon them. But we know that the mako can prevail. In 1864 Captain Nathaniel E. Atwood presented the lower jaw of a large mako to the Boston Society of Natural History which body in its *Proceedings* for that year noted: 'In the stomach of this specimen, nearly the whole of a full grown sword-fish was found, and some ten to twelve wounds in the skin of the shark, giving evidence of the contest which must have occurred. . . .'

The outcome of a more one-sided encounter was recorded in May of 1939 at Bimini in the Bahamas. A 720-pound mako caught there on rod and reel had in its stomach a 110-pound swordfish intact except for the tail.

But we know too from the late William E. Young, for many years and in many places a commercial shark fisherman, that the swordfish can prevail. 'It was,' Young relates, 'while we were shark-fishing around Warimos Island near Djibouti on the Red Sea. One morning a native came to me to report that a dead shark was on the beach. I ordered the men to drag it up to the station and skin it, since shark skins were what we were after. When they had the skin partly off, a man came running to bring me to see what they had found . . . 18 inches of a Broad-Billed Swordfish sword in the vital organs of the shark. . . . The sword had entered the right side of the shark in the space behind the last gill-slit and just in front of the base of the right pectoral fin. The sword entered to the very hilt and obliquely penetrated the vitals of the shark.'

Young does not identify the shark as a mako. However he and his co-authors incorporate the story with a discussion of the mako in their book about sharks, *Shadows in the Sea*, which was published in 1963.

Throughout its habitat the mako has attacked both boats and swimmers and it may have been a mako that behaved with such pleasing logic at Concega Beach near Rincon, Puerto Rico in the fall of 1956.

One morning a fisherman caught a ray and, near the water's edge, cleaned it. Small waves lapped at the discards and by mid-afternoon two sharks were seen 20 to 30 feet from the beach. Hooks and lines were cast out, but the sharks departed. About an hour later, though, they reappeared and when one, 7 to 8 feet long, moved close inshore, Robert Strong of San Juan shot it with his speargun.

The shark broke the cable to the spear, sped toward deep water, jumped—the mako is one of the very few sharks that, whatever the circumstances, jumps—dislodged the spear, sped back toward shore, launched itself from the water and landed on the beach directly in front of Strong. Then, decamped by a fortuitous wave, it swam away before anything more could be done to or about it. Strong, backed by three corroborative witnesses, described the shark as blue above, white below with prominent teeth and a 'definitely pointed' snout.

The mako's vernacular names include the sharp-nosed mackerel shark (the United States and South Africa), the bonito shark (the west coast of the United States), the snapper shark (South Africa and Australia), the blue pointer shark (Australia), the blue porpoise shark (South Africa) and there are no doubt more. Scientifically, there is little to choose from. *I. glaucus* is still at times applied to Pacific makos, but they and Atlantic makos have proved identical and *I. oxyrinchus* enjoys seniority in the nomenclature. In 1967, however, the picture was somewhat enlivened by the description of a new mako, *I. paucus*, from specimens captured off Cuba and in the central Pacific. Unlike *I. oxyrinchus*, the pectoral fins of which are usually 70 per cent the length of its head length, the pectorals of *I. paucus* equal its head length. Unlike *I. oxyrinchus* which is pure white below, *I. paucus* on the underside of its snout and around the mouth is a dusky colour. There are, to be sure, other differences—*I. paucus* has slightly larger eyes suggesting that it may habituate deeper waters—but the difference in pectoral fins and colour are easy to see and permit identification without having both sorts of mako on hand.

It has been proposed that *I. oxyrinchus* be called in the vernacular the short-finned mako and *I. paucus* the long-finned mako. But whatever the destiny of the proposal, the word mako itself is a gift from New Zealand's Maori who in bygone days valued the teeth of the creature and about which R. H. Matthews reminisced in 1910 in the *Transactions and Proceedings of the New Zealand Institute*. 'The teeth of the *mako* shark were greatly prized. They were called *ngutukao* and were worn suspended from a hole bored in the lobe of the ear. If sold they always fetched a high price, and I saw two bullocks given for a pair of medium size in 1855.'

Matthews also told of how the teeth were obtained and it gives pause to thought. 'In the north the *mako* is usually caught at or near the North Cape. The canoe pulls out to the *mako* ground,

The mako is splendid in form and the fact that it may
jump splendidly when hooked also commends it to the
sportsman.

when a lot of fish is thrown overboard as a *poa* (attraction). The *mako*, which is a tame fish, is attracted alongside by the bait, when a strong *mahanga* (noose) is passed over its head . . . and then pulled tight around the small of the body. It was never caught with a hook, for fear of injuring the teeth. Four teeth only were considered of special value. . . .'

A 'tame fish' the mako patently is not and it would be interesting to know if the worth of its teeth reflected their scarcity and if their scarcity reflected the perils of snaring the beast Maori fashion. Nevertheless, the mako when hooked may jump furiously and that commends it to sportsmen among whom were once Ernest Hemingway and Zane Grey, authors of a different stripe, certainly, but with a shared devotion to catching fish.

Hemingway, in June 1935, caught a 786-pound mako at Bimini and it stood for a while as the Atlantic record. Zane Grey, who was actually christened Pearl Grey, set no mako records but he did catch a great many makos of up to 580 pounds, all in New Zealand, and in 1928 in the American magazine *Natural History* he wrote: 'The *mako* . . . is the aristocrat of all sharks. It is really unfitting to call him a shark at all. I seldom use the word with regard to him. . . . His leaps are prodigious, inconceivably high. The ease and grace . . . is indescribable. It must be seen.'

But in 1934 and also in *Natural History*, in writing about a mako that did not jump but fought hard, Grey pulled out all adjectival stops. 'At last he showed, broadside, limned dark against the blood-stained water . . . gaping, his terrible jaws spread,-his wide, weary tail churning the water. He was overcome but not beaten. He had the diabolical eye of a creature that would kill as he was being killed. And as Reuben lassoed that waving tail, the mako lurched out with snapping jaws, half way up to the gunwale, to sink his teeth on the side of the boat. That was his last gesture.'

That, however, was not Grey's last word on the shark. 'I never loved sharks,' he continued, 'but at that moment I repented of my lust to kill these death-dealing engines of the deep. If he had only leaped, I would have let him be the last mako to fall to my rod! But he would not leap. He was the ninetieth mako for me and that should be enough. He weighed 510 pounds and was the second largest I had caught. No doubt, however, he came first in exemplify-ing the claims I had made . . . that he was New Zealand's premier sporting fish, as game as he was beautiful, as ferocious as he was enduring.'

Grey was a missionary fisherman. He caught many record fish in as many oceans and he had decided opinions about tackle and technique, opinions he wasn't in the least reluctant to express and bluntly. So he was forever embroiled in squabbles and his first visit to New Zealand predictably got one going. 'As for the tackle used here by New Zealand and English anglers,' he commented in an article for the *Auckland Herald*, 'it is hopelessly inadequate, and unsportsman-like in the extreme.' The *Herald* cancelled the rest of what had been planned as a Grey series.

However, Grey later took solace from his role of missionary novelist. 'I found my books, mostly the 3/6d English edition, everywhere that we went, even in the remote Maori homes, far out in the bush; and I found them read to tatters. This surely was the sweetest and most moving of all the experiences I had; and it faced me again with the appalling responsibility of a novelist who in these modern days of materialism dares to foster idealism and love of nature, chivalry in men and chastity in women. Yet how potent the knowledge for renewed hope and endurance!'

In 1939 Grey died. Today his fishing books are out of print. But not his novels of derring-do in the Wild West.

The current I.G.F.A. all-tackle record mako measured 12 feet in length, weighed 1,000 pounds and fittingly enough was caught, in March 1943, at Mayor Island, New Zealand. The British record, 491 pounds 8 ounces, was taken at Looe in 1966. The record British porbeagle, 311 pounds, was also caught at Looe and in 1916. The I.G.F.A. all-tackle record porbeagle was taken at Fire Island, New York in May 1965. It was 7 feet 9½ inches long and weighed 400 pounds 8 ounces.

There is one more species in the family Isuridae and it is also ranked a game fish. But we have placed it in the next chapter not only because it is a bellicose cavern of a shark but also because the three largest sharks seemed to deserve a chapter to themselves.

CHAPTER 8

The
Leviathans
Three

In September, 1964 on Georges Bank east of the Maine coast, the commercial fishing boat *Explorer* dredged up a fossil shark tooth 4 inches long and $4\frac{1}{2}$ wide at the base which, as measurements go, is not appreciably smaller than a medium sized human hand. Teeth of the same sort and size have also been retrieved from submerged or dry land beds in the West Indies, South America, Europe, Africa, eastern Asia and New Zealand and they once graced the jaws of a shark with the name *Carcharodon megalodon*, a name that translates to rough-toothed, huge-toothed.

The shark complemented its teeth. Scientists estimate that it may have reached 60 feet and more than 50 tons. Sadly, if one is an admirer of sharks, this splendid animal has been extinct for some 20,000,000 years. However, one is comforted by the fact that a near relative of *Carcharodon megalodon* is among the living. It is *Carcharodon carcharias*, the great white shark or man-eater, the fourth species in the family Isuridae and a creature of substance. Only two shark species are larger, but the teeth of both these are tiny and non-functional, the diet is planktonic minutiae and the nature ordinarily placid if not torpid. The teeth of the great white shark—or, more simply, the white shark—are large and functional, the diet takes in food like whole seals and the nature is emphatically aggressive. So while there is much of interest about the two larger species, *C. carcharias* is the most redoubtable of sharks.

There has always been conjecture about the maximum size of the white shark. Guesses and sightings have put it at 40 feet but the

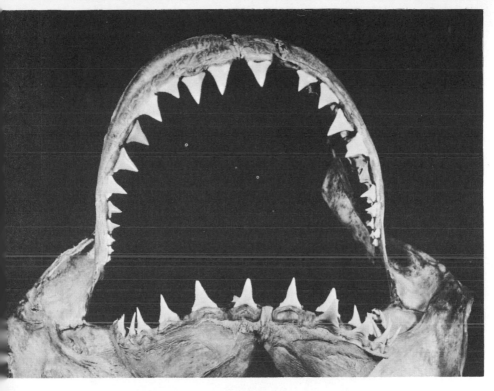

The jaws of a white shark, *Carcharodon carcharias.*

largest thus far actually measured and weighed was taken off Cuba
in the middle 1940's. It measured 21 feet and weighed 7,302 pounds
and 1,005 pounds of that was the liver alone. At a given length,
though, there can be a marked variation in weight. A white shark
harpooned off Montauk at the eastern tip of Long Island, New
York in 1964 measured 17 feet 6 inches and weighed 4,500 pounds.
Another, taken off Ceduna, South Australia in 1959 measured
about the same, 16 feet 10 inches, yet weighed a comparatively
modest, 2,664 pounds. This variation probably reflects physical
condition—meaning that the 2,664-pound shark was on the slim
side, not necessarily ailing—and it extends to smaller white sharks
too. At 8 feet, for instance, they can weigh from 350 to 600 pounds.

As to maximum size, our own guess is that a very few white
sharks reach or pass 25 feet. But, until one such is caught, white
sharks of verified sizes small and large are sharks enough.

Two white sharks, one 15 feet long and the other 11, at the presently inactive Tory Channel Whaling Station in New Zealand.

In the tenth edition of *Systema Naturae*, 1758, which has been called the international date line for the scientific classication of life, Linnaeus appended a note to his description of the white shark. '*Jonam Prophetam, ut veteres Herculem trinoctem, in hujus ventriculo tridui spatio, baessise verosimile est.*' Or: 'It is likely that the prophet Jonah remained in the belly of this animal for a space of three days, as Hercules of old did for three nights.'

Linnaeus was not the first to conjoin Jonah and the shark. At least 16 earlier scholars opted for the shark rather than the whale and the earliest seems to have been Heinrich Herman Frey who in 1594 in his *Biblisch Fischbuch*, or *Ichthyobiblia*, devoted 20 of 66 pages to *Jonah and the Great Fish*.

We find the facts of the matter somewhat elusive. There is no doubt, however, that large white sharks can swallow prophets whole. There is no doubt either that white sharks of varied size attack less blessed swimmers. Tooth fragments left in many of those unfortunates have adequately confirmed that. But after an attack in Australia on February 26, 1966, there was confirmation in rare surplus.

The place was Coledale Beach on the south coast of New South Wales. The weather was clear. The water was murky from days of wind and its temperature was 71·2°F. The swimmer was Raymond Short, 13 years old, of Sydney who was 30 yards from shore in a depth of five feet. The time was two o'clock in the afternoon.

The shark first took the boy by his left thigh and next by the lower portion of his right leg. The boy tried to beat the creature off. He even bit it on the snout. It would not let go. The boy screamed and the shark warning bell was rung.

Raymond Joyce, a member of the Coledale Surf Club, was first on the scene. The boy said: 'Help me please, the shark is still there.' Joyce did not believe it. He saw no shark in the murky water. But neither could he move the boy towards the shore.

Almost immediately five more men joined Joyce. The boy kept insisting that the shark still had hold of his leg. Joyce ran a hand down the leg and he then felt the shark. A man lifted the leg to the surface. With it came the shark. Another man clubbed the shark on the head with a surfboard. The shark stayed fast and finally it and the boy were half-carried, half-dragged onto the beach. There the jaws of the shark were pried open and the boy's leg freed.

During the rescue, which occupied only about one minute, the boy bled profusely. His left thigh and hands had been deeply lacerated. The back of his right leg had been denuded of calf muscles and all other muscular tissue. The exposed shinbone had tooth marks along its entire length.

The boy very nearly died, but he did survive and his leg was saved. Coledale District Hospital was, providentially, just 300 yards from the beach and he was got there in seven minutes. It was thought, however, that the leg probably would be withered and might require a brace.

The shark, which did die on the beach, was an immature white shark 8 feet 3 inches long and it had itself been hurt. On its belly and hindquarters were multiple healed and partially healed cuts, parallel scratches and elliptical wounds all of which indicated that it had been attacked by another shark of like size though unknown species. X-rays revealed no tooth fragments.

That the shark may have attacked the boy because it was too crippled to catch more normal food, and that it may have been too crippled to resist being manhandled onto the beach, are a pair of possibilities. But the shark had in its stomach two pieces of squid and the vertebrae of a small fish. Further, sharks do at times lock to an object with great tenacity and only a few seconds of the minute-long rescue were involved in hauling the boy and the animal shoreward. Possibly then, the shark attacked from happenstance, not hurt, and succumbed to its own obstinacy.

Be that as it may, the attack had something odd about it as did the rescue. In contrast, an attack in California in 1959 was elementary. On the afternoon of June 14, a Sunday, Robert L. Pamperin, 33, and Gerald Lehrer were diving for shellfish in La Jolla Cove near San Diego. They were about 200 feet from shore in four fathoms of clear water when Pamperin called for help and went under. Lehrer looked down and through his face mask saw Pamperin, wreathed in blood, protruding trunk-first from the mouth of a shark he, Lehrer, calculated to be 20 feet in length. The shark was not caught and Pamperin was never found, but from Lehrer's description scientists agreed that the shark was likely *C. carcharias.*

The species also attacks boats and without discernible provocation. On July 9, 1953 to take one case, at Fourchu on the north-east coast of Cape Breton Island, Nova Scotia, a shark about 12 feet long gnashed an 8-inch hole in a 12-foot dory which sank and set adrift two fishermen. A piece of a tooth left in the dory identified the shark as a white shark.

There were intriguing features about this attack too. First, neither fisherman, both of whom were in the water for several hours and one of whom drowned, were molested by the shark. Second, a large shark had been in the area a few days before and whenever seen had been following the ill-fated dory, the only one of many in use at Fourchu that was painted white.

But white shark feeding can be a source of frustration as well as calamity. In August 1952 a porpoise hunter, in the south-west Bay of Fundy off New Brunswick to collect specimens for Canada's Atlantic Biological Laboratory, was about to shoot a full-grown common porpoise, the species *Phocaena phocaena* which reaches 6 feet and 125 pounds, when a shark abruptly bit it in two. The shark ate the back part. The hunter gaffed the front part. The shark then circled close by the hunter's skiff, but swam off when the hunter loosed a round at its head. The hunter guessed the shark to have been a trifle longer than the 14-foot skiff and since no other aggressive shark of such size ranges the Bay of Fundy, the assumption was that the shark was a white shark.

Guesses and assumptions are not always necessary. In July, 1959 off Rockport, Maine, Harry Goodridge indignantly harpooned a white shark 11 feet 9 inches long. The shark had discovered Goodridge's pet seal Basil swimming about Goodridge's boat. It had bit Basil in half, and it had swallowed Basil half by half. In its stomach was another seal it had not troubled to halve.

Actually, a white shark can bolt creatures half its own size. One, 15 feet 6 inches long and caught in Florida in 1939, contained two whole sandbar sharks, the species *Carcharhinus milberti*, between 6 and 7 feet long. Still, the white shark does not ignore smaller edibles and sometimes indulges in that random sort of browsing— the vacuum cleaner syndrome if you will—which yields a bellyful of the miscellaneous. The late J. L. B. Smith in his book *The Sea Fishes of Southern Africa*, 1950, refers to a white shark of 18 feet that had in it: '. . . the foot of a native, half a small goat, 2 pumpkins, a wicker-covered scent bottle, 2 large fishes quite fresh, a small shark and unidentifiable oddments.' Considering the variety of artifacts mined from other sharks, Smith's informant about this collection should not be discounted solely on the grounds that he was an 'old sailor'.

It now must be evident that the singularity of the white shark does not rest upon militance alone. Other shark species attack boats and swimmers and swallow animals whole. What makes the white shark singular is its incorporation of militance and mass. 'The White

Shark', wrote Couch in 1868, 'is to sailors the most formidable of all the inhabitants of the ocean; for in none besides are the powers of inflicting injury so equally combined with eagerness to accomplish it'. Couch may be liable for a modicum of hyperbole, but only a modicum.

Available information, little of it as there is, suggests that *C. carcharias* is not an abundant species. To illustrate, out of every 100,000 sharks caught in the Florida shark fishery just 27 were white sharks. In that same fishery, however, hooked white sharks often parted chain and wire rope which had a breaking strength of 3,800 pounds and Springer has commented: 'Since many white sharks weigh as much as 3,800 pounds, this does not seem unreasonable.' So while the Florida catch ratio is suggestive of white shark abundance it is that and no more.

We cannot, though, put much stock in the proposal, sometimes advanced, that *C. carcharias* is on the way to extinction because it has far greater difficulty in finding food enough than have smaller, more abundant shark species. In point of probable fact, sharks need not constantly consume to survive. They will, to be sure, stuff themselves if necessity dictates and chance affords. But if they must, they can exist for a long stretch on their liver fats alone. Sharks new to captivity can fast for weeks and even months before demonstrating the faintest interest in food. Moreover, sharks adjusted to captivity remain in good health on a weekly food intake totalling only from 3 to 14 per cent of their own body weight and, usually, the larger, more mature the shark the lower its metabolism and the smaller its intake. 'These figures . . .', explains Eugenie Clark, who had addressed herself to the discouraging fact that captive sharks tend to pine away, 'may be less than normal to keep a shark alive in its natural habitat where energy used in swimming is probably greater. On the other hand, these figures may represent more food than a shark obtains when it has to find its own. . . .'

At the time of writing no white shark has been held captive—but 50-odd other species have and they have survived for a matter of weeks to 25 years—and Clark's figures thus are, like the Florida catch ratio, only suggestive. There is ample reason to suppose, nevertheless, that *C. carcharias*, whatever its food requirements, is well able to earn its wild keep and persevere as a species. After all, to say that white sharks are not abundant is not to say that they are scarce. Abundance is relative and if there are lots less white sharks than, for example, blue sharks, there are still white sharks enough so that year in and year out a fair number are taken by anglers and commercial fishermen, are involved in attacks on boats and people and are observed while attending to such affairs as the Bay of Fundy porpoise or Basil the luckless seal.

The range of the white shark is worldwide, inshore and off, from the tropics to cool temperate zones. Britain's coasts should fall comfortably within that range—as do the coasts of the Mediterranean, South Africa, Australia and many more—and early British naturalists did record the British presence of *C. carcharias*. Pennant in 1769, Low in 1813 and Couch in 1868 are three who did and, it seems, accurately. But it also seems that there is no recent account of the sighting, catching or washing ashore of a single white shark along the coasts of Great Britain.

The white shark travels with the season and in *The Australian Zoologist* for August 2, 1967, G. P. Whitley gave some regional particulars. 'In view,' he wrote, 'of Postel's (1958) observation that the white shark appeared regularly off the coast of Tunis in the latter half of May, I have drawn up a rough, and admittedly incomplete "calendar" of occurrences off Australia's coasts from which the following picture emerges.

'Most of the big-game specimens are taken in South Australian waters in January, although September and November to April captures have been made there. In Victoria it has been taken in April and July; in New South Wales in October and from January to June; in Queensland in May and June. Perhaps a leisurely and not very direct migration is indicated ... Mr A. Dean, who has caught many large South Australian specimens, states [in the June, 1966 issue of *Australian Outdoors*] of *Carcharodon*, "Despite a proved capacity for long migrations, individuals favour a particular area and will repeatedly return to it". One female shark he recognized from a characteristic scar after 13 years; her weight had apparently not increased.'

Whitley's calendar could help the sportsman who is anxious to add a white shark to his bag. More white sharks are caught on rod and reel in Australia than anywhere else though other localities, Cape Cod Bay and its contiguous Massachusetts Bay in the United States being two, might be productive if the angling effort were applied. Still, it was the angler quoted by Whitley, Alf Dean of Ilrymple in Victoria, who caught—on April 21, 1959 at Ceduna, South Australia—the 2,664-pound white shark mentioned early in this chapter. It is not only the I.G.F.A. all-tackle record for the species, but is also the largest fish of any sort ever taken on rod and reel.

It is likely that *C. carcharias* reaches sexual maturity at some point between 11 and 14 feet. But knowledge of white shark reproduction is wanting, so wanting that the reference to white shark young most often repeated, and most often repeated without question, dates from 1934 and has a brood of nine 2-foot pups weighing 108 pounds each. The number and length of the pups are reasonable. Their reported weight is unimaginable and Bigelow and Schroeder expressed doubts about it in 1948. Yet the reference in all its originality persists. As recently as 1967 it was again repeated without question, this time in a paper in a well known Australian journal of marine science.

The white shark—in Australia also called the white pointer and in South Africa the blue pointer—is not always the white its name implies. A large one may be dun coloured or lead-white, but one in the category of 12 feet may be grey, blue, brown or even black on the topsides and shade more or less abruptly to a dirty white below.

If not from its colour, a free-swimming white shark can on occasion be recognized either from sheer weight and isurid conformation or from its markings. Usually there is a black spot on the trunk in the axils, or armpits, of the pectoral fins and the pectorals themselves are black at the tips with, usually, several adjacent black spots. The tail and dorsal fins are dark on the after edges. The pelvics are darker still, but on the forward edges, which are olive and fade tailward to white.

However the teeth of the white shark leave no margin for error

A. Dean of Aldgate, South Australia with a white shark weighing 2,166 pounds. Dean also holds the world record white shark catch of 2,664 pounds.

about species. They are more equilaterally triangular and more roughly serrate than those of any other large sort of shark. In fact, owing to their size and symmetry, they once served Florida Indians as arrowheads.

A first encounter with the second shark in the triumvirate of leviathans is certain to be remembered and ours was not a chance one. Several of the creatures had been reported nearby and since this was an uncommon turn of events the three of us—one of the authors, his elder boy then 11, and a yellow Labrador retriever— set out on a July day in 1966 to see what might be seen.

Woods Hole, a port village and centre of marine science, dropped behind. The 13-foot skiff skimmed on smooth water and the island of Martha's Vineyard, minutes to the east, grew large to meet us. On our left hand lay the south shore of Cape Cod, on our right the Elizabeth Islands which reach a few miles southward to touch the fringes of the open Atlantic. The place-names—Cape Cod, Martha's Vineyard, Elizabeth Islands—the legacy of the English explorer Bartholomew Gosnold who in 1602 explored the cape and islands and about which his fellow voyager John Brereton remarked: '. . . the schools of Mackerell, herrings, Cod and other fish, that we daily saw . . . were woonderfull. . . .'. .

The shark we found, about a mile off the Vineyard, was wonderful too. The distance between the projecting portions of its dorsal and its tail equalled the length of the skiff and the shadow beneath was appreciably longer. But it was a while before we saw the shark entire. We came too close too quickly and it sounded.

When the fins reappeared we tried to guess the creature's course and detoured to put the skiff athwart it. Two or three times the shark wandered off on tangents and we had to reposition ourselves. The next time it slowly swam right up to the skiff, swept its tail and tipped down to slide under the bow.

We were in no way ready for what we saw and it was not only that we saw a shark almost twice the length of our skiff. It was the magnificently proportioned heft of the beast; the enormous lunate tail, the fusiform body which was grey with lateral streaks of lighter grey, the dorsal from four to five feet tall, the long and

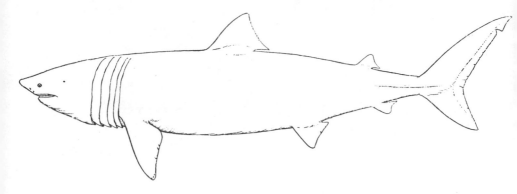

The basking shark, *Cetorhinus maximus.* **For all its great size the basker feeds on tiny planktonic creatures which it strains from the water by swimming along with its mouth wide open.**

wing-like pectorals. We were utterly dwarfed and appalled by three tons or more of shark for a very few moments just a very few feet away.

The retriever must be excepted. True to his Labrador genes he had ignored the shark in favour of a gull which bobbed nearby and, as so often happened, it got the better of him. Over the side he went before man or boy, still reflecting upon the shark, could lay hold of his tail. The gull flew off. The retriever paddled back to be hauled aboard and the usual price was paid for missing his tail. He shook drenchingly, but on an unusual day.

The shark we had seen, and we had not seen the last of it, was a basking shark of medium size. This species, *Cetorhinus maximus*, grows to over 30 feet and possibly an occasional Methuselah to 40. In pieces, however, a basking shark 30 feet long scales out impressively. The head weighs 2,000 pounds; the liver 1,850 pounds; the fins 2,000 pounds; the tail 1,000 pounds; the skin 2,000 pounds; the meat 3,000 pounds; the innards 1,000 pounds; the contents of the stomach and intestines 1,000 pounds. The total is 13,850 pounds.

C. maximus is likely the one species in the family Cetorhinidae— if a species does not fit into an existing family science makes one for it—but is related to the Isuridae. It is also a caller in all temper-

The basking shark, *Cetorhinus maximus.*

ate to boreal or subarctic waters, the Baltic excluded, and sometimes in schools of hundreds.

First to describe the basking shark, in 1765, was the Norwegian
naturalist and cleric Johann Ernst Gunnerus, the Bishop of
Trondheim and he proposed that the basking shark had swallowed
Jonah. Within a few years, though, *C. maximus* caught the attention
of Thomas Pennant. 'This species', he wrote, again in *British*

Zoology, 'has been long known to the inhabitants of the south and west of *Ireland* and *Scotland* and those of *Caernarvonshire* and *Anglesea*; but . . . has till this time remained undescribed by any English writer; and what is worse, mistaken for and confounded with the *luna* of *Rondeletius*, the same that our *English* writers call the *sun-fish*. The *Irish* and *Welch* give it the same name, from its lying as if to sun itself on the surface of the water; and for the same reason we have taken the liberty of calling it the *basking shark*. It was long taken for a species of whale, till we pointed out the branchial orifices on the sides, and the perpendicular site of the tail.'

Pennant notwithstanding, in British waters the basking shark is still known to some as the sunfish or, in acknowledgement of the tall dorsal, sailfish. In the Hebrides the creature is also called muldoan and in the Orkneys hoe-mother or homer which means the mother of the dogfish.

After the Labrador's excursion to retrieve the irretrievable we took up with the shark again and it was an enterprise of strange incongruity. Within plain view were all the trappings of summer civilization; sailing boats, motorboats, beach umbrellas, dots that were people. Also within plain view was the basking shark, a living relic of prehistory and a monumental one at that and here we were tagging after it in a ridiculously small skiff. Supposedly, it was a harmless, sluggish sort of shark the minute teeth of which had no function in its garnering of minute zooplankton. But the very size of the creature, and our lack of it, discouraged complete comfort and reservations were being entertained about sluggishness. When we first approached and startled the shark it had sounded with surprising alacrity and when the shark first swam under our bow it had shown a good turn of speed with economic motion. Some months later, a letter was found in *The Proceedings of the Zoological Society of London* for 1951. It had been written by a Captain Harry Thomson, who was then engaged in the basking shark fishery, and it reads in part:

'During June, 1948, whilst hunting in Loch Brolum-Shiant islands area I recorded the following incident. The weather was fine with bright sunshine and a light southerly wind and excellent visibility. I was in the wheelhouse "conning" the catching vessel and leaning out of the open side window conversing with a member of the crew. . . . Suddenly, at no more than 30 yards range a huge shark (*i.e.* 25 ft. to 29 ft. class) leapt into the air, the entire fish being clearly outlined against the sky. Whilst in mid air the shark gave a pronounced twist or wriggle of his entire rear portion from the dorsal fin tailwards whereupon he fell back upon his flank into the sea with a resounding smack and splash. He disappeared in a shower of spray and foam. . . .'

Captain Thomson continues: 'The sight is indelibly imprinted on my memory and at such close quarters was indeed a most impressive sight. The fact that the fish was clearly silhouetted against the sky and the height of the observer's eye being known and also the range, clearly demonstrated that the shark's tail was at least six feet clear of the water and of course his head would be considerably higher than this. I have often been puzzled by the fact that such a heavy and slow moving fish could attain sufficient momentum to eject itself into the air. In this connection I would point out that of the many sharks which I have seen "leaping" I have never seen one do so in shallow water. This aerobatic performance always takes place outside the 40 fathom line. From this I have formed the opinion that he must start his "take off" from a very considerable depth. . . .'

Lastly, Captain Thomson notes the behaviour that is sometimes associated with jumping basking sharks: 'When "stooging" around an area where a shoal was known to be present and awaiting the shoal to surface times without number, I have seen a shark, or sometimes more than one fish, leap into the air followed soon afterwards by the shoal rising to the surface. However no hard and fast rules can be applied to this phenomenon. During the season of 1948 I counted as many as eleven "leaps" in one day in widely separated areas and yet no fish appeared on the surface. . . .'

Had we been treated to a jumping basking shark that July morning off Martha's Vineyard we surely would have fled. As it was we were then ignorant of such a potentially shattering habit so we stayed on and watched our shark feed in the peculiar way basking sharks do.

In keeping with the great bulk of the animal, the basking shark has extremely long and large gill slits or clefts. They, five of them to the side, reach so far around the neck as to almost meet above and below and on their insides on each gill arch, the structure that carries the gills, are 1,000 to 1,300 gill rakers. These resemble long bristles and are stiff though flexible derivatives of the dermal denticles. When the shark's mouth is shut the rakers lie flat on the arch, but when the mouth is opened they spring erect across it to form a sieve for the straining of copepods and other virtually invisible planktonic animals.

The mouth of a basking shark.

The mouth of our basking shark was almost continuously wide open and its gill clefts were greatly distended as it swam at a deliberate 2 knots, 2·3 miles per hour, simultaneously browsing and breathing. That rate of speed, 2 knots, seems to be the usual one for a feeding C. *maximus* and it has been the basis for some rather astonishing quantitative calculations. If the shark is of average size, around the 23 feet which ours was, the area of its open mouth is about 3 square feet and swimming at 2 knots the shark will strain, each and every hour, almost 4,000,000 pounds of sea water. How much food is strained would depend upon how much is present, but it is likely that our basking shark had in its stomach at least 300 pounds of plankton and another 700 pounds of its own mucous. For what purpose the latter, is not known.

With the onset of winter C. *maximus* sheds its gill rakers and an explanation of why and what might happen next has been offered by L. Harrison Matthews of the Zoological Society of London. 'During the warmer months,' wrote Matthews in *The New Scientist* in March, 1962, 'the fish feed luxuriously on the rich summer plankton, gulping it down by the ton; but in winter the pastures of the seas are bare and there is little nourishment to be found. The power needed to propel a feeding shark of average length at its feeding speed of 2 knots is about 0·33 h.p.—the heat equivalent of this is 212 calories per hour. Allowing 40 per cent efficiency to the shark's muscles in doing work, and 80 per cent to its tail as a propeller—a very generous allowance—a shark 7 metres [about 23 feet] long would need to take each hour food with a calorific value of 663 calories to give merely the energy required in swimming to collect the food. Even if we multiply the recorded density of plankton in the North Sea in November by three, the shark's intake could be only 410 calories per hour under the most favourable conditions, and it would be losing on the deal. So it solves its problem by throwing away its rakers worn by a season's use, refraining from feeding, sinking to the bottom and hibernating. At this moment there are probably great schools of these enormous fish quietly resting on the bottom of the sea, perhaps in the heads of the canyons at the edge of the continental shelf, with their metabolism running at its lowest level while they grow their new gill rakers ready for browsing on next summer's crop of plankton.'

Matthews' may be the answer and it may be just part of the answer. Off the coast of central California *C. maximus* is present throughout the year, but is least abundant in June and July there when it is most abundant off northern British coasts and also when the water temperatures of the two regions are very much alike. And, the paradox is almost complete. When the basking shark is most abundant in central California waters, from October through April, it is all but gone from northern British waters. However, during winter the relevant water temperatures part company and Britain's drop much lower.

It could easily be that the paradox reflects nothing more than copepod availability. But while it is logical that where there are enough copepods there will also be basking sharks, it is not so logical that central California basking sharks go the whole winter without gill rakers.

The difficulty is that no one knows how often the gill rakers are shed and how rapidly they are replaced. Possibly the wear and tear of feeding dictate. Thus with a short feeding season, British basking sharks may need to shed and replace their rakers just once a year and may well retire to deep water, if not to hibernate in the strict physiological sense, at least to slow their metabolism and wait out the barren winter. The basking sharks off central California, on the other hand, with an apparently long feeding season, may need and get several sets of rakers every year. But there is also the possibility that the loss and replacement of gill rakers, like the loss and re-placement of most shark teeth, is a continuous process. Should that be the case, basking sharks everywhere could feed the year around. Those in latitudes of poor winter pasturage, British ones among them, could simply shift offshore to deeper water, a shift made by many shark species as a matter of seasonal course, and balance any calorific deficit by drawing on their livers.

With one possible exception, a gravid female basking shark has yet to be seen and the exception comes by way of Pennant who reported two hundred years ago: '. . . a young one about a foot in length being found in the belly of a fish of this kind.'

The smallest of observed basking sharks are 5 to 6 feet long and they are considered the young of the year. Probably they are whelped well offshore, but at what size and in what number is not known. It is known, though, that basking shark egg production is not typical. The ovary of most sharks produces a few large, yolky eggs. The ovary of *C. maximus* produces millions of tiny eggs, upwards of 6 million no larger than birdshot, and they are not very yolky. This is reminiscent of spawning bony fishes, but it does not suggest that the basking shark spawns. Shark eggs are fertilized internally through copulation.

As we watched the shark feed off Martha's Vineyard we talked about the fact that its liver would yield anywhere from 80 to 600 gallons of oil. Once the oil was considered the equal of sperm oil for lamps and candles and by the middle 1700's New England's local stock of basking sharks had followed its stock of right whales (the family Balaenidae) into the try pot. But as long as whaling men rode the seas they lowered for the basking shark which they called the bone shark because its gill rakers put them in mind of the baleen, the plankton-straining structures, of the whalebone whales.

Today, basking shark oil has some industrial applications and the great carcass can be reduced to meal, but the market is uncertain and except for local fisheries such as those in north-west Britain the creature is not much hunted. Hopefully, nothing will change that, though something could.

We turned for home. The boy, hair bleached and skin browned by school-free days, curled drowsily in the bow. The dog stood on a thwart and the wind we made tossed and tumbled his ears. Nature had privileged us that day, and the following year G. P. Whitley would write and we would concur; 'For cosmetic purposes, the ladies of Japan are anxious to obtain squalene, an oily preparation from basking sharks and dogfishes. Since, however, the ladies of Japan are already beautiful it seems a pity to sacrifice such uncommon and interesting animals as basking sharks and the less known squaloids like *Centrophorus* for this purpose. In the past, seals have been decimated for their pelts, egrets and other birds have been slaughtered for their plumes, and many rare and lovely creatures have vanished in the fleeting course of fashion.'

The last of this chapter's species is the largest of sharks and the largest of all fishes too. It is *Rhincodon typus*, the whale shark, and the sole species in the family Rhincodontidae. It is known to reach 50 feet and thought to reach 60 or more. A length of 35 feet and a weight of 10 tons seems the average, but comparatively few specimens have been taken. Size and the handling of it discourages zoologists and the animal has never been commercially important.

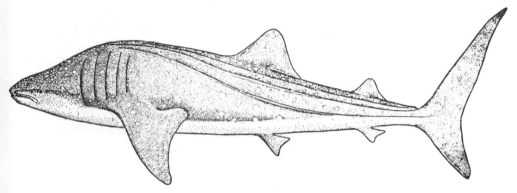

Rhinocodon typus, **the whale shark, which exceeds 50 feet in length and which is the largest of all fishes. Fortunately, it feeds on plankton and small fish and is, generally, inoffensive.**

R. typus ranges all tropic waters and infrequently strays into temperate ones. Most often it is solitary though sometimes it is seen in small groups. In any case, there can be no confusion about what it is. The mouth, unlike that of any other large shark, is at the very front of the head and it is cavernous. The eyes, just above and behind the corners of the mouth, are minute. The top of the blunt head is flattened. The body, stoutly streamlined, is traced with lateral ridges a pair of which originate close together and high on each shoulder. The lower ridge extends down and aft onto the forward part of the tail to form a caudal keel. The upper ridge

125

divides well ahead of the first dorsal and both branches terminate in the vicinity of the second dorsal. There may be another ridge between the back of the head and the first dorsal.

The colour of the whale shark is usually reported as a dark reddish or greenish brown on the back and sides to white or yellow below and the body is strikingly and distinctively marked. From stem to stern, except for the undersides, it is covered with a profusion of white or yellow spots. Also the body is striped with vertical lines, again white or yellow, and since many of these transect the dermal ridges, *R. typus* has, from above, the look of a monumental checkerboard with the checkers on it. To Captain H. Piddington in the Philippines, however, it once had the look of something else entirely. 'In December, 1816,' Piddington related in 1835 in *The Journal of the Asiatic Society of Bengal*, 'I commanded a small Spanish brig, and was lying at anchor in the Bay of Mariveles, at the entrance of the Bay of Manilla. One day, about noon, hearing a confusion upon deck, I ran up, and looking over the side, thought, from what I saw, that the vessel had parted and was drifting over a bank of white sand and coral . . . I called out to let go another anchor, but my people, Manilla men, all said "No Sir; its only the *chacon*!" and upon running up the rigging, I saw indeed that I had mistaken the motion of the spotted back of an enormous fish passing under the vessel, for the vessel itself driving over a bank! . . . From the view I had of the fish, and the time it took to pass slowly under the vessel, I should suppose it not less than 70 or 80 feet in length. Its breadth was very great in proportion; perhaps not less than 30 feet. The back was so spotted, that, had it been at rest, it must have been taken for a coral shoal [reef], the appearance of which is familiar to seamen.'

Piddington admitted to being shortsighted and that may account for the seemingly exaggerated dimensions of the spotted fish, the breadth in particular. But had he committed himself to paper a bit sooner, his would have been history's first mention of the whale shark. As it was, the species had been described and named by Dr Andrew Smith of Cape Town, South Africa in 1829 in *The Zoological Journal*. 'Length of the specimen . . .' Smith noted, 'fifteen feet; greatest circumference nine feet. Was caught by fishermen in

This view of a harpooned whale shark shows the distinctive markings of the creature.

Table Bay during the month of April, 1928, and the skin was purchased for £6 sterling, and forwarded to the Paris Museum.'

Smith's specimen of *R. typus* is one of the smaller ones on record and no drawing of it was published with his 1829 description. Between 1838 and 1850 however, he brought out his five-volume work *Illustrations of the Zoology of South Africa* and in the fourth volume—*Pisces*, 1849—is that handcoloured rendering of his discovery which is also the first published rendering of the whale shark.

The torpid ways of *R. typus* are legendary and in recent years have led to a rash of accounts such as the following by Conrad Limbaugh. 'One encounter involved a specimen estimated to be 35–42 feet long. This large fish was seen 200 miles west of Magdalena Bay, Baja California, Mexico. The dorsal fin and tip of the sculling caudal fin and occasionally portions of its back projected above the water surface. . . . It had lateral ridges that projected sufficiently to be used as hand-holds for the inspecting swimmers. When first observed, it was surrounded by a cloud of black- and silver-banded pilot fish, which swam away as we approached. Large, whitish shark suckers, which were scattered over its body, took cover in the mouth, gills, and on the opposite side. The entire body was rigid, except for the tail, which swung back and forth. The mouth opened and closed with very slow, mechanical regularity. By swimming fast, our group of four swimmers, equipped with swim fins, could keep up with this shark (approx. 2–3 m.p.h.). We clambered over it, examining it closely, even looking in its mouth. It showed no concern, except that when we examined its head, it slowly dived out of sight. But it soon returned to the surface and allowed us to climb aboard again.'

This indifference, sadly, also means that with fair frequency the creature is rammed by ships and E. W. Gudger, who had a lifetime preoccupation with *R. typus*, catalogued dozens of such collisions. Here are two, the first from *The Illustrated London News* of February 11, 1905. 'During a recent voyage of the "Armadale Castle", when the vessel was in latitude 3 deg. south, the stem's perpendicular struck a large fish close to the head, and held it prisoner for about fifteen minutes. The monster was not less than fifty-seven feet in length, and must have been eight feet in diameter. It was beautifully marked, and Captain Robinson was sorry he could not lasso and preserve it. . . . As Mr. Rudyard Kipling was on board and saw the sight, it has been suggested that the creature should be called "Piscus Rudyardensis".'

The second account comes from the report, published by Gudger, of the captain of the schooner-yacht *Navigator* who on May 8, 1938 was in the offings of Cape San Lucas, Mexico. 'The vessel was struck on the starboard side by an immense shark. The wheel was wrenched out of the hands of the man at the wheel. The tail of the fish rose eight feet above the rail of the ship and about 14 feet above the waterline. . . . The fish was distinctly seen as it went astern, was of a mottled colour and was at least 30 to 35 feet long. After going into drydock, it was found that considerable damage had been done to the hull and rudder.'

This last incident raises a question. The report states that the vessel was struck by the shark, not the shark by the vessel, and mindful of the whale shark's bumbling nature that is certainly possible. The question is whether it is possible that the shark struck the vessel on purpose. The earlier literature makes occasional mention of belligerence on the part of *R. typus*, but it always has been discounted. Among the *Ichthyological Notes* in *Copeia* in March 1967, however, there was a communication from J. L. B. Smith that would seem to leave the question open.

'The monotypic *Rhincodon*,' Smith writes, 'is perhaps most abundant in the western Indian Ocean. . . . It appears to be particularly well known in the Mauritius-Seychelles area. . . . As with large whales, the whale shark appears to be generally inoffensive, certainly all reports of its habits have stressed this character. Divers and people in small boats have repeatedly approached close to this animal in the surface without eliciting any hostile response. Generally . . . the whale shark had completely ignored them and even divers or swimmers who have touched or clambered on the animal. . . . It has therefore been all the more surprising to receive a recent report of a different nature. Mr. J. Maurice Jauffret, noted angler and observer of marine life, of Port Louis, Mauritius, has written as follows: "As you are aware, RHINCODON TYPUS, the whale shark, is very common in our waters, and, whilst fishing, I have had many occasions to take my boat very close to them. They had showed no particular interest in the boat. Since last year, however, three fishing boats (cabin cruisers) belonging to members of our club have been attacked by three sharks whilst members of the crew were playing fish hooked in a shoal [school]. Fortunately the boats sustained no damage. The last attack was made on my boat in which my son, Maurice, aged 23, was fishing. He reported that he saw the shark near a shoal of tunny, and whilst one of his friends was bringing in a 30 lb. fish, the monster (about 50 ft. long) raised his head out of the water and came straight for the boat. He hit the boat astern and turned her around. The shock was so hard that all the crew were thrown down. My son then put the engine in full throttle and the shark did not follow." '

'In response to queries,' Smith concludes, 'Mr. Jauffret has assured me that there is no question of the identity of at least the shark that attacked his launch. From long experience he and others mentioned know this shark well and they clearly saw on this particular animal the light markings characteristic of the species. It is significant that the circumstances of attack in all the cases reported by Mr Jauffret were identical. Each attack was directed at a boat in which an angler was playing a large fish hooked from a shoal.'

Like the basking shark, the whale shark feeds on plankton. Unlike the basking shark, it also feeds on small squids, sardines, anchovies and such and the fact that tuna do too tells why whale sharks and schools of tuna are so often mixed together.

An additional difference between the two largest of sharks is in their devices for straining plankton. *C. maximus* has erectile gill rakers. The whale shark has much more the true sieve. Each of its gill arches is joined to the next one by numerous lateral bars of cartilage which support masses of spongy, very finely meshed tissue. Water taken in by the shark is forced through the mesh and out through the gill clefts leaving the plankton behind. It is not known what part, if any, that the whale shark's 3,000-odd tiny teeth play in feeding.

Now, there is further controversy about *R. typus* in addition to its possible belligerence. First, the gullet of the creature is small, too small, it is thought by some, to accommodate any but very small fish. Second, the creature often feeds in a most extraordinary manner. Third, when it does so, an extraordinary thing is often seen to happen. But, if Stewart Springer did not entirely quench the controversy, he virtually did in January 1957 in the journal *Ecology*. 'The feeding habits of whale sharks, *Rhincodon typus*,' he begins, 'are discussed in considerable detail by Gudger (1941) and include a series of observations attributed to fishermen. . . . Some observations made in September 1951 from the *Oregon* off the coast of Mississippi at the 500-fathom curve were similar to those reported by Gudger in all essential details. "Breezing schools" of blackfin tuna, *Thunnus atlanticus* (Lesson), were first sighted at about 4:00 P.M. in a glassy smooth sea. From that time until nightfall a great many of these schools were continuously in sight. . . . The principal food being sought by the tuna were apparently schools of small fishes estimated at less than 3 inches long. . . . In the center of almost every actively feeding school of tuna there was one whale shark, its head at or above the surface and tail straight downward. The whale shark carried on a kind of pumping action in a 15 to 20 second cycle. The head of the shark would rise about 30 inches above the surface and slowly sink downward, stopping as its open terminal mouth reached the surface. At this point we could see the water pouring into the open mouth of the shark. We could not see the small fish on which the whale sharks were presumably feeding because the cascading water at the whale shark's mouth set off a flurry of tuna strikes. The tuna churned the water right around the shark and we saw several of the tuna leap into the shark's mouth at each cycle. The sea surface near each whale shark was the scene of considerable confusion and the whole sea surface as far as we could see from the *Oregon* was sparsely studded with whale shark heads at intervals of perhaps a quarter of a mile. The whale sharks looked like black oil drums slowly rising and sinking in a long swell, only there was no swell, just a choppy sea ten to a hundred yards in diameter stirred up by the tuna around each whale shark. As the whale shark's mouth filled with water it swam upward until the water had poured out of its gill slits and then started to repeat the cycle.'

Here Springer gets to the heart of the matter. 'Dr. Gudger says of a similar observation . . . "All this phenomenon then, to a non-scientific and non-critical observer at some distance, would appear as if the bonitos were leaping into the mouth of the great shark."'

'Although,' Springer says, 'I attempted to preserve a scientific and critical attitude and was aware of Dr. Gudger's admonition, I still saw the blackfins leap into the shark's mouth, even when at my urging the captain managed to get the vessel within a boat length of a pumping shark. . . . Only a few blackfin tuna were captured [by us], these by trolling. They weighed from 4 to 6 pounds. We hit one of the sharks, apparently of average size, while moving at less than 5 knots. . . . The unexpected shock was quite notable even for the 259 ton vessel.'

Springer draws his conclusion. 'I am inclined to believe that the whale sharks did swallow a considerable number of tuna although

I would be much more certain if we had caught one and had found tuna in the whale shark's stomach.'

On July 2, 1953 Captain Odell Freeze of the shrimp trawler *Doris* was fishing in 31 fathoms in the Gulf of Mexico about 130 miles south of Port Isabel, Texas, his homeport, when in one haul of the net he noticed an egg case. 'I saw this thing in the net,' he later said, 'and, on picking it up, felt something kicking around in it. When I opened it with a knife, out flopped this little shark, very much alive.'

The embryo shark measured $14\frac{1}{2}$ inches overall; the egg case measured 12 inches long, $5\frac{1}{2}$ high and $3\frac{1}{2}$ thick and science is deep in debt to Captain Freeze for keeping both and for delivering them to an ichthyologist. The embryo, a male and almost full term was, down to the spots, obviously a whale shark and until the finding of it, and its egg case, whale shark reproduction had been a total mystery. No whale shark pup or egg case had been seen before and, to date, none has been seen since. But from that lone, fortuitous discovery, science now knows something of *R. typus* young and knows the species to be a layer of eggs.

The only egg case and embryo of the whale shark thus far found. It is interesting that the $14\frac{1}{2}$-inch embryo looks so like the adult, which may be 50 or more feet in length.

CHAPTER 9

Sand, Threshers, Nurses, Carpets, Cats and Dogs

The sharks we turn to now may be less surpassing than some which have gone before, but they have a claim to attention and among them are the sand or sand-tiger sharks of the family Odontaspidae. The family name is quite new. Until quite recently, the usual family name was Carchariidae and the generic name was *Carcharias*.

There are six nominal species of Odontaspidae, but they are so closely related that several may well prove synonymous and we will therefore let *Odontaspis taurus*, the sand shark, speak for the family.

In South Africa the sand shark is also known as the ragged tooth shark and in Australia, where its trivial name is *arenarius* not *taurus*, as the grey nurse. This shark is a common one in water of five feet or less out to 30 feet in tropic and temperate zones, though it is not a member of Britain's shark fauna. The maximum size of the species is about 11 feet and 700 pounds. A length of 6 to 7 feet however, and a weight of 200 to 250 pounds would be close to the mean.

'Proverbially voracious', wrote Bigelow, and Schroeder in 1948, 'the Sand Shark, feeds chiefly on smaller fishes, for the capture of which its slender raptorial teeth are admirably adapted. Large specimens have been taken with as much as 100 pounds of fish in the stomachs, and by eyewitness accounts, schools of them may surround other fish or even those imprisoned in fishermen's nets.'

One eyewitness was the Russell J. Coles whom we quoted in connection with the behaviour of hammerheads. 'They occasionally arrive in large schools,' Coles observed of sand sharks in 1915 in *The Proceedings of the Biological Society of Washington*, 'especially on the shoals extending out beyond Cape Lookout [North Carolina], where they proved very troublesome to the blue-fish [the species *Pomatomus saltatrix*] fishermen. This shark works in a more systematic way in securing its food than any shark of which I know. On one occasion I saw a school of a hundred or more surround a school of blue-fish and force them into a solid mass in shallow water, and then at the same instant the entire school of sharks dashed in on the blue-fish. On another occasion with a large school of blue-fish in my net, a school of these sharks attacked it from all sides and ate or liberated the school of blue-fish, practically ruining the net. Again in July, 1914 on Lookout Shoals, I had a large net filled with blue-fish attacked by a school of about 200 of these vicious sharks and the net ruined. I killed about twenty of them with harpoon and lance. Their average length was slightly in excess of eight feet.'

A shark with these proclivities would not seem to commend itself to aquariums, but the fact is that aquariums like to exhibit *O. taurus*. Its teeth are long and crooked and since several rows are functional they give the creature a menacing, bristly countenance which is the sort of countenance that aquarium visitors expect of a shark. But aquariums also like the sand shark because the sand shark, in a manner of speaking, likes aquariums. It may live for several years, perhaps ten, and even though it seldom stops swimming about the tank, is content with a fraction of the food it seems to need in the wild. Sand sharks of 5 feet at the New York Aquarium are fed about 1½ pounds of mackerel a day and one of 11 feet and something over 300 pounds at Taronga Park Aquarium in Sydney, Australia, subsisted on a yearly 170 to 200 pounds of fish by eating at the most 48 pounds some months and at the least 3 to 4 pounds other months.

The sand shark, the grey nurse to Australians, is an abundant fish and its liver oil at one time lit the lamps of Sydney. 'These sharks', commented Edward Smith Hill in 1864 in *The Annual Report of the Acclimatisation Society of New South Wales*, 'are caught in October, November, and part of December, for their oil alone. . . . During these months they yield a considerable quantity,

The sand shark, *Odontaspis taurus*, is a popular aquarium exhibit. It does well in captivity and has a toothy and fierce look about it, the last in keeping with its temperament.

the quality of which is good, and excellent for burning in lamps. These sharks used to be caught in Botany Bay, at regular "nurse" grounds, near to the Seven-mile Beach, and what is known as "Doll's Point", where they could be seen of a calm day during the months of October and November, lying on the bottom in regular rows like logs of timber, and each row apparently as if they had been selected of one length. . . . The fact is also very curious that when fishing for these sharks you will, with a rare exception, catch them all of one length—no variation which can be detected by the eye, and out of twenty-eight caught in 1857, at one fishing, there was not the slightest perceptible difference.'

Since many species of sharks segregate by size, and we will

subsequently return to this phenomenon, what Hill took to be curious is really not.

The sand shark can be readily identified and not only from the prong-like teeth that are flanked by one ore more basal cusps. The first and second dorsal, the pelvic and anal fins are all about the same size. The tail is not lunate and its upper fork is nearly thrice the length of the lower. Lastly, abaft the pectorals on the sides of the light grey-brown trunk, and on the dorsal and tail fins, are upwards of 100 distinctive oval or round spots from a fifth to three fifths of an inch in diameter and yellowish in colour.

The sand shark migrates offshore as the water temperature nears 67°F. As to pups, the reproduction of *O. taurus* is so unusual that the particulars will be reserved for chapter 11, which has to do with reproduction.

The abundance of *O. taurus* is not confined to Australia and it can be quite extraordinary. During the summer of 1918, by way of example, over Horseshoe Shoal, a few miles off the south shore of Cape Cod in Nantucket Sound, three fishermen caught 1,900 sand sharks. Despite this abundance, though, and despite the creature's edacious feeding habits, *O. taurus* in United States waters has yet to mount an unprovoked attack against a swimmer—in July of 1961 there was a minor incident of provocation in Long Island Sound, New York—and that is indeed curious. In both South Africa and Australia the species has been held responsible for several un-provoked attacks. We have no explanation for the disparity but since *O. taurus* has the potential to do harm wherever it is found, it warrants respect.

In *The Zoologist* for December of 1866, Harry Blake-Knox remarked on Irish ichthyology. 'If Ornithology and Entomology are badly worked out in Ireland how very backward must our Ichthyology be? and so it is. . . . Many book ichthyologists there may be . . . but there are very few of the real true hard-working teach-myself sort, who work the sea themselves, and do not trust to chance sea-shore waifs and market stalls; yes, these are very few, and is it not a pity? . . . still I predict that if I could meet with assistance from various parts of Ireland, Yarrell or Thompson would be no books of reference for the Irish ichthyologist in the future.'

Blake-Knox, apparently, met with no such assistance. Under his name in Bashford Dean's exhaustive *Bibliography of Fishes*, first published in 1917, are listed only two short papers including the one just quoted. So the works of William Thompson (1805–1852) and William Yarrell (1784–1856) are still works of reference for ichthyologists and not Irish ones alone. Ichthyologists who study and write about sharks, however, think kindly of Harry Blake-Knox and it is because of something he saw in Dublin Bay in 1865 and reported along with his lament for Irish ichthyology. First, he notes what Thompson had to say about the thresher shark: 'Can be announced only on circumstantial evidence as frequenting the Irish coast. . . .' Then, he appends his own irreverent note: 'Is often very common in this Bay. Last winter I saw one rise and kill a wounded diver [loon] with a slap of its tail, and then swallow it.'

Blake-Knox was clearly unawed by Thompson. In fact he devotes a good part of his paper to quoting from Thompson's *Natural History of Ireland*, 1856, and then, as he did with the thresher shark, flatly contradicting the quote. But if it seems improbable that a shark would swat a bird with its tail, it can only be said that the thresher is an improbable sort of shark.

To see a thresher, as to see a hammerhead, is to recognize it then and there. The upper fork of its tail is slim and scythe-like and is nearly if not equal to the creature's body length. Thus, since some thresher species reach a length of 20 feet or more, 10 of that 20 feet is a tail fin. To mention that the thresher is of handsome build or to mention that when freshly caught it reflects a lovely lavender tint from its back and a steel-blue from its flanks, is quite all right but unnecessary. No other species of shark has a tail like the thresher's.

That the thresher uses its tail to thresh at or herd together herring, mackerel and the other small fishes on which it feeds, has been long accepted. Nonetheless, in 1916 in the *Brooklyn Museum Science Bulletin*, the deservedly prominent American zoologists John Treadwell Nichols and Robert Cushman Murphy, while they did not doubt that the thresher herded with its tail, they did doubt that it threshed. 'Formerly it was believed that they killed their prey by furious slashes of the flexible tail, but this theory has not been well borne out by observation, and it is at least improbable.'

Next, in 1927 in *Zoologica*, Nichols, this time along with Charles M. Breder, Jr., equally prominent and deservedly so, doubts it once again. 'The thresher's elongate tail is not sufficiently rigid or muscular to strike an efficient blow.'

This is the sort of armchair ichthyology which so annoyed Harry Blake-Knox. For if the literature of science is not rich with accounts of feeding threshers, neither is it barren of them. Blake-Knox's is one and there is no reason to question it. And there are others. In 1915, a year before Nichols and Murphy expressed their doubts, Russell J. Coles, in the same paper in which he described the depredations of sand sharks, reported as follows: 'Late in July, 1914, I saw a shark of this easily identifiable species in the bight of Cape Lookout. Although I was very close to it, I did not have my harpoons at hand and could not capture it. At the time of observation, it was feeding in shallow water by throwing the fish to its mouth with its tail, and I saw one fish, which it failed to seize, thrown for a considerable distance, clear of the water.'

Then, in July 1923, four years before Nichols and Breder expressed their doubts, there was, in *Science*, this note from W. E. Allen of the Scripps Institution of Oceanography at La Jolla, California: 'While taking my plankton collection at about 7.25 a.m., April 14, 1923, I heard a splash near by. Turning, I saw about one hundred feet distant a swirl in the water like that made by a California sea lion. A moment later a long, slender, compressed tail (about three feet long) flashed above the surface and lashed about like a coach whip. . . . At about 7.45 . . . I saw about fifty feet from the pier what appeared *at first* to be a "soup fin shark". . . . It was coming diagonally toward the surface and swimming rapidly. Almost immediately I noticed a small fish (possibly California smelt . . . about ten inches long) frantically swimming just in front. A moment later the pursuer, a six-foot thresher shark, passed partly ahead of the victim (probably half its own length) when it turned quickly and gave the coach-whip lash with the tail which I had seen before. . . . The whip stroke was instantly repeated with very confusing speed, and it then became evident that the victim was seriously injured. It was, however, almost under the drip from my net, at which the shark was apparently frightened. The shark darted away. . . . The victim sank, swimming feebly, then came to the surface and lay on its side awhile. . . . Finally it sank again until out of sight . . . I was much impressed with the speed and skill with which the shark worked and with the accuracy shown in its strokes at a single flying target.'

The thresher shark, *Alopias vulpinus*. The colloquial name derives from the fact that the very long, perhaps 10 feet, upper lobe of the tail fin is used to thresh at small fishes.

In classical times the thresher was called *alopex* by the Greeks and *vulpes* by the Romans because the animal was credited with cunning. Both words mean fox and Aristotle wrote: 'The so-called fox-shark, when it finds it has swallowed the hook, tries to get rid of it . . . it runs up the fishing-line, and bites it off short. . . .'

However in more recent years, the thresher's vernacular names, even those involving the word fox, are tribute to the tail. In his *De Aquatilibus, Libri Duo*, 1553, Pierre Belon, who seems to be the first naturalist to make modern mention of the thresher, gave it the name *simia* from the Latin *simius* for monkey or ape. The first Englishman to describe the thresher, Dr Joannes Caius, again, in 1570 in *De Canibus Britannicis*, called it *cercus* which is a latinization of the Greek *karcos* for tail. Since then—in one place and in one tongue or another—the thresher has been given names to spare; the thrasher shark, the fox shark, the sea fox, the sea ape, the swingletail, the swiveltail, the long-tailed shark, the rat fish, the mouse fish, the peacock shark and there are doubtless more.

There are now six scientifically named species of thresher sharks in the family Alopiidae but, like the sand sharks, species relationships are somewhat muddled. *Alopias pelagicus* and *Alopias profundus* were described and named in 1935 from two specimens caught off Suo on the east coast of Formosa. The literature about these species is very slim although Formosan shark fishermen say that when *A. profundus* is brought aboard it often has mud in its mouth.

The trivial name of *Alopias superciliosus* and its colloquial name, the big-eyed thresher, refer to eyes that, in a 10-foot member of the species, measure some 4 inches in diameter. This thresher is not normally found at the surface of the sea. It frequents the deeps of the tropical and subtropical Atlantic and that accounts for the enormous eyes and the paucity of specimens. For *A. superciliosus* was described and named in 1840 from a specimen taken off the island of Madeira and was not seen again until 1941 when a 12-foot one was landed at Salerno on the Florida west coast. A few more have been caught since and the big-eyed thresher is thought to be, within its range, a reasonably abundant shark.

Many ichthyologists believe that the two Australian threshers, *Alopias caudatus* and *Alopias greyi*, are actually the common thresher, *Alopias vulpinus*. We then are going to proceed on the assumption that the three are one and we are also going to drop the word common from thresher. Henceforth, in this chapter, thresher will mean the common thresher and that is what it meant earlier in the chapter before we took up the subject of species.

Even if it is half tail, the thresher is a large shark. A length of 13 to 16 feet and a weight of 400 to 700 pounds is not an unusual size. At the species' near-maximum length of 20 feet, it probably weighs over 1,000 pounds.

In range, the thresher is a pelagic cosmopolitan in warm temperate and subtropical latitudes and is most often encountered at least a few miles off the coast. Still its excursions close to shore are not infrequent. The normal poleward limits of its seasonal range, a range always exceeded by some individuals, include Ireland, New England on the east coast of the United States, and Oregon on the west, southernmost South Africa, Western Australia and Queensland and so on around the world wherever summertime water temperatures are comparable.

A. vulpinus is probably not sexually mature at much less than 14 feet. Its litters are small, two to four pups, but the pups are very large. One female 14 feet 6 inches long was found to be carrying an embryo 5 feet 1 inch long. Another female, 15 feet 6 inches long was carrying two 5-foot young. That length, however, is probably the near extreme. Free-living threshers of 4 to 5 feet are not at all uncommon and some have been taken smaller still.

The thresher is not commercially important, but it makes for good table fare and good sport too. It often breaches (jumps) in the wild and often when hooked and that, and its size, commends it to anglers. The present I.G.F.A. all-tackle record was taken at Bay of Islands, New Zealand in March 1937 and weighed 922 pounds. The present British record, 280 pounds, was caught at Dungeness in the Straits of Dover in 1933. Neither of the sharks, it seems, was measured for length or girth.

So far as is known, the thresher has never been involved in an attack on a swimmer. But having been known from antiquity, it is no wonder that it got involved in folklore and many are the versions of the tale about how the thresher and the swordfish (*Xiphias gladius* again) together attack the whale. The following, however, is from *Hakluytus Posthumus or Purchas His Pilgrimes*, a continuation of *Hakluyt's Voyages* compiled by Samuel Purchas and published in 1625.

The tale: 'Now of the fight betwixt the Whale and his contraries; which are the Sword-fish and the Thresher . . . the Sword-fish placeth himself under the belly of the Whale, and the Thresher upon the Ryme [the surface] of the water, and with his tayle thresheth upon the head of the Whale, till he force him to give way, which the Sword-fish perceiving, receiveth him upon his sword, and wounding him in the belly forceth him to mount up again: (besides that, he cannot abide long under water, but must of force rise up to breath) and when in such manner they torment him, that the fight is sometimes heard above three leagues distance, and I dare affirme, that I have heard the blowes of the Thresher two leagues off, as the report of a peece of Ordnance, the Whales roaring being heard much farther.'

Whatever the roots of this fable, we did say elsewhere in this book that the swordfish has not got the equipment to feed on a whale and therefore has not reason to attack one; and that the broken off pieces of swordfish swords which are sometimes found in whales probably got there from adventitious collisions.

The thresher is little better equipped than the swordfish. Its small teeth and mouth are suited to small fishes and it is not known to feed on anything else. Fables, though, do have deep roots and as late as the 1880's Francis Day in *The Fishes of Great Britain and Ireland* could still entertain the possibility that the fable of the thresher, the swordfish and the whale might not be fable after all.

The family Orectolobidae is the family of carpet sharks and nurse sharks. There are about a dozen genera—Bigelow and Schroeder, 1948, recognize 11—and some 30 species nearly all of which inhabit the warm shallows of the Indo-Pacific and Red Sea. Most are small, from 2 to 4 feet long, but a few reach 10 feet or a bit more. Some lay eggs, some bear live young. All have two dorsal fins set far back on the body and an anal fin. The caudal trails aft with no lower fork worth the mention. However the most definitive characteristic of the family is the barbel or feeler near each nostril and the deep groove which connects each nostril with the mouth.

The carpet sharks are called so because they are spotted and striped with a variety of brilliant colour on a frequently colourful background. How the word 'nurse' came to be applied to certain orectolobids, and to some other sorts of sharks as well, is an etymological puzzle but the word and its variants are old to the English tongue. Writing of his voyage to Novaya Zemlya in 1556 Stephen Burrough said: 'Munday, we doubled about Caninoze and came at an anker there, to the intent that we might kill some fish if God would permit it, and there we gate a great Nuse, which Nuses were there so plentie, that they would scarcely suffer any other fish to come neere the hookes: the said Nuses caried away sundrie of our hookes and leads.' John Collins in 1682 in *Salt and Fishery, a Discourse Thereof* wrote about the Icelanders: 'Their

Bread is also another sort of Fish, called Hokettle, or the Nurse-Fish, which hath a sharp Ridge on his Back that cuts asunder Fishery-Tackle.'

Possibly, some bygone observer watched a shark giving birth to live young and thought the shark was giving nurse. Possibly the use of the word sprang from the old notion that a shark would protect the young by taking them into its mouth. But the *Oxford English Dictionary* points to another possibility. In medieval times the *n* of *an* was frequently transferred to a following word that began with a vowel. *Huss, husse* and *hurse* were long-ago names for dogfish and with a prefixed *n* they came close to *nuse, nusse* and *nurse*, also long-ago names for dogfish and other sharks as well. *Nurse* survives and so does *huss*. Incidentally, Burrough probably and Collins certainly were writing of the spiny dogfish, *Squalus acanthias.*

Etymological speculations aside, carpet shark patternings serve to match the creatures to the rock or coral bottom on which they live. Moreover, a species that lives on bottom which is also weedy may be further camouflaged by weedy fringes of flesh at the front and sides of its head.

On the top of carpet shark heads behind the eyes are a pair of apertures connecting to the throat. These are called spiracles—many sharks have spiracles although some species have very small ones—and through them carpet sharks can deliver to their gills a steady stream of oxygenated water. Carpet sharks, then, need not swim to breathe so they need not swim to hunt. They can simply lie as a disguised bit of bottom until crab, lobster or fish chances within reach.

The carpet sharks have been described as gentle and inoffensive which they are not. Some of the large species have attacked without provocation and with fatal result. But many of the small sorts have attacked and most often with good reason. Being more or less sedentary they invite spearing or simply bothering and if well hidden they may be accidentally walked on by waders.

In Australia the carpet sharks are called wobbegongs (an aboriginal word) and the English settlers of that land had hardly dropped anchor in 1788 before there was trouble with one. Captain

Arthur Phillip of the Royal Navy, the leader of the settlement expedition and Australia's first governor, recorded the incident in his *Voyage to Botany Bay*, 1789. 'This fish,' said Phillip, 'was met with in Sydney Cove, Port Jackson, by Lieutenant Watts, and is supposed to be full as voracious as any of the genus, in proportion to its size; for having lain on the deck for two hours, seemingly quiet, on Mr. Watt's dog passing by, the shark sprung upon it with all the ferocity imaginable, and seized it by the leg; nor could the dog have disengaged himself had not the people near at hand come to his assistance.'

Wobbegong teeth are sharp and erect and there are several rows of them and the animal does have a penchant for hanging on. In April 1960, for instance, at Rottnest Island off Fremantle in Western Australia, a diver speared a wobbegong. The wobbegong laid hold of the diver's arm. The diver tried to force the wobbegong's jaws with a knife and failed and he next tried to kill the wobbegong and failed. Another diver managed to separate the pair and the bitten diver swam to his boat towing the wobbegong. But as he began to climb aboard, the wobbegong clamped down on his rear and it was not until both were in the boat that the wobby could be dispatched.

Quite obviously, the diver had not read the aforementioned Edward Smith Hill, he who wrote of the grey nurse sharks at Sydney. As Hill would have it, the only time to free oneself from a wobbegong was when it momentarily relaxed prior to taking a still tighter hold and one could tell that opportune time because the wobbegong then went 'gruff-chuff'.

Ginglymostoma cirratum, the nurse shark, is the only species in the family Orectolobidae to inhabit the Atlantic where, to the east, it ranges from tropical West Africa to the Cape Verde Islands and, to the west, from southern Brazil to the Carolinas. It is also the one orectolobid to be found on the Pacific coast of the Americas and there it ranges from Ecuador to Baja California.

G. cirratum is known to reach 14 feet, but may mature quite early. One 5-foot female caught in Bermuda was carrying six well developed embryos 3 to 6 inches long. The usual nurse shark brood, however, counts 20 to 30 foot-long pups.

The nurse shark, *Ginglymostoma cirratum,* **and its fellows
often rest in water so shallow that their dorsal fins stick
above the surface.**

Nurse sharks are decidedly inshore animals and groups of them often rest on the bottom in water so shallow that their dorsals stick above the surface. Gudger remarked that they then '. . . much remind one of well-fed pigs in a barnyard. . . . They lie with heads on each other's pectorals or tails, or one will have his snout elevated on another's flank, or they will lie heads and tails together or in a confused herd'. The analogy with pigs need not end there. Nurse sharks are lazy though greedy feeders and will take pretty much what they can find from sea urchins to crabs, from squid to small fishes.

   G. cirratum also lingers in the caves and under the ledges of reefs, but wherever it is seen in the Atlantic it can be identified from one feature alone. No other Atlantic shark has barbels.

There are two other species of *Ginglymostoma* in the Pacific. *G. ferrugineum*, which grows to 8 or 10 feet, occupies warm waters from the Red Sea to Australasia. *G. brevicaudatum*, which grows to 3 feet, is a member of the Indian Ocean fish fauna and J. L. B. Smith says of it, in *The Fishes of the Seychelles*, 1963: 'Noses about reefs and breaks fish traps.'

Neither of the last two species—nor those species of nurse shark in the allied genus *Nebrius*—are known to be dangerous but *G. cirratum* is. It has attacked with and without provocation and, while there have been no fatalities thus far, the creature is every bit as obdurate as any wobbegong. In April 1958 off Miami Beach, Florida a skin diver grabbed a 5-foot nurse shark by the tail. The shark grabbed the diver by the right thigh. Another diver shot a spear into the shark. The shark persisted. Diver and shark were then helped into a boat where it took ten minutes to part the shark's jaws.

The cat sharks, the family Scyliorhinidae, number 12 genera and some 60 species and they are quite like the carpet sharks. They are decoratively marked with stripes, spots and bars, most of them are small, and, in the main, are creatures of the tropical shallows. Virtually none, however, has barbels or a groove connecting mouth and nostrils.

While the centres of cat shark abundance may be tropical, two of the most common of British and Western European sharks are cat sharks and both figure in the commercial catch of food fish. *Scyliorhinus caniculus*, the lesser spotted dogfish, the rough-dog or rough-hound, grows to 3½ feet and is liberally covered with dark spots of yellowish-grey. When hooked on rod and reel, according to Hugh Stoker in *The Modern Sea Angler*, 1958: 'It cannot be called a fighter, but some have a disconcerting habit, when caught from a boat, of spinning round and round in the water.'

Scyliorhinus stellaris, the greater spotted dogfish, the nursehound or bull huss grows to 5 feet. Its spots are larger than those of *S. caniculus* and dusky red in colour. This species says Stoker, '. . . favours a rocky locality, and is frequently caught, both from the shore and afloat, on hooks and baits intended for conger [eel]. Like the conger, it also takes a lot of killing, and with its blotchy, leathery skin it is a rather ugly brute. For all that, it is quite good to eat. . . .'

Early on in history, several small shark species acquired the vernacular name of dogfish because they hunt in packs like dogs or hounds do. But in the vernacular names of *S. caniculus*, rough-dog and rough-hound the meaning of the word rough is not at all plain. One source has it as descriptive of the sort of sea bottom the species prefers. *S. caniculus*, however, seems to prefer a sandy bottom. Perhaps rough refers to the skin although the skin of both species is rough enough to have been once used as an abrasive.

Like other cat sharks, *S. caniculus* and *S. stellaris* subsist on a variety of small fishes, crustaceans, mollusks, urchins and worms. And like other cat sharks, they lay eggs the cases of which resemble the mermaid's or pixy purses—the egg cases of skates—so familiar to those who comb the beach.

The only cat shark found near the United States east coast is *Scyliorhinus retifer*, the chain dogfish, and it takes its colloquial name from a pattern of lines that give it the appearance of being wrapped in chains. It is a bottom resident between the 40 and 125-fathom contours from New Jersey to the Carolinas.

On the west coast of the United States the only common cat shark is the swell shark, *Cephaloscyllium uter*, of the middle and southern California kelp beds. As a defence mechanism, *C. uter* and other members of the genus can inflate their stomach with air

The swell shark, *Cephaloscyllium uter*, **so-called because it and other members of the genus can, as a defence mechanism, inflate themselves with air or water.**

or water and the corners of their mouth are accordion pleated to allow for this ballooning. It has been said that in New Zealand the swell shark barks like a dog and possibly it does. But the barks must result from the intake and exhaust of ballooning for all sharks now known are, if the word is appropriate, speechless. Many teleosts, however, do have the ability to make purposeful sounds.

In South Africa cat sharks are called *skaamoogs* or *shyeyes* because, when caught, they cover their heads with their tails and this family propensity may account for the name cat shark itself. Cats often sleep with tails covering their heads.

On February 8, 1883 at Amagansett, Long Island, New York, there washed ashore a strange and slender sort of shark 9 feet 8 inches long which in due course proved to be a rare gift of the sea. It was only the second specimen of its kind, the first having been seen in Portugal in 1867, and it differed from other sharks most obviously in the long and low first dorsal, seven times longer than high, or almost the length of the tail.

Since 1867 less than a dozen of these creatures have been taken, all of them by chance and most of them at depths from 1,000 to 5,000 feet. Three, including the first, are recorded from Portugal, one from the Cape Verde Islands, three from Iceland, one from an unspecified locality in the Atlantic, two from the United States and one from Japan for a total of 11.

It would seem, then, an everywhere uncommon shark that uncommonly wanders inshore and it is known as the false cat shark with the one genus and two species, *Pseudotriakis microdon* in the Atlantic and *Pseudotriakis acrages* in the Pacific, occupying the family Pseudotriakidae. The choice of scientific names, however, was a poor one. The false cat sharks are closely allied with the true cat sharks of the family Scyliorhinidae, not with the sharks of the family Triakidae to which we next move.

The Triakidae are yet another large family of small sharks very few of which exceed 5 feet. Smooth dogfish is the all-inclusive vernacular name for the family and here the adjective notes the absence of dorsal spines. Since, though, the triakids populate the shoals and moderate depths of all temperate and tropic oceans, local names are many. On the United States east coast the triakid species *Mustelus canis* is called the smooth dog. In Great Britain *Mustelus mustelus* is called the smooth hound, or, in ironic salute to its redolence of ammonia, Sweet William. In the Canary Islands *M. mustelus* is called *tollo* which means spotted dogfish, a blind for hunting or a bog. In Australia *Mustelus antarcticus* is called the gummy shark and it is commercially exploited as a food fish. In South Africa *Mustelus punctulatus* is sometimes called *spierhaai* or the spear-eyed shark. Granted, *Mustelus* is only one of seven triakid genera, but it contains some 20 species and that is half or more of the family.

Mustelus canis **is known on the United States east coast as the smooth dogfish. In Britain, the closely related** *Mustelus mustelus* **is called the smooth hound. Both species are abundant in the shallows and are frequently caught by anglers.**

The triakids are related to the carcharhinids and in form are much like them. The chief differences are the small size and the teeth of the triakids. The teeth are short and little, but there are many rows and they fashion a rough pavement for holding and crushing the invertebrates, the crabs, lobsters and other crustaceans, and the small fishes which are triakid staples. The entire family bears live young and those species in temperate zones migrate with the season. Abundant is a proper term for the triakids and ranging shoreward to the low water mark as they do, they are often taken by anglers. Harmless, it would seem, is not an invariably proper term. In February 1955 in Trinidad Bay in northern

California a shark with no provocation attacked a skin diver. The shark was about 3 feet long, had black crossbars on its back and black spots on its sides and that identified it as the leopard shark, *Triakis semifasciata*, a species which reaches a length of 5 feet and is found from Oregon to Magdalena Bay in southern California. Fortunately, if not unexpectedly in this instance, the diver was able to beat the little creature off and he was not seriously hurt.

Having given them rather short shrift, we here take leave of the Triakidae. Some will re-emerge further on. The departure is necessary, however, to afford what is due to a quite interesting dogfish and a quite interesting family of sharks.

CHAPTER 10

A Very Mixed Bag

The Squalidae is a family which goes to remarkable extremes. It contains the only polar sharks, the smallest of sharks, the only luminous sharks, the deepest caught of sharks and the shark with the longest gestation period of any vertebrate creature, *Squalus acanthias*.

In North America *S. acanthias* is known as the spiny dogfish and while there are other species with the same vernacular name, spiny dogfish in this chapter refers only to *S. acanthias*.

In Great Britain the spiny dogfish is known as the spurdog or the picked or piked dogfish; in the Faroe Islands as *háur;* in Iceland as *háfur;* in Norway as *pigghå;* in France as *aiquillat;* in South Africa as spiky jack, and they are names that call attention to the animal's mildly poisonous spines, one in front of each dorsal fin. By bowing its body this small shark—not often larger than $3\frac{1}{2}$ feet and 10 pounds—can lash out with these spines and many are the incautious fishermen who have been painfully punctured. Taxonomically, spines are characteristic of several squalid genera and the absence of an anal fin is characteristic of the entire family. In colour, *S. acanthias* is nondescript. It is a slate-grey above, sometimes tinged with brown, which pales to grey-white on the sides and perhaps to pure white on the belly. Usually there is an irregular row of small white spots on the sides, but they fade with age.

It is difficult to be categorical about spiny dogfish distribution. Many ichthyologists in many places have in the past described and named many species of spiny dogfish, and the number of these that are in reality *S. acanthias* will not be known until revision of the genus *Squalus*, a revision the genus begs for and which will take years of comparative study. It is quite possible, however, that there are only a few species of spiny dogfish, so it seems reasonable to say that *S. acanthias*, or a very similar species, is distributed worldwide in waters from the temperate to the subpolar, from the shallows of the shore to the 100-fathom curve.

The spiny dogfish is a migrant and its travels—north and south, from this depth to that, from inshore to offshore or conversely— seem to be keyed to avoiding water that is cooler than about 40°F. or warmer than about 60°F. For the most part, the species winters offshore on the bottom.

Some spiny dogfish travel far and wide. One, tagged off St John's Newfoundland in July of 1942 was recaptured in November off Cape Ann, Massachusetts having travelled a straight-line distance of about 1,000 miles. Another, tagged off Willapa Bay, Washington in 1944 was caught again eight years later near the northern end of Honshu Island, Japan. Here, if the fish kept within its normal depth range and followed the coast, and that seems likely, it travelled much farther than the straight-line distance of 4,700 miles.

There is, however, record of a journey that had to be oceanic. A spiny dogfish tagged off Newfoundland in June of 1947 was recaptured in August 1957 some 1,300 miles away in Faxa Bay, Iceland.

Although it has its numerical ups and downs, *S. acanthias* is by every measure an abundant species and this together with its feeding behaviour has stimulated more heartfelt profanity than any other creature in the entire western Atlantic Ocean. 'The Spiny Dog', noted Bigelow and Schroeder in 1948, 'is as voracious as any fish of its size, and its wanderings on the coast are no doubt chiefly in pursuit of food. Its recorded diet in the Western Atlantic includes capelin, herring, menhaden (*Brevoortia*) mackerel, scup (*Stenotomus*), silver hake (*Merluccius*), cod, haddock, pollock, blennies and croakers (*Micropogon*). . . . Even when newly born they have been seen attacking herring much larger than themselves, as adults do cod and haddock. . . . They also prey on squid and to some extent on worms, shrimps, prawns, crabs. . . . They occasionally feed on

The spiny dogfish or spurdog, *Squalus acanthias*, has become an important ingredient in Britain's fish and chips. In North America, however, the creature is considered to be a destructive pest.

gastropods [snails, slugs and the like] and jellyfish (*Aurelia*), and even red, brown and green algae have been found in their stomachs.'

Next, Bigelow and Schroeder explained the stimulation of profanity: 'From a practical aspect the Spiny Dog in the western Atlantic is chiefly important because it is undoubtedly more destructive to gear and interferes more with fishing operations than does any other fish—shark or teleost. Its habit of taking the bait is proverbial. In fact, when Dogfish are plentiful, hook and line fishing for cod, haddock and other ground fish is often actually prevented. . . . Still more serious is the damage they do by tearing and biting nets, biting snoods off long lines, attacking netted or hooked fish and by driving away better fish.'

We do not, and Bigelow and Schroeder did not, have any latter-day figures to illustrate the cost of spiny dogfish pilferings. However, in the early 1900's in Massachusetts waters alone the estimate was $400,000 annually and, in a *Report of the Commissioners on Fisheries and Game Upon the Damage Caused to the Fisheries of Massachusetts by Dogfish During the Year 1905*, there are these notes:

'September 5—Schooner "Emilia Enos" of Provincetown . . . arrived at Boston . . . with a broken trip [a trip cut short] of 5,000 pounds of fresh haddock and 5,000 pounds of fresh codfish, the whole stock amounting to about $250. The broken trip was the result of the ravages of the dogfish . . . an average catch would have been about 50,000 pounds of fish and stock $1,000.'

'September 7—Schooner "Alena L. Young" of Rockport, Mass., arrived at Boston. . . . This vessel was out on the voyage ten days, and the crew of 10 men shared [earned] only 34 cents each, owing to the fact that dogfish were numerous on the fishing ground. Broken trips like this discourage the men, and often they leave the vessel. . . .'

'October 12—Schooner "Louise Cabral" reports catching a dogfish with a rubber band around its head. . . .'

The North American fisherman still pays dearly for damage done by *S. acanthias* and, at the time of writing, there is little in the way of a compensatory market for the beast. There are technological problems in reducing it to meal or fertilizer, and there is difficulty in overcoming unwarranted prejudice about sharks as food fish. In northern Europe and the British Isles the situation is quite otherwise. There the spiny dogfish is no less destructive, but it is at least counted among the more worthwhile food fish species.

In Britain the spurdog is sold under the name of flake or rock salmon and a great deal of it is served in fish and chip shops. However, since *S. acanthias* accounts for about 99 per cent of Britain's dogfish catch, by the mid-1960's the fish and the fishery were showing signs of stress. In 1952 about 14,000 tons of spurdog were landed. By 1965 this had fallen to about 5,500 tons. Norwegian

A commercial haul of spiny dogfish or spurdog. Although once considered abundant, the spurdog in European waters is showing signs of depletion.

landings had similarly fallen, from 30,000 tons in 1963 to below 19,000 tons in 1965.

The truth is that *S. acanthias* may be abundant if undisturbed or properly managed as a resource, but it is sensitive to fishing because it simply is not fecund. Tagging studies have revealed that the creature has a life span of 25 to 30 years. Still, the male does not reach sexual maturity until the age of 11 and the female does not until, remarkably, the age of 19 or 20. Litters, furthermore, are small, four to seven pups generally, and they are whelped after a gestation period of 20 to 24 months, the longest among vertebrates.

We might add, nonetheless, that a sea fishery has yet to threaten a sea fish with extinction. The point may be reached where a particular stock of fish becomes so depleted as to make further exploitation unprofitable. But that point is reached before the stock is too depleted to renew itself sooner or later. This is not to speak in behalf of unbridled fishing. It is to say that in the long run the fishery suffers more from overfishing, given the present state of the art, than does the fish.

The function of *S. acanthias* in the laboratory is unenviable but of consequence. Sharks represent a primitive vertebrate type which is simple yet has most major features of higher forms, or of their embryos, human ones included. The spiny dogfish and the smooth dogfish, the genus *Mustelus*, are small convenient sharks which, if needs be, do nicely in captivity and they therefore lend themselves to a broad spectrum of basic physiological research, the outcome of which could well advance such fields as human cardiology or immunology. At a more mundane level, every year and the world over, dogfish in multiples of thousands are dissected by students training in zoology or vertebrate taxonomy.

On June 8, 1908 in Batanga Bay on the island of Luzon in the Philippines a shark was trawled up from 170 fathoms. It was a squalid new to science and since it fitted no existing family genus, Hugh M. Smith and Lewis Radcliffe of the United States National Museum set up the genus *Squaliolus* and named the shark *Squaliolus laticaudus*. They described its colour, in the museum's *Proceedings* for 1912, as jet black with white fins and its form as graceful and cigar-shaped. But what was most significant about the shark, a

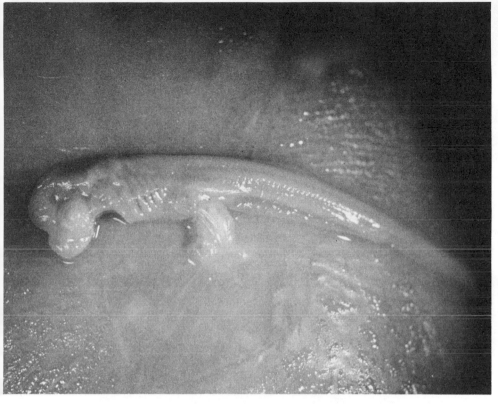

A spiny dogfish embryo in the oviduct. It is 19 mm in length and in the fourth month of a two-year gestation period, the longest such of any vertebrate creature.

male, was that it measured 15 centimetres or just 5·9 inches in length, yet was fully mature. *S. laticaudus*, then, is the smallest of known sharks or, to put it a bit more conservatively, the smallest of sharks for which the length at maturity is known.

About a year later, another *S. laticaudus*, this one a female 11·5 centimetres or 4·3 inches long, was taken in the same place and for many years thereafter the two Philippine specimens stood alone. On the night of June 2, 1961, however, Japanese shrimp fishermen in Suruga Bay on the south central coast of Honshu caught no less than five, all measuring between four and five inches, and the ichthyologist Tokiharu Abe gave the species the vernacular name

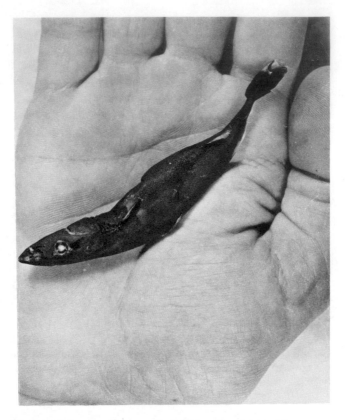

Squaliolus laticaudus, **the smallest of known sharks. The Japanese know it as tsuranagakobitozame which means the dwarf shark with a long face.** (*Actual size*)

tsuranagakobitozame meaning the dwarf shark with a long face or head.

The Atlantic dwarf shark may be a second species of the genus or it may be synonymous with *S. laticaudus*. Early in the 1920's, though, a shark about 9 inches long was taken at Madeira and on reading the paper wherein it was described and named *Squaliolus sarmenti*, one discovers why Madeira has always been so productive of new species of fish including such sharks as the big-eyed thresher *Alopias superciliosus* and the false cat shark *Pseudotriakis microdon*.

'In the present paper,' wrote Adolfo Cesar Di Noronha in the *Annals of the Carnegie Museum*, 1925–1926, 'I give an account of a deep-sea shark taken in Madeiran waters during the month of September, 1923, by fishermen from the village of Coma de Lobos, with the lines they use for the capture of the common "*Peixe espada preto*" or Black Swordfish (*Aphanopus carbo* Lowe). These long lines have procured for me, from the horizon of that fish, many interesting deep-sea species, some of them unknown to science, others rare, or at least not yet recorded from these waters.'

The horizon of *Aphanopus carbo* is from 500 to 800 fathoms and few commercial fisheries extend to those depths. *Aphanopus carbo*, incidentally, is not a swordfish in that it has a beak or bill. It is a teleost that grows to about 6 feet and it belongs to the family Trichiuridae, the members of which are also, and more often, called cutlass or scabbard fish because of their long, straight-sided bodies.

To the best of our knowledge the Madeiran black swordfish fishery has yet to yield another specimen of *S. sarmenti* or, as the case may be, *S. laticaudus*. However, a second specimen has been caught and in curious circumstances. Slightly smaller than the first, though also a female, it was taken in April of 1935 near Arcachon, France, on the Bay of Biscay, not from hundreds of fathoms as might be expected, but from among eel grass in very shallow water.

The most brilliantly luminous of the Squalidae, which are the only light-emitting sharks, is *Isistius brasiliensis*, a pelagic species which attains a length of about 20 inches and ranges the tropic and subtropic belts of all seas. The creature was first described in 1824, but the earliest notice of its luminescence dates from 1840 and the publication of *Narrative of a Whaling Voyage Round the Globe, from the Year 1833 to 1836* by Frederick Debell Bennett, a naturalist and Fellow of the Royal College of Surgeons, London.

'Two examples of this fish were accidentally taken, at different periods of the voyage, by a net, towing on the surface of the sea. The first . . . was ten inches in length. It was captured in the daytime, and consequently . . . its phosphorescent power was not then noticed. The second specimen was taken at night. . . . Its entire length was 1½ foot. Both fishes were alive when taken on board. They fought fiercely with their jaws, and had torn the net in several places.

'When the larger specimen, taken at night, was removed into a dark apartment, it afforded a very extraordinary spectacle. The entire inferior surface of the body and head emitted a vivid and greenish phosphorescent gleam, imparting to the creature, by its own light a truly ghastly and terrific appearance. . . . The only part of the under surface of the animal which was free from luminosity was the black collar around the throat.'

Bennett remarked that his *Isistius brasiliensis* lived and luminesced out of water for more than three hours and he then came to a conclusion. 'It was my first impression, that the fish had accidentally contracted some phosphorescent matter from the sea, or from the net in which it was captured; but the most rigid investigation did not confirm this suspicion . . . did not leave a doubt in my mind but that it [the luminosity] was a vital principle, essential to the economy of the animal.'

Finally, Bennett allowed himself to speculate. 'The small size of the fins would appear to denote that this fish is not active in swimming, and since it is highly predaceous, and evidently of nocturnal habits, we may perhaps indulge in the hypothesis, that the phosphorescent power it possesses is of use to attract its prey, upon the same principle as the Polynesian Islanders, and others, employ torches in night fishing.'

Phosphorescent is not the proper term for *I. brasiliensis*. Something that is phosphorescent gives off light only after it has itself been exposed to light. The luminosity of *I. brasiliensis* derives from hundreds of light-producing organs called photophores and the proper term for the creature is therefore bioluminescent. Apart from that, Bennett was not wide of the mark and scientists are still speculating, as they have been for centuries, about the function of bioluminescence. In 1957 in *The Physiology of Fishes*, a two-volume collection of papers, E. Newton Harvey, the American scientist who devoted a long and distinguished lifetime to bioluminescence, ended his contribution thus: 'Although the purpose of luminescence in fish can hardly be considered a physiological subject, and definite answers are apt to be mere guesses, the extensive evolution of diverse and complicated luminous organs among both elasmobranches [sharks, skates and rays] and teleosts must have some meaning. The previous comparison between chromatophore and photophore systems is of special import. The chromatophore or color distribution of surface fish undoubtedly often supplies the recognition pattern by which individuals of one species recognize each other, or male recognizes female during the daytime. In the dark depths of the sea, the photophore pattern, different for each species and in some cases different in male and female, may be thought of as supplying the recognition pattern. Even if the distribution of male and female photophores is similar, it is quite possible that a different pattern of control of the lights by male and by female allows the sexes to be identified. This appears to be one important and likely use of fish photophores.

'Luminescence of surface fish,' Harvey continued, 'can be of value only at night and the above reasoning would apply to any species with nocturnal habits. It has also been suggested that light organs of fish may actually be used to illuminate the surroundings, to attract the sexes, to attract food, a lure as in the illicium [the stalk with a lighted tip] of deep-sea angler fishes, a warning that the species is distasteful, or a means of defense, for confusing an attacking fish. A sudden flash of light might blind a predator while the prey escapes. Such uses are reasonable but very difficult to prove, and the whole subject must be left for future observation and experiment.'

In 1964 a mature female shark some $16\frac{1}{2}$ inches long was collected about 100 miles south of Dauphin Island, Alabama, in the Gulf of Mexico and that same year J. A. F. Garrick and Stewart Springer, in *Copeia*, described and named it as a new species, *Isistius plutodus*. They observed that it has fewer photophores than *I. brasiliensis*, and commented that they are 'restricted to lower abdominal surface and sparse.' Still, it is only the second known species of the genus.

It is often impossible to precisely fix the depth at which a fish has been caught. Most specimens are trawled and few trawls are either self-closing or remotely closeable from aboard ship. As a consequence, scientists cannot be certain what the trawl may have netted at trawling depth and what it may have netted on its way down or its way up. About the squalid *Centroscymnus coelolepis*, however, scientists are certain.

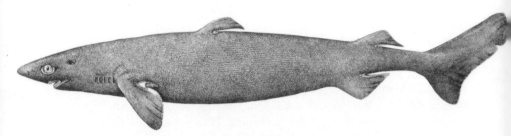

The small Portuguese shark, *Centroscymnus coelolepis,* **has been taken at a depth of 8,922 feet, the deepest that any shark has yet been caught.**

C. coelolepis—it was once fished commercially in Portugal hence its colloquial name, the Portuguese shark—inhabits the western Mediterranean and both sides of the North Atlantic. The species is an abundant one with adults averaging 3 to 3½ feet in length, but what is noteworthy is the depth at which Portuguese sharks have been caught. They have been caught as deep as 8,922 feet and the depth is certain because they were caught in traps set on the bottom. No other species of shark has been taken from deeper water although off West Africa an odd looking 6-foot shark with bulging eyes was seen from the French bathyscaph *FNRS 3* below 13,000 feet.

In this chapter we have thus far touched upon sharks that are small to tiny, bizarre and, with the exception of *Squalus acanthias*, more or less secluded. But among the 11 presently recognized genera of Squalidae there are two that include bizarre sharks which are neither small nor lead secluded lives.

The genus *Echinorhinus* has in it several named species but all are thought to be one and the same with *Echinorhinus brucus*, another of the few sharks which pose no problems in recognition. Its body and fins are generously scattered with large button-like dermal denticles from each of which sprouts one or more curved spines. Logically, the animal is known as the spinous, spiny, briar or bramble shark and it may be met with almost anywhere from tropic waters to temperate ones, from 10 fathoms or less to 100 fathoms and beyond.

A bottom resident, *E. brucus* is often unintentionally caught on hook and line and the largest on record in Great Britain seems to be one reported by Day; 'a female, 9 feet long, containing 17 eggs, was taken on a conger line January 1st, 1869, off the Eddystone, inside it were several dog-fishes, some 3 feet in length.'

Day also remarked on a very determined bramble shark: 'On June 2nd, 1881, one, 6 feet long, was caught 16 miles off the Deadmans on a hook and line when fishing near the bottom for congers. The bait used was a piece of mackerel; the creature showed considerable violence before capture, and after being taken into the boat and it took a deal of mauling before the hook could be extracted, when it was thrown aside and left for dead; ten hours after, on being landed, it was found to be still alive.'

Strange it may be, but in the western Atlantic *E. brucus* is a true rarity. A bramble shark drifted ashore at the tip of Cape Cod in 1878. Twenty years later, one was caught off Buenos Aires, Argentina. A third and, to date, the last was taken off Virginia in January 1968.

The genus *Somniosus* contains the only sharks that inhabit polar waters all the year round and, as the generic name implies, they are a torpid lot. Some, in fact are notoriously so, and it is an aspect of their nature that makes them not only interesting but also puzzling. First, though, to species.

There are five nominal species. *Somniosus rostratus* ranges the Mediterranean and to some extent westward of it. *S. longus*, which is probably *S. rostratus*, ranges Japanese waters. *S. antarcticus* was described and named from a specimen stranded on Macquarie Island, almost 1,000 miles south of Australia, in 1912 and none has been seen since. *S. pacificus* ranges from Japan to the Bering Sea and Alaska south, now and then, to California. *S. microcephalus* ranges both sides of the North Atlantic; on the one side from east and west Greenland periodically south to the Gulf of Maine, on the other side from Spitzbergen south to the southern North Sea.

Somniosus microcephalus, **the Greenland or sleeper shark, which is remarkable, among other things, for its seeming lethargy. Also, the genus contains the only sharks,** *S. microcephalus* **being one, to inhabit polar waters all the year round.**

Beyond mentioning that *S. rostratus* does not seem to exceed 3 feet, we are, for the most part, going to confine ourselves to *S. microcephalus*. It is by far and away the best known shark of the genus and at least some of what can be said about it can be said also about the closely related *S. pacificus*.

S. microcephalus, the Greenland or sleeper shark, is a large animal. Ones of 8 to 14 feet are not unusual and some are larger still. But considering that the species is very abundant within its arctic range and is heavily fished there for liver oil, it is somewhat startling to find that the largest of Greenland sharks was caught in 1895 off May Island in the Firth of Forth, Scotland. It was 21 feet long and weighed 2,250 pounds. On the other hand, *S. microcephalus* is not uncommon in northern British waters.

Ove Bøje, in 1939 in *Meddelelser om Grønland*, made the following observations about the Greenland fishing and the fish. 'Every year large numbers of this shark are caught with hook and line, with blubber for bait, from boats in the summer months, from the ice in winter. At Angmagssalik there is a special method; the Eskimo makes a hole in the ice and, from a groove at the edge of this hole, allows blood to ooze out into the water; sharks that are lured by the blood are harpooned or simply caught by the eyes and dragged out of the water—a form of sport devoid of all danger, for this shark is incredibly apathetic. I myself have caught a live, unwounded shark from a boat, simply by seizing its tail.'

The puzzling part to this well-documented apathy is how *S. microcephalus* catches its prey. The creature will eat almost anything —New England fishermen named it the gurry shark, the word gurry being a nautical version of garbage—but its stomach frequently yields active animals of the order of squid, herring, halibut, salmon and seals. Furthermore, the frequency is such as to make unwarranted any presumption that the Greenland shark is dependent on the halt and the dead. Seals, in fact, are said to become scarce when the shark is about.

In whatever way it manages—one plausible conclusion is that if it needs food it can muster energy enough to catch it—*S. microcephalus* still labours under a handicap. Attached to the cornea of each eye of most Greenland sharks is a parasitic copepod. There are two species, *Ommotokoita superba* and *O. elongata* and they range in length from 3 or 4 millimetres to nearly three inches. The rule is one copepod to one eye and rarely are there more than two. They are whitish-yellow in colour and adults with large egg sacs are particularly conspicuous.

Vision may not be of paramount importance in the feeding of sharks, but it is certainly of considerable importance and the vision of Greenland sharks would seem to be seriously impaired for even uninfested ones usually have scarred and opaque corneas from past copepod presence. There is, though, a belief that the copepods are useful to *S. microcephalus* and a Norwegian biologist who spent several months in the Greenland shark fishery reported on it in *Nature* for August 19, 1961. 'The sluggishness of this shark,' commented Bjørn Berland, 'is proverbial, and it is to many a puzzle how such a sluggish fish is able to capture live prey.'

But he goes on to say: 'The information received from the

fishermen tends to show that, besides many other marine animals, the char, *Salmo alpinus* [a lively fish], has been repeatedly found in the stomach contents of this shark, even so freshly swallowed that it could be used for human consumption on board. According to information received from several skippers, some of the chars found in shark stomachs had been cut by the shark's teeth when captured, and in such cases their tail parts were invariably missing in the stomach contents. This naturally leads to the assumption that the char has been swallowed head foremost by the shark. It is believed very strongly by Norwegian fishermen, who have been fishing for Greenland sharks, that its potential prey is lured to swim toward it by the "white things", that is, the copepod. . . . The copepods are said to be luminous by some fishermen.'

Berland had strong reservations. His copepod specimens did not luminesce and he emphasized that in E. Newton Harvey's exhaustive 1952 book, *Bioluminescence*, their family was not cited as luminescent. Still, the conspicuousness of the copepods kept him from discarding out of hand the possibility that they could attract prey and that the relationship between copepods and *S. microcephalus* could therefore be one of mutual dependence or symbiotic.

As if there were not enough of the peculiar about the Greenland shark, its flesh, unless dried or boiled in several changes of water, is highly toxic. It causes symptoms similar to those caused by too much alcohol and the Eskimos refer to someone who is drunk as shark-sick. Sledge dogs are fed prepared shark meat, but when they get hold of fresh meat and actually become shark-sick the Eskimos refer to them as *silaerupok* or drunk.

Eskimos will not eat Greenland shark meat except out of necessity and coming from a people who consider fish eyes, old seal fat and botfly larvae as delicacies, this is a recommendation of the lowest order.

S. microcephalus, which bears its young alive, is dark brown or grey in colour and the back and sides may be faintly crossed with darker bands or faintly spotted with white. Its fins are small, its snout short, and therefrom *microcephalus*. Its teeth are smooth-edged but those in the upper jaw are tapered like slender thorns while those in the lower jaw are squarish and overlapping with the cusp bent so much to the side as to form an unbroken cutting edge. Of these lower teeth the Eskimos once fashioned barbering tools. Superstition would not let iron touch Eskimo hair.

The shark itself has a place apart in Eskimo mythology. All other Greenland fishes were created from chips of wood. But the shark smelled so strongly of ammonia that it was given quite a different genesis. Long ago, the legend would have it, an old woman had washed her hair with urine and was drying it with a cloth. A gust of wind carried the cloth to sea and there it turned into *skalugsuak*, the Greenland shark.

The four species in the family Oxynotidae are much alike. They are small, no longer than 3 feet, and they live in the ocean's moderate depths between 30 and 300 fathoms. They are also among the unloveliest of sharks. The little head could have been borrowed from a beaver. The body is plump and in cross-section triangular. The tall dorsals are each pierced by a spine and could pass for sails. The mouth is tiny with fleshy lips and it is a thicket of tiny, sharp teeth. The skin is so prickly that it puts one in mind of a bundle of barbed wire. There is, however, about the sum of these parts, a certain jauntiness, even winsomeness.

While some taxonomists group the single genus *Oxynotus* with the *Squalidae*, those who treat it as a separate family have seemingly good reason. For the odd arrangement of the upper teeth sets the oxynotids apart from both the squalids and all other sharks. In the first row there are just two or three teeth. But in each succeeding row more teeth are added until the six or so functional rows form a triangular patch on the roof of the mouth.

Oxynotus centrina frequents the Mediterranean and neighbouring eastern North Atlantic north, regularly, to the Bay of Biscay and in 1877 one was trawled in 26 fathoms off the Cornish coast of England. 'As I have said', wrote Thomas Cornish in *The Zoologist* of that year, 'these large standing dorsals at once distinguish this fish, and if it ever gets common enough to require an English name it should be called the Spritsail Shark.'

It did not become that common. The 1877 *O. centrina* was the first caught in British waters and seemingly the last.

O. paradoxus is another eastern North Atlantic species and it ranges from Morocco north to Ireland. British waters have yielded several specimens. In Australian and New Zealand waters where the oxynotids are represented by *O. bruniensis*, Australians know it as the prickly dogfish.

In October of 1960 an oxynotid was caught at 250 fathoms off Venezuela and by scientific lights the event was a rare one. First, until then the western North Atlantic had been thought devoid of oxynotids. Second, the catch was a new species and the Venezuelan ichthyologist Fernando Cervigon described and named it *Oxynotus caribbaeus*. Knowledge of the species' distribution, though, awaits the taking of more than that single specimen and it may be some time. Oxynotids seem nowhere very abundant.

The higher sharks have herein had the higher priority. Thus, there is not the space, nor in most instances the information, to dwell long upon four shark families which are generally considered to be the exotic remnants of ancient and perhaps slowly dying stocks. Nonetheless, the Hexanchidae, the Heterodontidae, the Scapano-rhynchidae and the Chlamydoselachidae do deserve attention.

The six-gilled shark, the seven-gilled shark, the comb-toothed shark, the cow shark, the mud shark, the one-finned shark, the grey shark, the bullshark, the bulldog shark, the griset and the perlon are all vernacular names for the Hexanchidae.

The sharks in this family cannot be mistaken for those in any other. They have either six or seven gill slits rather than the customary five. Also the lower teeth are distinctive. Each one has several parallel, more or less erect cusps which give it the look of a little comb.

The three hexanchid genera are *Hexanchus*, *Heptranchias*, and *Notorynchus* and their range is worldwide from the shallows to deep water. The number of species is in dispute. There are more than a dozen nominal ones, but some scientists lean toward the belief that there may be only three, one in each genus. We will do likewise because even if the belief proves illfounded, the three species probably typify their respective genera.

Heptranchias perlo, in Australia *H. dakini*, is a seven-gilled shark with a narrow head and sharp snout. It is mature at about 3 feet and grows to near 7. In the western Atlantic it has been taken only off Cuba, but the Mediterranean is one of its centres of abundance and in Spanish waters the creature is said to destroy great quantities of food fish, hake in particular.

Notorynchus maculatus, in Australia *N. cepedianus*, is a seven-gilled shark with a broad head and round snout. It reaches 10 feet in length, possibly more. The creature is best known in the Indo-Pacific and in South Australia is considered dangerous. In California it has been characterized as pugnacious.

The six-gilled shark is *Hexanchus griseus*. Like the seven-gilled ones, it is mostly a bottom inhabitant. But it grows to a far greater size reaching 15 feet 6 inches and 1,600 pounds. The longest on record supposedly measured 26 feet 5 inches and while some investigators have questioned the record, they seem to have missed the evidence that invalidates it. What follows, then, exemplifies how errors can be unwittingly propagated time and again.

In *The Zoologist* for 1846 Jonathan Couch reported that: 'On the 19th of February of the present year (1846) there was caught by a fisherman of Polperro, and immediately brought to me, a specimen of a fish, which I recognized as the six-branchial, or Gray Shark: a species new to the Fauna of Cornwall, and until lately, to Britain .... The length of this specimen was 2 feet, 2½ inches. . . .'

In the *Fishes of Great Britain and Ireland*, in his intriguing discussion of *H. griseus*, Francis Day reported that: 'February 19th, 1846, one 26 feet 5 inches in length [was] captured at Polperro, in Cornwall.'

Now, Couch in his major work *A History of the Fishes of the British Islands*, 1862–1865, makes no mention of the large specimen mentioned later by Day. Rather, he referred again to his small specimen. 'The example from which the description is taken, measured in length no more than two feet two inches and a half; but it has been caught of the length of eleven or twelve feet.'

Polperro fishermen commonly brought specimens to Couch. So it seems very improbable that a six-gilled shark 26 feet 5 inches long, landed on the same day and at the same port as the one of 2 feet 2½ inches, would have escaped his notice.

There is, though, more. We propose that Day, who did make reference to Couch's 1846 paper, had every intention of giving the length of the small Polperro specimen. We also propose that Day converted 2 feet 2½ inches into 26·5 inches and that either Day out of inadvertence, or perhaps an editor out of misinterpretation, wrote it 26 feet 5 inches. Because, Day's last sentence is quite out of character. If he had indeed meant to give record of a shark which was extraordinarily large whatever the species, it is hardly likely that, one short sentence later, Day would finish with *H. griseus* by writing: 'It is said to grow to a large size.'

Logical as it all seems, the record cannot be put to absolute rights. Couch died in 1870 and that was some years before publication of the probable error.

The family Heterodontidae is a family of small sharks none of which outgrows 5 feet and all of which are creatures of the littoral Pacific. And they are an odd-looking lot. The head is big, broad and very blunt with rounded cheeks and a ridge over the eyes. The dorsals are tall and fronted by a spine. The body is robust forward and disproportionately slim aft. The pectorals are expansive and were they less so one suspects that heterodontids would be forever standing on their heads.

There is the one genus *Heterodontus* and perhaps seven species and the first to be described and named, *Heterodontus portusjacksoni* of Australian waters, was collected shortly after the arrival of Australia's settlers in 1788.

The heterodontids have been collectively endowed with a number of common names. Most often, and appropriately, they are called the Port Jackson sharks. But they are also called the oyster crushers, a name which reflects the family diet of mollusks and crustaceans, and they are also called the bullhead sharks, a name which reflects the obvious.

The only heterodontid species on North American shores is *Heterodontus francisci* and it is abundant southward of Point Conception, California. It is known as the hornshark, after the shape of the dorsal spines, and sometimes the pig shark after the shape of the head. The beast does well in aquariums and we will have more to say about it in the next chapter.

Late in the 1880's, Alan Owston, a shipmaster and naturalist living in Yokohama, got from a Japanese fisherman a 42-inch male shark with a most grotesque head. Its flat snout had, from above, the look of a mason's trowel and it stuck far out over a protruding beak-like mouth.

Since the shark was of an unknown sort, Owston gave it to Kakichi Mitsukuri, Professor of Zoology at the University of Tokyo, and when the professor visited the United States in 1897 he brought it along and asked David Starr Jordan to identify it. Jordan, a noted ichthyologist and president of what was then Leland Stanford Junior University, thought the shark 'very remarkable' and being unable to fit it into any known family he honoured the professor by erecting the family Mitsukurinidae wherein was the single genus *Mitsukurina*. Then, at the professor's request, Jordan honoured Owston by naming the shark *Mitsukurina owstoni*.

The honour to Mitsukuri, sad to relate, was short-lived. In 1899, in the *Annals & Magazine of Natural History*, Arthur Smith Woodward of the British Museum pointed out that *M. owstoni* was remarkable not for its peculiar appearance, but because it was a living relic of a family presumed from fossil remains in Syria, to have lapsed into extinction during the Cretaceous period 90 to 140 million years ago. In due course, Woodward's generic name *Scapanorhynchus*—meaning shovel-snout and which he had already given the fossil sharks—replaced *Mitsukurina* and Owston was left to survive in the new specific name *Scapanorhynchus owstoni*, the valid name still.

There may or may not be a second living species in the family

The goblin shark, the genus *Scapanorhynchus*, which name aptly means shovel-snout, is known mostly from Japan and until 1899 was thought to be long extinct.

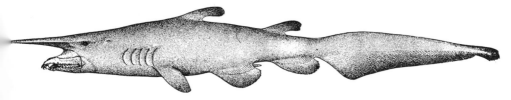

Scapanorhynchidae. In 1909 *S. jordani*, also from Japan, was proposed as new, but there is no certainty that it is and Jordan too might have to depart from the family.

S. owstoni is related to the sand sharks (Odontaspidae), grows to 11 feet at least, frequents deep water and probably bears live young. Beyond that, little is known about the shark but here is what Owston wrote of it in a letter to Jordan: 'This shark is taken mostly at Kozu near Odawara [on Sagami Bay about 60 miles south of Tokyo] where. . . . There is a bank with 53 fms. on it close to depths of 300 to 400 fms. . . . Mostly females are taken, and in the spring-time only. They are caught in *naname* (7-mesh nets), which are set at the upper edge of the bank, so catching the fish when they come up from the deep. Oil is extracted from the liver, but the flesh is used only for fertilizing purposes.

'This Shark,' Owston continued, 'appears to be fairly well known at this particular spot only, where they call it *Tengu-zame*, Goblin or Elfin Shark. I showed a figure of it to half a dozen fish-mongers at Odawara, only four miles away, and not one of them had even seen or heard of such an animal.'

Elsewhere in the world, catches of goblin sharks are few and far between. The species has been taken off Portugal, but its presence in the Indian Ocean is known only because one bit, broke and left a tooth in a telegraph cable at 750 fathoms.

The most primitively structured of sharks is *Chlamydoselachus anguineus*, the one genus and the one species in the family Chlamy-doselachidae, and it and the goblin shark are in some ways similar. Both are the sole living representatives of sharks long extinct with those represented by *Chlamydoselachus* being known from fossil teeth of 12 to 20 million years ago. Both were discovered by science at about the same time and both were discovered in Japan in the same region. Both are sharks of deep water and both are seldom caught elsewhere than in Japan. Similarities, however, end at looks. Even with its outlandish head, the goblin shark looks like a shark; *Chlamydoselachus* looks like a snake and this quite impressed Harvard's Samuel Garman who described and named the creature in 1884. 'Such an animal as that described', Garman wrote in *The*

Bulletin of the Essex Institute, 'is very likely to unsettle disbelief in what is popularly called the "sea serpent". Though it could hardly on examination be taken for anything but a shark, its appearance in the forward portion of the body, particularly in the head, brings vividly to mind the triangular heads, deep-cleft mouths, and fierce looks of many of our most dreaded snakes. In view of the possible discoveries of the future, the fact of the existence of such creatures, so recently undiscovered, certainly calls for a suspension of judgment in regard to the non-existence of that oft-appearing but elusive creature the serpent-like monster of the oceans.'

In the wake of that digression, Garman gets on with his general comment about the shark. 'A diameter of less than four inches to a length of five feet marks one of the slenderest of the tribe. . . . The delicate margins and filaments of the fins are those of an inhabitant of the open sea or considerable depths. . . . Rapidity of movement is suggested by the large amount of surface in the posterior fins. It is probable, however, that the large fins, being so far back, are important as support for the body when the anterior portion is quickly plunged forward to seize the prey; that is, they secure a fulcrum from which the animal may strike like a snake. The anterior fins (pectorals) being only of moderate size are yet ample for balancing or directing the body when in motion however rapid. . . . The teeth are constructed for grasping and from their peculiar shape and sharpness it would seem as if nothing that once came within their reach could escape them. Even in the dead specimen the formidable three-pronged teeth make the mouth a troublesome one to explore. . . . No other shark of which we know has the opercular flap free across the throat.'

No other shark does have a gill slit—in *Chlamydoselachus* it is the first of the six—that reaches from side to side uninterrupted. But neither does any other shark have prominent gill covers, the folds of which give the neck a cloaked or frilled look and which in part led Garman to name the creature as he did. The generic name *Chlamydoselachus* translates to cloak or frill shark while the trivial name *anguineus* means snaky, the other Garman impression.

Except in Japan the animal's colloquial name is the frilled shark.

The Japanese call it *rabuka* or the silk shark, possibly noting the delicate fins, sometimes *kagura* or the scaffold shark, noting, perhaps, the gill slit around the neck like a rope, and sometimes *tokagizami* or the lizard shark. The longest on record was taken, as most frilled sharks are, in Sagami Bay. It measured 6 feet 4 inches, but one caught at Bugonaes on Varanger Fjord, Norway in August of 1896 was very nearly that length.

Possibly, a few more than 15 frilled sharks have been collected outside of Japan and these in the main off the Iberian and North African coasts. Since 1935, however, at least four, from 4 feet 4 inches to the near record length of 6 feet 2 inches, have been caught, at about 300 fathoms, in Scottish and Irish waters.

The question of whether the frilled shark ranges the Indo-Pacific and other ocean areas is an open one. But it can be said of both the frilled shark and the goblin shark, and we said it earlier about deep water species, that more might be caught and their range perhaps extended if more commercial fishing were carried on at the depths they frequent. That accounts for Japan's yield of the new and the rare and, as we also said before, Madeira's. In fact, in March 1899, Madeira yielded the first of Atlantic frilled sharks. It was an immature female 23·7 inches long.

In Sagami Bay the pupping time for the frilled shark is reported to be from the end of April to the beginning of June. The young are born alive and, because the frilled shark is so primitive, that is a bit surprising. There are six to twelve pups in a litter and they are 12 to 14 inches long. Not much else, unhappily, is known about the life history of *Chlamydoselachus anguineus.*

The next two families also date from antiquity, but they are moré highly specialized.

The family Pristiophoridae, the sawsharks, resemble the family Pristidae, the sawfishes. But, the sawfishes are in reality rays of the order Batoidei and, although the skates and rays are closely related to sharks, they are also quite different animals.

There is, nonetheless, the resemblance. Both sawshark and sawfish have a modified snout in the form of a long flat blade set with teeth pointing sideways. Both have a slightly depressed body and a strongly flattened head. However, the basic structural plan of the sawshark is that of a shark not a ray and even the external differences outnumber the similarities. The upper eyelid of the sawshark is moveable; the gill slits are on the side of the head instead of beneath it; the pectoral fins are not joined to the head in front of the gill slits and so on. A further difference, but not one which differentiates sharks and rays as the foregoing do, is that the sawshark has, and the sawfish has not, two long barbels at about the middle of the saw.

There are, too, differences other than anatomical ones. The sawfishes inhabit the shallows of the tropics and subtropics. They penetrate fresh water. They reach a length of 20 feet and they can be dangerous.

The sawsharks have a similar albeit, seemingly, much less continuous geographical distribution, but they inhabit the sea alone and for the most part at depths of 10 to 200 fathoms. None reaches a length of more than 5 feet and nowhere are the sawsharks regarded as dangerous. They feed on small fishes and such, using their saw to flail about and, possibly, to poke edibles out of soft bottoms.

There are two genera in the family Pristiophoridae. There is *Pliotrema* with the one species *Pliotrema warreni* having six gill openings and there is *Pristiophorus* with five species having five gill openings. All of the species presumably bring forth living pups.

Pliotrema warreni is apparently restricted to South Africa. It grows to 3 feet and the pupils of its eyes are emerald green. J. L. B. Smith writes in 1949: 'Flesh excellent.'

Pristiophorus cirratus is found in South Africa, Australia, and the Philippines. It grows to 4 feet and in Australia is called the common sawshark. G. P. Whitley writes in 1940 that it makes 'excellent food'. J. L. B. Smith writes in 1949: 'The flesh is stated to be excellent.'

P. japonicus appears to be limited to Japan and Korea. It grows to 5 feet. In *Fishes of Japan*, 1955, Yaichiro Okada writes: 'The flesh of this shark makes a high grade of *Kamaboko*.' The dish referred to is one of paste or cakes.

P. nudipinnis seems native to Australia. It grows to 4 feet and is called the southern sawshark. We can find no comment on its palatability.

In June of 1959 a sawshark 14 inches long was trawled from 350 fathoms in the Bahamas. In June of 1958, and again in the Bahamas, two of the same sort, 25 and 31 inches long, were trawled at about 500 fathoms. They were, the three together, not only a new species, named *Pristiophorus schroederi* out of regard for William C. Schroeder and his work, but they were also the first sawsharks ever taken in the Western Hemisphere.

The case of *P. owenii* is a curious one. Albert Günther described the species in his eight-volume *Catalogue of the Fishes in the British Museum*, 1858–1870. Next, in 1941, it was placed in the synonymy of *P. nudipinnis*. Next in 1960, it was removed from the synonymy to again stand alone as a species and if that proves acceptable to science, then *P. owenii* is also again homeless. There is only the one 13-inch specimen and nobody has the faintest notion about when it was collected or where. For habitat Günther wrote, 'Hab.-?'

The last of the shark families is the family Squatinidae which includes one genus, *Squatina*, and 11 named species some of them, probably, synonymous.

In any event, *Squatina* is the angel shark or the monk shark, the fiddle-fish or mongrel skate and the names, generic and vernacular, are apt. The creature is very squat with great wing-like pectoral and pelvic fins which do suggest angel wings or monkish habit and which, together with a round head and slender tail region, do shape *Squatina* along the lines of a fiddle or a skate. The angel shark is, in fact, closer to the skates and rays than is the sawshark, but it is still a shark and for the same reasons the sawshark is. Its basic structural plan is essentially that of a shark, though less so than the sawshark plan, and its external characteristics, the ones earlier cited in connection with the sawshark, are those which serve to separate sharks from the Batoidei.

The range of the angel sharks is temperately and tropically global and they live at the bottom from, depending on the species, shoreline shallows out to quite deep water. However, the one taken in the fall of 1887 and 80 miles seaward of New York at 705 fathoms may have been a stray. Often angel sharks lie partially burrowed in mud or sand.

There is an angel shark species which may surpass 6 feet and 170 pounds, but 4 to 5 feet and 60 pounds seems near the family mean. All squatinids, in any event, bring forth live young and all subsist on a miscellany of bottom and near bottom animals with flatfishes —flounders and the like—skates, lobsters, crabs and whelks being everyday fare. They run otherwise true to shark form. An angel shark was once caught with a bundle of seaweed in its stomach. Another was caught with a hat in its stomach. Another was caught with a 2-pound can of mustard in its stomach. And one was caught with a piece of wood in its stomach and that would turn no heads if the piece of wood had not been 18 inches long, 10 inches wide and bristly with nails.

The nominal Australian angel sharks are *Squatina australis* and *S. tergocellata*, but there is the likelihood that they are conspecific and if such be the case the name *S. australis* takes precedence.

S. australis attains a length of 5 feet, is partial to water 10 to 50 fathoms deep and while the species was not scientifically described until 1879, and then as *Rhina squatina*, it had not gone unnoticed in the years before. William Dampier, again in *A Voyage to New Holland*, recorded that on August 23, 1699, the ship's company caught a monk fish and his drawing of the creature is the earliest illustration of an Australian shark.

The name monk fish was not of recent coinage even when Dampier used it. The French ichthyologist Guillaume Rondelet used it—in *Piscibus Marinus, in quibus verae Piscium effigies expressae sunt*, Lugduni—in 1554 and the name was probably in common currency then.

The ancients knew the angel shark as *rhina* or *rasp*, after its skin, or *squatina* and statements about it, often incorrect, can be found in the works of Aristotle, Pliny the Elder and others of the time.

Pliny advanced claims for the medicinal qualities of the beast. Applied topically, he said, its flesh would prevent swollen breasts and its incinerated hide was a fine cure for pimples. (Boils called for sterner measures. 'For boils', stated Pliny, 'the following remedies are prescribed; a spider, applied before mentioning the insect by name, care being taken to remove it at the end of two days; a shrew-mouse, suspended by the neck till it is dead, care being taken not to let it touch the earth when dead, and to pass it three times around the boil, both operator and patient spitting on the floor each time. . . .')

To return to the present day and age, *Squatina africana* ranges the east African coast from Delagoa Bay in southern Mozambique to Mossel Bay in southern South Africa. It is the usual squatinid size and is not too abundant; the same can be said of the angel sharks in United States waters.

S. californica ranges from southern Alaska to Mexico and possibly beyond. *S. dumeril* ranges from southern New England to south Florida and the northern Gulf of Mexico. During the warm months it seems to prefer the shallows, but it winters offshore and has been caught 75 miles off New York in February at 109 fathoms. However, the catch at 705 fathoms mentioned earlier, and also off New York, was made in September. *S. dumeril*, evidently, is given to wandering whatever the season.

Squatina squatina is the angel shark of Europe and Great Britain. This is the species which grows to at least 6 feet and 170 pounds and thus is the largest of angel sharks. Also it is relatively abundant. Francis Day, one autumn afternoon, counted 26 that seiners had left on the beach at Teignmouth in Devon. Today the creature is marketed. Abundant or not, the genus *Squatina* has a roomy mouth, several rows of sharp teeth and no patience when annoyed.

'It is', observed Thomas Pennant in the 1776 edition of his *British Zoology*, 'extremely fierce and dangerous to be approached. We knew of an instance of a fisherman, whose leg was terribly torn by a large one of this species, which lay within his nets in shallow water, and which he went to lay hold of incautiously.'

In the *Report, Commissioner of Fisheries of Maryland* for 1878, Otto Lugger commented: 'The not very inviting looks of this fish are not the only reasons why fishermen dislike it. It has, to some extent, the unpleasant habits of the snapping turtle, since it can open its mouth very suddenly, to an alarming extent, and not to play, either. In consequence of this biting propensity, it is called by the fishermen the "sand devil", and also the "fair maid"; the first name not without any reason and the latter certainly not out of politeness.'

Then there is a report that on February 17, 1961 at Mount Martha Beach in Victoria, Australia, an angel shark bit a woman without provocation. She survived.

With that we are done with species.

CHAPTER 11 | *Beginnings*

The foregoing survey of species makes it plain that knowledge of shark reproduction is inadequate, although we do know that shark reproduction is very different from teleost or bony fish reproduction even if precisely the very same ends are served.

Most teleosts shed a vast number of eggs, some species tens of millions, which are fertilized and hatched externally. The vulnerable hatchlings must face a multitude of natural hazards and a very few, but enough, survive to spawn themselves and maintain their kind.

In all sharks the eggs are fertilized internally and in many they are also hatched internally. The young are not born until they are physically able to make their own way and the litters are small. Just a handful of shark species bear more than 100 pups and the great majority bear far fewer. But because the littermates are so well developed, enough of the few survive.

Science lacks particulars: only a general notion exists about where and when many shark species breed, about where and when they pup and after how long a gestation period, about the time span from puppyhood to sexual maturity and so forth. On the plus side of the scientific ledger we are more sure of the mechanics or physiology of shark reproduction.

In a short talk on the subject in August 1871 Louis Agassiz, one of America's great naturalists, came to a long-belated conclusion. 'In', he said, 'reviewing the accounts given by various observers, we find that Aristotle really knew more about the process than all other zoologists since his time.'

A female hammerhead and her litter of pups. Shark litters are relatively small, but since the young are born quite ready to fend and forage, survival is high.

Aristotle, some twenty centuries before, had written that fish '. . . lie down side by side, and copulate belly to belly. . . . And among cartilaginous fishes are included . . . all the galeodes or sharks and dogfish. Cartilaginous fishes, then, of all kinds, have in many instances been observed copulating in the way above mentioned. . . . Again, in cartilaginous fishes, the male, in some species, differs from the female in the fact that he is furnished with two appendages hanging down from about the exit of the residuum, and that the female is not so furnished; and this distinction between the sexes is observed in all the species of the sharks and dog-fish.'

A few teleosts copulate, but Aristotle was correct in saying that all sharks do and that all male sharks possess a pair of reproductive appendages. These are the penis-like copulatory organs or mixopterygia and they came to be and still are called claspers because, Aristotle to the contrary, it was long supposed that with them male sharks clasped female sharks to breed somehow.

The claspers are a modification of the pelvic fins, the inner edges of which have rolled up and overlapped, though they have not fused, to form a groove or tube. Ordinarily the claspers trail aft but prior to mating they become swollen and erect and seminal fluid flows from the testes inside the body, out through the vent and into an opening or apopyle at the base of each clasper. During copulation the claspers are bent forward; this serves to close the apopyles, and muscular siphon sacs contract to discharge a spray of seminal fluid. The other functions of the twin siphon sacs—they are situated in the abdominal wall and open near the apopyles—have not been fully explained but they are thought to lubricate the claspers, to secrete some seminal fluid and to take in sea water to help in the forceful flush of seminal fluid.

There is considerable variation in claspers. Some are more flat than round. Some are naked and smooth. Some are covered or tipped with a few to a hundred or more denticles, spurs, claws or hooks which act as holdfasts during copulation and assist in the rupture of virginal female membranes. Interestingly, if logically, where the male shark has well-armed claspers, the female of the species has a toughly-lined genital tract.

The claspers of young males are short and soft and hardly reach the tips of the pelvic fins. But as the males approach maturity the claspers lengthen and stiffen from the calcification of cartilage and with relative rapidity. Past maturity, though, the claspers do not grow in proportion to the growth of the sharks and a male that matures at 10 feet with 9 inch claspers will not have substantially longer claspers at 12 or 15 feet.

Female sharks have paired oviducts which stretch almost the full length of the body cavity. But whether, in mating, they are penetrated by both claspers simultaneously or alternately or sometimes the one and sometimes the other is, at the moment, moot. Aristotle could comment that observations of mating sharks were many, but he was told of much more than he saw and is sparing of details.

The reality is that such observations are pitifully few and far between. From one, however, it would seem that one species uses one clasper and with a right-handed bias.

In 1961 Robert P. Dempster and Earl S. Herald, of the California Academy of Sciences' Steinhart Aquarium in San Francisco, wrote that staff interest in the copulatory ways of the hornshark, the species *Heterodontus francisci*, dated from December 30, 1949. 'A worried visitor', they said, 'reported a "terrific fight" taking place between two hornsharks in one of the large display tanks. One fish was about to kill another and "something should be done to prevent this tragedy". A quick check of the 1,043-gallon tank revealed that the "lethal battle" was actually mating and courtship. The pair were average size, and the male, measuring $27\frac{1}{2}$ inches, had seized a $28\frac{1}{2}$-inch female by the left pectoral fin and was firmly holding on to it with his mouth. The female was lying partially on her left side facing the male and did not appear to be making any great effort to get away from him. In a short time he had manipulated his body so that his tail occupied a position over her back immediately in front of the second dorsal fin. By using her second dorsal spine as an anchor and, at the same time, holding on to the left pectoral fin with his mouth—the mid-region of his body being in a position to move freely—he was able to thrust his right clasper into her vent.'

Dempster and Herald continue: 'The left clasper played no part whatsoever in the sexual act, it hung loosely in the water. . . . A garibaldi, (*Hypsypops rubicunda*), in the same tank was attracted by this unused clasper and from time to time nipped at it. The hornshark paid no attention to the garibaldi's harassing activity. Throughout the entire time of copulation (35 minutes), a gentle rhythmic motion was observed in the caudal region of the male and the female lay motionless on her side.'

All subsequent hornshark matings at Steinhart Aquarium were, according to Dempster and Herald, likewise executed with the right clasper alone.

The mating of a typical shark species seems, at the time of writing, to have been observed just once. It happened at the Mote Marine Laboratory in Florida and was described by Eugenie Clark in 1963 in *Sharks and Survival*. Clark had in captivity for experimental purposes a male and female lemon shark, the carcharhinid species *Negaprion brevirostris*, both about 9 feet long. 'Four times', she relates, 'we noticed that the female lemon shark had marks on her body that had not been seen the previous day. The marks were usually long scratches along one side and sometimes what appeared to be teeth marks. The scratches may have been from the oysters growing on the pilings of the pen, but such scratches were never seen on the male. Once, obvious teeth imprints were seen on the female's head, as if the male had taken a good portion of the left side of her head in his mouth and then released it without tearing the skin. When not feeding, the two lemon sharks frequently were seen swimming close together, one directly behind the other, or alongside each other with their bodies in contact or almost in contact. At midnight on May 1, 1959, Dr and Mrs Dugald Brown, who were working in the laboratory, walked out on the dock and saw the two lemon sharks in copula. The sharks were side by side, heads slightly apart but the posterior half of their bodies in such close contact and the swimming movement so perfectly synchronized that they gave the appearance of a single individual with two heads, as they swam in slow counterclockwise circles around the pen. . . . When the observers left the dock a half hour later, the sharks were still in copula.'

The sharks were closely watched day and night for a week but they did not mate again. Once, though, at dusk, Clark recounts '. . . the male lemon shark was seen swimming unusually close to the female and then suddenly sinking to the bottom in a curled position for periods as long as 4 minutes. When swimming or resting in this curled position, the claspers were noticeable . . . and they seemed enlarged and slightly pink.'

Shark courtship, particularly among the larger species, is both strenuous and potentially lethal. Fresh or partially healed cuts on pregnant females testify that males harass females, slashing the pectoral fins and the pelvic region of the back to encourage sexual co-operation. Rarely, if ever, are the wounds severe and it is considered probable that the males are restrained because of inherent courtship convention and because, until they have bred, they are inhibited from feeding. The latter probability is further enhanced by the slimness of ripe or recently spent males and by the depleted state of their livers.

The females demonstrate no such timely inhibition. Also, the females of many large shark species are, on the average, 25 per cent larger than the males. During courtship, then, some inhibited males may well succumb to larger, uninhibited and, on occasion, unreceptive and testy females.

The system of shark insemination may seem prone to leaks and the system of courtship fraught with peril, but they work nonetheless. Eggs do become fertilized and from subsequent developmental events most sharks can be assigned to one of three groups.

Among the *oviparous* sharks are the hornsharks of the family Heterodontidae, the cat sharks of the family Scyliorhinidae, and the whale shark of the family Rhincodontidae.

Oviparous sharks lay their eggs and leave the hatching to providence. But their eggs are hardy. All shark eggs, after fertilization, pass through a shell gland which manufactures and moulds an eggshell or case and the case enclosing the eggs of oviparous sharks is thick and rubbery. Usually it is also rectangular and has sticky tendrils at the corners to fasten it down. The egg case of the hornshark, though, is unexampled. From its cone shape to its threads it looks like a screw 5 inches long or longer with tip-end tendrils 7 feet long.

Oviparous sharks normally lay their eggs by the pair and some lay periodically for several months. Frequent insemination is not necessary since seminal fluid in the oviducts remains viable for some time. Embryos are nourished by the egg yolk and hatch, depending upon the species, roughly within six to ten months.

Among the *viviparous* sharks are some smooth dogfish of the family Triakidae, the blue shark, the whitetip and certain other species of the family Carcharhinidae, and probably all of the hammerheads of the family Sphyrnidae; viviparity is the most sophisticated mode of embryonic shark care. They do not lay eggs. The eggs hatch in the oviducts. But after the embryos have consumed the egg yolk a placental connection develops between embryos and the mother shark and further sustenance is provided through her blood. This placental relationship, strange to say, closely parallels that of the mammals, the highest creatures on the evolutionary scale.

The majority of sharks, however, occupy a sort of reproductive middle-ground. They are the *ovoviviparous* ones and they include, among many more, the sand sharks of the family Odontaspidae, the thresher sharks of the family Alopiidae, the makos, the porbeagle and probably the white shark of the family Isuridae, and the tiger shark and some other species, again, of the family Carcharhinidae. The precise number of ovoviviparous or viviparous carcharhinids is not known because the reproductive process of several species is not known and the same holds true of additional shark families. Still, none of the many carcharhinids is thought to be oviparous or egg laying.

The eggs of ovoviviparous sharks also hatch in the oviducts and the pups at birth are also living miniatures of the adult. Prior to birth, though, they have no placental connection with the mother. They subsist, most of them, through an attachment, on the yolk of their own egg.

Ovoviviparous and viviparous sharks may both have large litters of large pups. The ovoviviparous tiger shark may have upwards of 60 pups some 24 inches long and the viviparous blue shark upwards of 50 some 20 inches long. In general, however, ovoviviparous sharks whelp smaller litters and larger pups than do viviparous kinds and certain species are extraordinary in the way they go about it. There is, for one, the sand tiger or common sand shark, the species *Odontaspis taurus*, a creature of wide distribution in warm temperate waters.

The female is, say, 9 feet long. Only her right ovary is functional, the norm among the larger shark species, and it produces eggs about the size of a pea which is, among sharks generally, very small. Some species produce eggs that are larger than hens' eggs. In any case, 15 to 20 sand shark eggs are passed from the ovary to the shell glands and are there thinly packaged before entering the oviducts for fertilization. But after fertilization, just one egg in one package in each oviduct hatches an embryo and it and its twin proceed to utilize the yolks of their own and surrounding eggs.

The female *O. taurus* continues to ovulate. The embryos continue to forage on the eggs and by the time they reach a length of 10 inches the female's ovary contains 24,000 mature eggs and would fill a 10-quart pail. At 10 inches the twins are also lively and this quite surprised Stewart Springer, the ichthyologist who illuminated *O. taurus* reproduction. 'Examination of the embryos began', he reported in 1948 in *Copeia*, 'in a startling way. When I first put my hand through a slit in the oviduct I received the impression that I had been bitten. What I had encountered was an exceedingly active embryo which dashed about open mouthed inside the oviduct. The teeth were not strong enough to penetrate my skin but were sharp and hard enough to produce a pricking sensation.'

The boisterousness of the 10-inch twins is all the more remarkable because they are still far from being born. They keep on living freely in the oviducts, gobbling up eggs and facing forward. Then at a length of about 30 inches, nearly one third the length of the mother, the two young sand sharks turn around to face aft and are delivered into the sea, their respective bellies full with perhaps 28 ounces of egg yolk. They have spent a year in the oviducts.

Why the twins turn around is problematical. It may be that the turning coincides with a drop in egg production by the mother. It may be that since the twins are not sheathed in a shell membrane, as are the late embryos of many shark species, the turning is necessary to permit delivery with, rather than against, the grain of tailward pointing dermal denticles. Possibly both factors are involved.

O. taurus is not the only ovoviviparous shark to harbour free-living embryos until they are large in size and active. The porbeagle, *Lamna nasus*, does also and often rears two embryos in each oviduct, embryos which, in a female of 5 feet, may be 20 or more inches long at birth and grotesquely ballooned with egg yolk. The number of other ovoviviparous shark species that resemble *O. taurus* in reproduction just is not known. But the likelihood is that the number is small.

The possibility has been raised that sand shark embryos turn around in the oviducts to allow for birth with the grain of their hide. Other sharks have other facilitative mechanisms. The hammers of embryonic hammerheads are folded back against the body and the pups are born head first. The teeth that edge the jaws of saw sharks are prenatally soft, pliant and folded back and the pups are whelped head first. The sharp dorsal spines of embryo spiny dogfish and related squalids are capped with cartilaginous knobs. Here too the pups are delivered head first because the spines flex to the rear. After delivery the knobs are shed.

Despite their reproductive efficacy, however, sharks are not untroubled by genetic accidents and *Carcharhinus milberti*, the sandbar shark is an example. There will be one sandbar shark litter in perhaps every 500 to 1,000 normal litters in which each littermate, 10 of them give or take a few, lacks even the vestige of a mouth. The eyes, what is more, are set virtually touching together, behind the nostrils and on the underside of the snout.

It goes without saying that some shark species are more susceptible to observation than others. On the United States east coast, for instance, there are 20-odd migratory species which populate the shallows and nearshore waters. There are carcharhinids such as the bull shark, the dusky shark, the sandbar shark, the lemon shark, the blue shark and the tiger shark; there are sphyrnids such as the common hammerhead, the great hammerhead and the bonnethead; there are squalids such as the spiny dogfish and the smooth dogfish, and there are more.

Some of these species have been, in the past, the subject of much commercial attention. Some have been and continue to be the object of intensive field study by zoologists. A relative lot, therefore, is known about the migratory shark population on the United States east coast and the reproductive and associated habits of its member species can be to some extent generalized. Also wherever else these species occur under similar hydrographic conditions, the same generalities could apply.

In this generalized population, the pups are born in the spring or early summer, every year by some species and every other year by some, and on specific nursery grounds in somewhat shallower water than adults of the population usually frequent. Females may travel long or short distances to reach the grounds but do not move onto them until the pups are ready for whelping. The females do not feed while on the grounds, but neither do they stay there for very long. Soon after leaving they start to feed again, not necessarily far from the grounds though in deeper water. Adult males of the species rarely, if ever, visit the nursery.

The young of the generalized shark population stay in or close to the nursery area to feed and grow, but may gather to migrate as winter approaches. The gatherings comprise sharks of about equal size and both sexes and they are not normally found with or near adults. They are separated either geographically or by depth.

Gatherings of migratory adults are segregated by sex and males seem to favour slightly deeper or cooler water than do females. Between pupping seasons, sexually segregated gatherings of adults often occupy a great geographical range although at migratory terminal points sexual segregation may not be distinct. The range of the young is much more restricted.

In the springtime, the males move toward shore to mate and thus the generalized migratory shark population on the United States east coast completes one and begins another reproductive cycle.

The pattern of shark behaviour—the avoidance of nursery grounds by adult males, the feeding inhibition of mating males and pupping females, the segregation of adults by size and sex, the separation of young from adults—must serve to protect some shark species from their own cannibalistic tendencies. But certain facets of the behavioural pattern could also serve to distribute sharks in such a way that competition for food and living space is eased.

The factors at work in the pattern are poorly understood. Instinct, however, is certainly one and others may be otherwise automatic. It has been suggested that segregation by size could come about because sharks of different sizes move at different speeds. It has been suggested that segregation by sex could come about because the different sexes prefer different environments and, as noted before, male sharks frequent waters slightly deeper or slightly cooler than those which females frequent. Then again, sexual segregation could be simply a function of size segregation, that because male and female sharks grow at different rates a sorting out by size results in a coincidental sorting out by sex.

Among sharks, segregation by size is more nearly universal than segregation by sex, and, whatever the merit of various suggestions, there is good reason to believe that it is not a chance phenomenon. A shark invariably gives way to a larger shark and research indicates that the shark faculty for size discrimination is very acute. Indeed, in smooth dogfish, *Mustelus canis*, it is so acute that smooth dogfish will avoid other smooth dogfish only 7 per cent larger.

The natural devices which insure that a species survives and renews are balanced by devices which insure that a species is held in numerical check, that its survival and renewal do not tax the capacity of the environment to provide support. Mankind is an unhappy exception. The shark is not, even though it has no oceanic enemies and seldom faces starvation. The theory is that a healthy adult shark almost always finds food enough because it can do without for quite some time and in the interim take nourishment from its voluminous liver. So in the overlapping, interacting mosaic of species, the principal check on sharks is sharks themselves.

Natural devices such as segregation by size and sex may soften the struggle for survival, but they by no means eliminate it and an important element in the control of small shark species, those under 6 feet long, is their convenience as a dietary item for large shark species. Some large sharks also prey on other large sharks although not, it is thought, with a consistency that influences shark numbers. However, the possibly low fecundity of large species may have considerable influence. Samplings of *Carcharhinus obscurus*, the dusky shark, show that females often carry embryos in just one oviduct and this could reflect difficulties in mating. Samplings of *Carcharhinus milberti*, the sandbar shark again, show that the ratio of females to males can be a substantial 5 to 1 and a much higher than expected proportion of the females are not gravid. This could reflect greater male mortality—all females sharks bear both male and female pups in roughly equal numbers—and the mortality could be appreciably greater in the mating season when the female is, to the male, an occupational hazard.

Competition for nursery grounds is another significant mechanism in the regulation of a shark population and there are still others such as temperature changes or food shortages on the nursery grounds which force young sharks to leave prematurely and enter a habitat wherein they may be more vulnerable to predation.

The zoologist can only wonder about what to make of contrary species like the tiger shark, *Galeocerdo cuvieri*. It segregates neither by sex nor by size. Its nursery grounds, if it has any, are undiscovered. Yet a check-and-balance system must exist for this species too.

While, as we earlier emphasized, science lacks a multitude of particulars about shark reproduction, the particulars may well derive from human perversity. Mankind now seems generally unable or disinclined to control his own reproduction and he more and more thinks of the sea as the cornucopia from which a famished planet will be fed. It is, to many scientists, wishful thinking. There are limits to what even the sea can yield and the technology of farming its open reaches is many years away if attainable at all. Nonetheless, the sea's living resources will and should be harvested and sharks, out of necessity, will doubtless be among them. Doubtless too, sharks will be over-harvested and as this or that species goes into decline ichthyologists will be asked to launch an investigation into the life history of the species and propose measures to set things right again. Possibly the investigation would have been long since launched had funds been forthcoming but, often the availability of funds materializes only with unavailability of fish. The investigation, in any event, can be enormously demanding in time of if equally rewarding in particulars and such was the six-year long investigation of the school shark, *Galeorhinus australis*, a species important as a food fish in Australia and one which, in the middle 1940's, was an unmistakably declining one.

Between 1947 and 1952 a total of 600 school sharks were examined throughout the range of the species and in all seasons. A total of 5,862 were caught, tagged and released alive and 237 or 4 per cent were caught again. The percentage might seem small but in tagging programmes it is not considered so and by 1953 field and laboratory work had combined to give Australian zoologists quite a thorough knowledge of the school shark. They knew about its parasites, its food preferences, its distribution, its migratory paths and, of greatest value, they knew about its reproductive cycle and the reason for its decline.

Each gravid female *Galeorhinus australis*, the research demonstrated carries from 17 to 41 embryos. The average is 28 and the pups are whelped at an average length of 12 inches after a gestation period of six months. However, only half of the females bear pups in a given year and the growth rate of the species is very slow. The smallest mature males are 4 feet long and 8 years old, the smallest mature females 4½ feet long and 10 years old.

A slow rate of growth and a rate of fishing that caught more school sharks than school sharks could replace was a logical guess without an investigation. But a resource cannot be managed by guesswork. Particulars are needed. Australia got them and also the conservation programme which, if heeded, can keep both the commercial catch and *Galeorhinus australis*, the natural resource, at optimum levels.

CHAPTER 12

The Whole Animal and some of its parts

Ishmael, in *Moby Dick*, tells of sharks. 'When in the Southern Fishery a captured sperm Whale, after long and weary toil, is brought alongside late at night, it is not, as a general thing at least, customary to proceed at once to the business of cutting him in. For that business is an exceedingly laborious one. . . . Therefore, the common usage is to take in all sail; lash the helm a'lee; and then send every one below to his hammock till daylight, with the reservation that . . . anchor-watches shall be kept. . . .

'But sometimes, especially upon the Line in the Pacific, this plan will not answer at all; because such incalcuable hosts of sharks gather round the moored carcase, that were he left so for six hours, say, on a stretch, little more than the skeleton would be visible by morning. In most other parts of the ocean, however, where these fish do not so largely abound, their wondrous voracity can be at times considerably diminished, by vigorously stirring them up with sharp whaling-spades. . . . But it was not thus in the present case with the Pequod's sharks; though, to be sure, any man unaccustomed to such sights, to have looked over her side that night, would have almost thought the whole round sea was one huge cheese, and those sharks the maggots in it.

'Nevertheless, upon Stubb setting the anchor-watch . . . and when, accordingly Queequeg and a forecastle seaman came on deck, no small excitement was created among the sharks; for immediately suspending the cutting stages over the side, and lowering three lanterns, so that they cast long gleams of light over the turbid sea, these two mariners, darting their long whaling-spades,

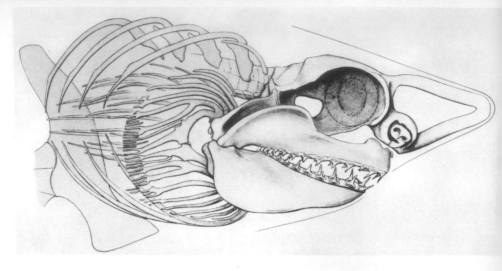

Section of the head of the mako shark, *Isurus oxyrinchus*.
Rib-like projections at the rear of the skull support
muscles between the gill slits. The other projections
support the gills.

kept up an incessant murdering of the sharks, by striking the keen
steel deep into their skulls, seemingly their only vital part. But in
the foamy confusion of their mixed and struggling hosts, the marks-
men could not always hit their mark; and this brought about new
revelations of the incredible ferocity of the foe. They viciously
snapped, not only at each other's disembowelments, but like
flexible bows, bent round, and bit their own; till those entrails
seemed swallowed over and over again by the same mouth, to be
oppositely voided by the gaping wound. Nor was this all. It was
unsafe to meddle with the corpses and ghosts of these creatures. A
sort of generic or Pantheistic vitality seemed to lurk in their very
joints and bones, after what might be called the individual life had
departed. Killed and hoisted on deck for the sake of his skin, one of
these sharks almost took poor Queequeg's hand off, when he tried
to shut down the dead lid of his murderous jaw.

' "Queequeg no care what god made him shark," said the savage,
agonizingly lifting his hand up and down; "wedder Fejee god or
Nantucket god; but de god wat made shark must be one dam
Ingin." '

The foregoing may be literature's most vivid description of what

194

zoologists term mob feeding or a feeding frenzy, a state of affairs wherein sharks become so lashed by the sight, sound, smell, taste and feel of abundant food and the seizing of it by others of their kind around them, that they lose all restraint. The phenomenon seems limited to the larger shark species and it might have a useful purpose. It might be a factor in population control since the larger sharks have few if any natural enemies which can effectively check shark production. Sharks, then, occasionally take leave of their senses. But they sooner or later return to them and shark senses are both acute and various.

The shark's sense of smell is celebrated and for good reason. The brain of a shark 8 feet long is about 7 inches long, but as much as two-thirds of its weight is given over to the olfactory function. At the large foreportion of the brain are the olfactory lobes and from them, like the arms of a Y, the olfactory tracts extend to olfactory bulbs just behind and connected to each nostril, or nasal capsule, by very short olfactory nerves.

The nasal capsules themselves do not open into the mouth. Rather, they are baffled so that, as the shark swims along, water flows in and out of the blind olfactory sac and over its profusion of sensory cells.

The importance of these receptors was first shown by a now classic series of simple experiments conducted in Woods Hole between 1910 and 1913 by George Howard Parker of Harvard and Ralph Edward Sheldon of the then United States Bureau of Fisheries.

Parker and Sheldon, who sometimes worked together and sometimes independently, tested the reactions of smooth dogfish, *Mustelus canis*, to freshly killed crabs which had been punctured to let the juices seep out.

The dogfish swam here and there in the tank until they got quite close to a crab. At that point their movements quickened and they swam in tighter circles around the crab. Finally, a dogfish would snatch up the crab, shake it and swallow it. Next, the crabs were disguised by wrapping them in cheesecloth or eelgrass. The dogfish found them with no difficulty. Next, the dogfish were presented with two packages, disguised crabs and disguised stones. The crabs

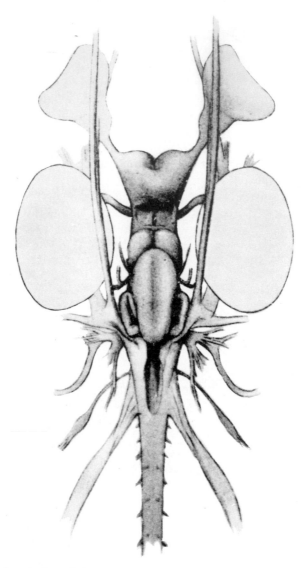

A dorsal view of the brain of the spiny dogfish, *Squalus acanthias*, the entire foreportion of which (see text) is given over to the sense of smell. The large ovals at the sides of the brain are the eyes.

were quickly taken, the stones ignored. As a last step, the nasal capsules of the dogfish were plugged with greased cotton wadding. Offered crabs went unnoticed.

It was also established that if one nostril was blocked, a dogfish would always turn toward the side of the unblocked one. This indicates that a shark turns toward the side where the scent is stronger and accounts for the familiar zigzag tracking movements of the creature as it follows a scent upstream. First, say, the right nostril gets the stronger scent and the shark swings to the right. Now the swing has brought the left nostril into position to receive the stronger scent and the shark swings to the left and so on left to right, right to left. Of course, when there is no scent gradient, when both nostrils are being equally stimulated, no turn is made.

Sharks do not seek out and catch only hurt animals. They catch active and unhurt ones too, animals that are not bleeding or releasing other attractive body fluids. But if the shark sense of smell and its role in catching the hurt has been paid considerable research attention, its possible role in catching the unhurt has not. The consequent imbalance of knowledge, however, was significantly redressed in April 1963 when Albert L. Tester of the University of Hawaii reported on his work in the journal *Pacific Science*, work which was done in 1959 and 1960 with several shark species in tanks and pens at the University's Hawaii Marine Laboratory and at the Eniwetok Marine Biological Laboratory on Eniwetok Atoll in the Marshall Islands.

Among other things, Tester and his graduate student co-workers found that sharks could sense 1 part human blood in 10 to 100 million parts water. They also found that some sharks were strongly repelled by human sweat, but a derivative repellent was not very effective as a feeding inhibitor. They found, too, that starved sharks were more excited by attractive smells than fed sharks were. While this last may not seem an earthshaking discovery, the fact is that until the experiment was made no one knew whether hunger modified shark behaviour. Indeed there was (and is) some speculation that it did not and we will come to it.

Tester's most ingenious and revealing experiments, however, were those in which uninjured food fish were held in one container or tank and sharks in another. Then water was periodically siphoned from the food fish tank to the shark tank. If the food fish were quiet, the sharks reacted to the 'quiet water' with mild hunting activity which soon stopped. If the food fish were distressed, as they were when threatened with sticks, the sharks reacted to the 'distressed water' with strong hunting activity in the course of which they circled about and even bit at the end of the siphon tube.

'These experiments', Tester concluded after many such, 'show that "quiescent" prey give off an odor which can be detected by sharks when it is first introduced into their environment but to which they soon become habituated . . . that when the prey becomes frightened and excited it gives off an additional or a new odor which again stimulates the habituated sharks, provoking the typical hunting response. Moreover it seems that shark activity, and thus presumably the amount of odorous material released, increases with increased agitation of the prey. . . . Whatever may be the source and nature of the attractant, we have presented evidence that olfaction is involved in the predation of sharks on normal healthy fish.'

Tester hypothesized that what pertained in the experiments pertained in the wild and the hypothesis was supported by the later experiments of Edmond S. Hobson Jr., a Tester graduate student, in the lagoon at Eniwetok. Water siphoned into the lagoon from a plastic container, in which was a large, agitated but apparently uninjured food fish, attracted wild sharks to the source, a hidden tube, within minutes.

Shark vision was once dismissed as poor. Research, however, has overturned that judgement. Probably, at some point in shark hunting, shark vision is the predominating sense.

The shark eye is rich in rods, those cells which are sensitive to dim light, and poor in bipolar and ganglion cells which help in the transmission of optic impulses to the brain. This makes for shark vision of low acuity, but high sensitivity, in dim light. Moreover, the sensitivity in dim light is greatly enhanced by the so-called *tapetum lucidum*. This layer is situated in the choroid underlying the retina and consists of silvery plates which reflect light back to the retina to stimulate further the rods therein. Thus, the shark eye, while not at all well suited for seeing an object in sharp detail, is admirably suited for separating an object, particularly a moving one, from its background.

The delicate, sensitive rods would probably be damaged by bright light, so there are protective devices. The iris of the shark eye is mobile and can expand to reduce the aperture of the pupil to a small point in many sharks, to a narrow slit in several pelagic sharks and rays, or to a series of tiny points in the Scyliorhinidae (cat sharks) and skates. Also in many sharks and in some rays, when the light is bright, cells of black pigment move out onto the silvery tapetal plates and, in a manner of speaking, draw the blinds. In dim light or darkness the cells retreat and this cyclical ability to occlude and clear the *tapetum lucidum* is unique to elasmobranchs.

The shark eye in general has upper and lower eyelids which are somewhat moveable, but do not altogether cover the eyeball. Many sharks, however, have a second lower lid, called the nictating membrane or nictitans, which does move freely and does altogether cover the eye. The functions of the sturdy and opaque nictitans are not entirely clear, though the evidence is that it serves as a shield against abrasion and traumatic injury and not as a shield against light of which the shark eye has a sufficiency. Perry W. Gilbert, whose work on the shark eye has been extensive, shone intense light at several shark species and the nictitans was not moved. On the other hand, when he probed near their heads with a pole, the nictitans was straight away pulled up.

With the relevant muscles at rest, the shark eye is adjusted for seeing objects at a distance. With their contraction, the eye is adjusted for seeing objects at close range. And the musculature of the eye is such that the eyeball can be rotated to afford a constant field of vision whether the shark is turning or twisting or simply swimming in a straight line.

There are a number of differences between the shark eye and the teleost eye, but a most conspicuous one is that the latter is rich in cones, not rods, and cones are associated with colour vision. A very few shark species are known to have cones. Still no species has been yet shown to have colour vision.

At what point vision becomes the predominant sense of a hunting shark is conjectural and depends largely on variables like water clarity and light. In favourable circumstances then, vision is probably useful to the shark up to a range of about 50 feet. In the shark's rush at prey, vision is probably the overriding sense and this probability is supported by tests in which wild sharks were attracted by a 4-inch cube of fish 3 feet away from and suspended at the same depth as a 4-inch cube of wood. In 20 trials over a period of two days the fish was struck first 11 times and the wood 9. So it would seem that in the final phase of approach, vision was the dominant sense for, if olfaction were, the fish should have been struck every time. When, incidentally, a shark mouthed the wood, it spat it out and this shows that gustation or taste, and perhaps touch too, are functional shark senses even though the creatures do at times swallow oddments.

Shark hearing like shark vision was also once thought poor and the reality is more the opposite. Shark hearing is excellent and on many occasions first senses the presence of prey.

All fishes have inner ears which are housed in the side of the head behind the eyes. Each ear or labyrinth rests in a fluid bath and is itself filled with fluid. The upper section of the ear is called the utriculus and that of sharks and bony fishes harbours three semi-circular canals. The utriculus communicates through a narrow neck with the lower section of the ear, called the sacculus, and the sacculus has an annex called the lagena. The inner ears of bony fishes are completely enclosed, but the sharks' are open to the sea through a small duct.

In each of the three ear chambers—the utriculus, the sacculus and the lagena—there is a calcified ear stone or otolith that is coupled to a cluster of hair-like sensory cells. In the widened portion or ampulla of the semicircular canals there is a cluster of sensory cells capped with hair cells which are set in a gelatinous substance called, after its shape, the cupula. The whole structure, less the cupula, is called a neuromast.

Research has determined that the upper ear, the canals and the utriculus, are concerned with gravitation and orientation of the body. As the shark yaws, pitches or rolls, ear fluid rocks the cupulae in the canals and moves the otolith in the utriculus. Thereby, the sensory cells are stimulated to convey impulses to the brain through branches of the auditory nerve. The brain then activates nerves which, in turn, activates the muscles controlling fins and eyes. Thus fins are flexed to keep the shark on an even keel and eyes are shifted to maintain a constant field of vision. Thus too, muscle tone is regulated.

Since the tissues of a fish are largely water, they are more sound transparent, as it were, than are the dense otoliths in the sacculus and lagena of the lower ear or seat of hearing. So when sound reaches the ear it causes a vibratory interplay between the dense otoliths and their less dense cushion of sensory cells. The brain, through the auditory nerve, takes information about the nature of the interplay and reacts accordingly and this is the way sharks, and most teleosts, hear and decipher sounds.

In 1961 the American scientists Henry Kritzler and Langley Wood obtained the first shark audiogram. Their subjects were bull sharks, *Carcharhinus leucas*, and they found that the hearing of the species ranged from about 100 cycles per second, or about two octaves above the bass end of a piano, to about 1,500 cycles per second, or about one octave below the treble end of a piano. There is evidence now that hearing ranges may vary from species to species, but it seems safe to assume that a shark can detect most of the sea sounds which should be of moment to it.

Certain sounds are of indisputable moment to certain if not all sharks and that was demonstrated at the Institute of Marine Science of the University of Miami in Florida in 1963 and 1964.

First, investigators recorded the sounds generated by a speared and struggling 25-pound fish. Second, they played back underwater, separately, the high and low-frequency sound pulses of the struggle as well as a continuous, unpulsed, low-frequency sound. Each 15-minute playback period was preceded by a 15-minute quiet period.

During 28 quiet periods one shark was seen. During 12 periods of low-frequency continuous sound no shark was seen. During 15 periods of high-frequency pulsed sound, 400 to 600 cycles per second, two sharks were seen but the investigators later found reason to doubt that they had been attracted by the test frequencies.

However, 22 periods of low-frequency pulsed sounds, 20 to 60 cycles per second, attracted 18 sharks, from 5 to 10 feet long and mostly carcharhinids, and they mostly swam directly toward the sound source or transducer.

In 1964 sharks were watched from an aircraft, and they homed on the transducer from a distance as great as 600 feet so, while there may be much more to learn about the hearing of sharks, there is no question that the shark ear is alive to low-frequency pulsed sounds and no question that it is serviceably directional.

The lateral lines of fishes are regarded as a sensory array intermediate between hearing and touch and the phrase 'acoustico-lateralis system' is often encountered. In any event, most fishes possess lateral lines which, typically, run the length of the body with branches on the head. Actually, the lines are subcutaneous canals or tubes and they are filled with fluid, lined with neuromasts having dome-shaped cupulae and are open to the surrounding water by way of pores. There is one line to a side and the name 'lateral line' alludes to the fact that in many fishes the special arrangement of scales over the organ does trace a visible line. In fishes with no scales, the line is traced by the pores.

Physiologically, the lateral line canals are quite like the semicircular canals or labyrinth of the inner ear. External forces, through lateral line pores, cause canal fluid to deflect canal neuromasts and pertinent messages are sent to the central nervous system.

Just what the lateral line canals do sense has long been and still is a subject of controversy. Some physiologists believe them to have an acoustical function and some do not. It has been shown, though, that whatever else they may sense the canals are perceptive to close by or near-field water disturbances. In laboratory experiments, blinded fish quickly learn to associate small water disturbances in their vicinity with the presence of either food or punishment, and they can locate the centre of disturbance with, in the words of Otto E. Lowenstein, a British authority on the lateral line, 'astonishing accuracy.'

This function of the canals has been likened to a sense of 'distant touch', an analogy often attributed to the Dutch physiologist Sven

Dijkgraaf although he credits William John Crozier, an American, as having drawn it, in the form of 'touch at a distance', in 1918 in the *Journal of Experimental Neurology*. Nevertheless, the lateral line alerts sharks and other fishes to the presence of prey or predators and, to a lesser extent, obstacles and it may be a factor in species and sexual recognition.

Sharks and other fishes are generously scattered with free neuromasts or pit organs, and while they are integral to the lateral line system, they are not connected to the canals. In sharks, the free neuromasts and their long cupulae are sunk between modified denticles and, unlike the canal neuromasts, are directly exposed to water disturbances. The presumption is that free neuromasts act in sensory concert with canal neuromasts and the presumption is made necessary because so little research has been done on the organs. The free neuromasts of sharks were, for years, thought to be taste buds.

The fourth and last components of the lateral line system or, if you will, the acoustico-lateralis system, are the ampullae of Lorenzini. All elasmobranchs have them—some teleosts have something similar—and they are quite different from the other neuromasts of the system. They are clustered, by the hundreds in active shark species, on the head and each ampulla consists of a vesicle beneath the skin with a duct leading to the outside. The vesicle has sensory cells in its walls and both it and the duct are full of a jelly-like substance.

The ampullae of Lorenzini were in reality discovered by Marcello Malpighi in 1663, but they were first described in detail by Stefano Lorenzini in 1678. They are sensitive to pressure and temperature and they are also sensitive to alternating electrical fields and that was nicely and lately demonstrated by A. J. Kalmijn, a colleague of Dijkgraaf's at the University of Utrecht and like Dijkgraaf very involved in lateral line research.

The English scientist R. W. Murray had already found that the ampullae were sensitive to electrical stimuli. And Dijkgraaf and Kalmijn had already found that if the ampullary network was denervated on one part of the head of *Scyliorhinus canicula*, the lesser spotted dogfish, the part was rendered insensitive to electrical stimuli. There was, then, no question that the ampullae were electro-receptors. The question was whether the electroreceptors were employed in hunting and Kalmijn provided the answer in *Nature* for December 10, 1966.

Step 1 of the experimental procedure: Kalmijn recorded the normal electrocardiogram of the thornback ray, *Raja clavata*. Next, he exposed the test animals to electrical stimuli. The result was a marked slowing of the heartbeat. Eventually—with an electronic arrangement which could correctly calculate heartbeat variations to a fraction of one per cent and trace the data on paper—Kalmijn determined that the threshold of electrical stimulation in *R. clavata* was one tenth of a microvolt per centimetre. Suffice it to say, of the sensitivity of the ampullae, that a microvolt is one millionth of a volt.

Step 2: Kalmijn knew that, in sea water, the gill movements of a plaice, or flatfish, or flounder, *Pleuronectes platessa*, generated electrical potentials of more than 1,000 microvolts per centimetre. So he put a plaice in one basin and a ray in another and electrically connected the basins. The ray was situated in such a fashion that it could sense the plaice electrically or not at all. The gill movement potentials were transmitted to the ray and its heartbeat slowed distinctly. The same occurred when the potentials of a burrowing plaice were transmitted.

Step 3: Kalmijn conditioned rays, dogfishes and topes (*Galeo-rhinus galeus*, a carcharhinid) to an electrical field generated by two electrodes buried 4 inches apart in sand in basins. With the field switched on, the animals were offered food directly over the electrodes and after some 50 feedings they would hunt about and snap at the electrodes even though no food was offered. The strength of the field was four tenths of a microvolt.

The sum of Kalmijn's work is that elasmobranchs do employ the electroreceptive ampullae in close range hunting—close range because potentials on the level of microvolts dissipate within inches—and at the moment of bite when vision straight ahead is likely impaired, and particularly at night, the ampullae of Lorenzini may be the controlling sensory apparatus.

Such is the array of shark senses and, bearing in mind that some guesswork and many variables are involved, it might be well to estimate their useful range. Since sound intensity diminishes slowly as it travels through water, shark hearing, depending on the intensity of the sound at its source, might be measured in 1,000's of yards; shark olfaction, depending on the strength of the scent and the velocity of wind, wave or current dispersing it, in 100's of yards. The utility of the lateral line canals and free neuromasts is thought limited to about 100 feet from the stimulus and, as we said before, vision, in favourable circumstances, to about 50 feet from the object. The utility of shark ampullae is a matter of inches and touch and taste require contact. Of course, the shorter the useful range of a sense, the greater its precision in fixing the source of stimuli.

The shark brain shows little development of centres for inter-comparing data simultaneously received by the several senses. In other words, shark senses are not, apparently, well integrated. But while scientists are curious about the degree of integration, it seems not to matter much to the natural history of the beast whether the integration is none, a little or a lot. The shark, quite clearly, makes its way.

Scientists are also curious about what stimulus or combination of stimuli triggers shark feeding or attack. It simply is not known, but Stewart Springer had this to say in *Sharks, Skates and Rays*, 1967: 'It is clear from observations in the field and experiments with sharks in tanks that olfactory and visual cues play a part as stimuli that cause sharks to feed and that vibrations and noise (however perceived by the shark) have important roles as feeding stimuli. I find no indication, however, that the kind of internal drive that men know as hunger operates or even exists for sharks. I have no evidence to offer that a hunger drive does not exist for sharks, but suggest that it may play a minor role acting perhaps at a nearly constant but low level. My chief reason for suspecting that hunger is not very useful in describing the shark's urge to feed is that in the commercial fishery the best and largest catches I have seen were of sharks with stomachs partly or nearly full of freshly eaten fish, turtles, and invertebrates, not obtained from baited hooks, whereas poor catches included, for the most part, sharks with empty stomachs.'

Although the shark brain is considerably less complex than that of higher vertebrates, teleosts included, sharks are not, as is widely believed, wholly without intelligence and beyond learning. They can be taught, through conditioning, to discriminate between objects of different sizes or shapes; between patterns like circles, squares and diamonds and, on the basis of either hue or brightness, between colours. Sometimes they learn quite quickly and in one case there were unexpected ramifications.

In 1965, Lester R. and Frederick R. Aronson of the American Museum of Natural History and Eugenie Clark of Mote Marine Laboratory undertook the conditioning of a young female nurse shark, *Ginglymostoma cirratum*, 12 inches in length and 2 pounds in weight, to discriminate between two targets. The targets, about 4 by 2 inches, were transparent and behind each were lights. However, at any given moment only one target was lighted.

Food was positioned in such a manner that to get it the shark had to push one or the other of the targets. If it pushed the correct target, in this experiment the lighted one, it would be rewarded with more food. If it pushed the incorrect target, there would be no reward. Light would be automatically shifted, or not shifted, in a programmed random sequence whenever the shark pushed the correct target.

Training sessions were held every day in a dark room and continued until the shark had eaten about an ounce of food or from 7 to 16 minutes. Shark pushes per session varied from 28 to 65.

Within five days the shark was pushing the correct target 88 per cent of the time and thereafter, one day excepted, it pushed the incorrect target less than ·01 per cent of the time. At the end of two weeks, sessions were reduced to five days weekly and conducted for almost a month. In the final 17 sessions the shark pushed the incorrect target not once even though on a number of occasions it disregarded the food award.

The significance of the experiment is not just that the little shark learned quickly and well, but that it learned as quickly and well as two higher animals. 'The light-dark discrimination,' reported the investigators in the *Bulletin of Marine Science* in 1967, 'was learned as rapidly as mice learned the same problem, and as *Tilapia* [a small bony fish] learned a related visual discrimination. Thus, despite small eyes, a limited neural optic system and a primitive brain, the nurse shark mastered a simple visual problem as effectively as did a teleost and a rodent. This, of course, does not equate the learning abilities of the three vertebrate classes, but it does indicate that differences must be looked for by using more complex problems.'

The overwhelming majority of fishes are cold-blooded, which is to say that their body temperature is about the same as the temperature of the surrounding water. Marine mammals, on the other hand, even though many of them inhabit frigid polar waters, maintain a body temperature of about 37°C. or 98·6°F. But, marine mammals breathe air and it requires little heat to warm a lung filled with air from environmental temperature to body temperature. Fishes, however, in a manner of speaking, breathe water and the heat capacity of water is 3,000 times as great as an equal volume of air. Moreover, the amount of oxygen dissolved in water is small and fishes must therefore process 40 volumes of water to obtain the oxygen in 1 volume of air. So, cooling during respiration is 100,000 times greater in creatures that breathe water than those that breathe air.

The dynamics of the cooling have to do with circulation and diffusion. The blood of a fish, warmed by metabolism, flows from heart to gills where it absorbs oxygen from the water. Then, it flows on to the tissues. Since, though, heat diffuses 10 times more rapidly than oxygen, by the time the blood absorbs oxygen enough for respiratory purposes and leaves the gills, it has been cooled to, or near to, water temperature and, in turn, cools the body tissues.

Nonetheless, despite the inherent difficulties of heat conservation in fishes and despite the lack in fishes of such helpful mammalian insulation as blubber or fur, it has for years been common scientific knowledge that certain tunas and bonitos of the fish family Scombridae have a body temperature which is 10°C. (18°F.) or more above water temperature. Actually, some sailing men were aware of it for, in *The Cruise of the Cachalot Round the World After Sperm Whales*, 1902, Frank T. Bullen remarked on what was probably the oceanic bonito, *Katsuwonus pelamis*. 'These fish . . .' he wrote, 'love to follow a ship, playing around her, if her pace be not too great, for days together. Their flesh resembles beef in appearance, and they are warm-blooded. . . . The struggles of these fish [at the end of a line] are marvellous. . . . Such is the tremendous vibration that a twenty-pound bonito makes in a man's grip, that it can be felt in the cabin at the other end of the ship. . . .'

If, however, the fact of hot-blooded Scombridae has been long established, the discovery that another family of fishes shares the phenomenon is a recent one. In 1966, Francis G. Carey and John M. Teal of the Woods Hole Oceanographic Institution on Cape Cod in Massachusetts, while investigating the physiology of high temperature in the bluefin tuna, *Thunnus thynnus*, took the temperature of certain sharks and found it also high.

Thus far, Carey and Teal have proved only the porbeagle, *Lamna nasus*, and the short-finned or common mako, *Isurus oxyrinchus*, to be warm-blooded. Both species, though, are members of the family Isuridae, and since there are only four species in the family (the other two being the newly, 1967, described long-finned mako, *Isurus paucus*, and the great white shark or maneater, *Carcharodon carcharias*) and since the four species are quite similar, the family as a whole is likely warm.

Being warm has decided advantages. Digestion, transmission of nerve impulses and metabolism are quickened by warmth. Further, with each 10°C. rise in body temperature, muscle contraction and relaxation will be triply quicker although the force exerted by the muscle won't change. In short, by raising its temperature 10°C. a fish triples the power of a muscle mass.

The powerful tunas may well be the fastest of fishes. The bluefin, for one, which grows to more than 1,000 pounds, has been scientifically clocked, in bursts of 10 to 20 seconds, at 43·4 miles per hour and a legion of author-anglers, in the manner of Bullen about the bonito, have extolled its virtues as a game fish. The isurid sharks are also powerful, also fast, also regarded as game fish and the mako is almost unique among sharks for its prodigious jumping when hooked. Estimates are that it can clear the surface by 15 to 20 feet, an achievement which requires a starting velocity, in the water, upwards of 22 miles per hour.

At the root of this power and speed are warm muscles. Obviously, though, to keep warm a fish must have a thermal barrier between tissues and gills, a barrier which permits the passage of blood, but prevents the passage of heat. The tunas and the isurid sharks, Carey and Teal have determined, do have such a system and it derives from a common feature of vertebrate circulation. Typically, arteries and veins follow the same pathways and frequently they lie side by side in actual contact. Also, blood in arteries and veins flows in opposite directions. If, consequently, arterial and venous blood are of a different temperature, and arteries and veins are in contact, heat will pass from the warmer vessel to the cooler one and be carried back to whence it came. That, then, is a thermal barrier which works to conserve heat and many animals have developed it. Industry has too, which is not a case of art imitating nature, but rather the application of basic thermodynamic principles. In any event, the mechanism is known as the countercurrent heat exchanger and it has a number of workaday uses. It is, for instance, a component of most modern marine diesel engines.

There is a crude sort of heat exchanger in the human arm, but in some other creatures the system is highly refined and transfers heat from arterial to venous blood with great efficiency. Its salient characteristic is, in the deeper muscles, masses of small, parallel, contiguous arteries and veins arrayed alternately and called by early anatomists the *rete mirabile* or 'miraculous net'. Such animals as sloths, lemurs, porpoises and whales have the refined sort of *rete mirabile* and so have the hot-blooded tunas and sharks.

Because warmth is the advantage it is, the natural prospect is that many fishes would have developed heat exchangers. Seemingly, however, they have not. Carey, Teal and others have taken the temperature of many active species and almost invariably it has been within one degree of water temperature. Some marlins of the family Istiophoridae may also prove to be warm, but the evidence is not now conclusive. Regardless, the presence of heat exchangers in both tunas and sharks is an oddity in itself, a case, in scientific terms, of convergent evolution. The tunas, which are teleosts, and the sharks represent distinct lines of evolutionary development and they share no recent common ancestor. Yet, a few species of each line independently evolved nearly identical ways of conserving heat.

209

We have already spoken about other aspects of shark anatomy—teeth, liver, eyes and whatnot—but one more merits attention.

The stomach of a shark is a bag shaped in the form of either a U or a J. It is rough and reddish on the inside, very distensible, very loosely hung in the body cavity and it is drained by a complicated intestine most of which is taken up by a structure unique to elasmobranchs, the spiral valve. In many shark species the valve looks like a spiral staircase or ramp. Its pitch is gradual, its turns are many and the whole of it is enclosed within a tube. In other shark species the valve is more like a scroll of many windings, but is also within a tube.

The spiral valve does not really function as a valve. What it does, is enormously increase the absorptive surface of the intestine in little more space than a short straight pipe would occupy. Therefore, the food in the stomach of shark doesn't have to traverse long loops of intestine. It spirals instead through the compact ramp or scroll and leftover waste moves on into the cloaca, the same pocket to which lead the oviducts and tubes from the testes, and via the vent to the sea.

The ramp sort of spiral valve, incidentally, can be appreciated by slitting the intestine lengthways and we think it worth the slitting. It will show the ingenuity and nicety of natural engineering and also, in this instance, a bit of beauty in an unexpected place.

V. C. Wynn-Edwards in 1965 in *Science*, defined a society as an organization of individuals that is capable of providing conventional competition among its members. 'This definition,' writes Stewart Springer, 'is sufficiently broad to include the simplest of animal societies and is especially apt for sharks in drawing attention to one of the primary functions of a society—the regulation of intraspecies competition so as to permit natural selection to operate without excessive waste.'

Among sharks, the regulatory social conventions are those given in the previous chapter: the more or less universal tendency of sharks to segregate by sex outside of the mating season; the development of feeding inhibition in males during courtship, particularly in the larger species with formidable teeth; the habit of females to cease feeding while on the nursery grounds; and the use by some

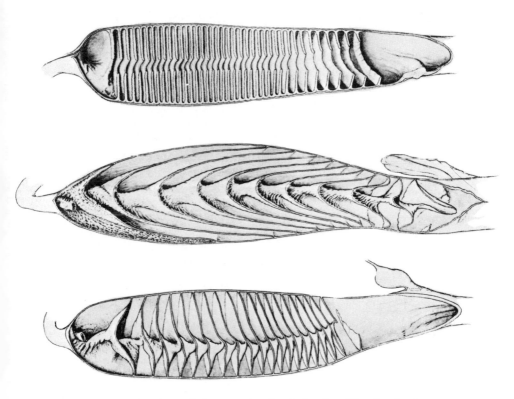

Sections of three sorts of spiral valve. The structure, unique to elasmobranchs, enormously increases the absorptive surface of the intestine in a very short space thus making long loops of intestine unnecessary.

species of nursery grounds beyond the normal geographical or habitat range of mature males.

There is another facet to shark behaviour and shark population dynamics which, like the foregoing, has been paid scant notice except by Springer. The total population of certain species, Springer theorizes, is divided into two populations. The principal population is the main breeding population, the core of the total population, that part of the total population that maintains its numbers and follows regular patterns of distribution and habit. The accessory population is the lost part of the total population. Its members have wandered away from the principal population to inhabit unaccustomed waters.

The accessory population of a given species is small. It may be out of phase in the reproductive cycle as well as out of the principal population's normal range so its breeding, if any occurs, is probably without gain. Out-of-phase and out-of-range young would seem to have little chance of surviving.

The accessory population is far less predictable than the principal population. It feeds far more indiscriminately and behaves far more erratically. It seems, in many cases, to be made up of either young sharks or quite old ones, and they are more often inshore than are the sharks of the principal population. Possibly, therefore, sharks of accessory populations—inshore white sharks may afford a good example—are disproportionately dangerous to man and with that in mind we will examine the problem of attack prevention.

CHAPTER 13

Sharks and the Discouragement Thereof

Mankind's ways of dealing with shark attack have been, and are, sometimes pathetic, sometimes whimsical and usually unavailing. Even today there are Japanese fisherfolk who rely on a long red sash to protect them from sharks although Dr Tohru Uchida of Hokkaido University at Sapporo took pains to report in 1958 that: 'This method . . . was not successful in actual practice.'

Today too, there are Ceylonese pearl divers who place great confidence in shark charmers, something recorded by Marco Polo in 1298 and by Sir James Emerson Tennent, an acquaintance of Byron and Colonial Secretary of Ceylon, in 1861 in his *Sketches of the Natural History of Ceylon*. 'The only precaution,' noted Sir James, 'to which the Ceylon diver devotedly resorts is the mystic ceremony of the shark charmer, whose exorcism is an indispensable preliminary to every fishery. His power is believed to be hereditary; nor is it supposed that the value of his incantations is at all dependent upon the religious faith professed by the operator, for the present head of the family happens to be a Roman Catholic. At the time of our visit this mysterious functionary was ill and unable to attend; but he sent an accredited substitute, who assured me that although he himself was ignorant of the grand and mystic secrets, the mere fact of his presence, as a representative of the higher authority, would be recognized and respected by the sharks.'

The warm spaciousness of the Pacific with its myriad island cultures has been since time immemorial the cradle of shark worship and Sir Harry Luke gave a delightful glimpse of it in 1946 in *From a South Seas Diary*.

In 1938 Sir Harry, then Governor and Commander-in-Chief of Fiji and High Commissioner for the Western Pacific, was making a tour of the Solomons and late in June visited Auki, the main village on the island of Malaita. His entry for June 22: 'It is really beautiful, and in the pearly flush of dawn reminiscent of the lagoon of Venice . . . the shark is the sacred or totem animal of the place, and on occasions the particular tutelary fish of the neighbourhood, the "steady" so to speak, who is marked with a smudge of tar on his back to be easily recognized, comes along, perhaps accompanied, as today, by a mate, to be fed by three dreadful-looking old priests of the cult. The sharks come swimming slowly from the open sea into a little cove or canoe camber, where the old men feed them with the entrails of a dead pig—the pig on this occasion provided by me. The water in the camber is quite shallow—barely a foot or so—and the old men tickle the sharks and scratch their backs. The sharks seem quite tame, at all events with the old men, and the natives of the village not only have no fear of them and swim in the shark-infested waters unconcernedly, but actually regard them as their protectors. . . .'

Three years later in the Phoenix Islands, Sir Harry discovered another sort of shark deterrent. His entry for November 28: 'One of the Americans owns a terrier of dubious ancestry but dauntless spirit called Snodgrass, who goes into the lagoon after young sharks, which he finishes off with the help of a lady friend of his. Unfortunately, Snodgrass has recently been rather badly bitten by one of his victims and for the moment is laying low.'

World War II soon made it distressingly clear that while venerable priests and small dogs might serve local purposes, the problem of shark attack called for something with a far broader application. 'We know now,' wrote George A. Llano, an American authority on survival in hostile environments, in 1963, 'that the absence of information on animals hazards caused no great loss in survival on land, for, although there were rare encounters between survivors and dangerous animals (wild elephants, crocodiles, and snakes), chiefly on the continent and islands of Southeast Asia, there is little evidence that fear of these potentially harmful land animals ever deterred men when they saw ways to escape prisoner-of-war camps and lose themselves, in the trackless jungles. The latent hazards of the sea aroused far more apprehension, and it was most pronounced when men were cast into the water without the benefit of lifeboats or life rafts. Of all the undersea animals, none was so consistently suspect nor so universally dreaded as the shark. After ship sinkings or abandonment of aircraft at sea, when loss of life was expected and accepted, death by shark attack evoked a horror that had no equal among the evils faced on land.'

Under the circumstances, a nation's navy, or the air arm of the navy, might be expected to have a more than casual interest in developing a shark repellent or deterrent, but, at least in the United States, this was not so. The air arm of the Navy in 1942 issued a *Technical Note*—four pages long and entitled *Protection of Personnel Afloat in Life Rafts*—wherein the Navy's position was stated. 'From experience . . . or lack of it—it is believed that sharks constitute a negligible danger to Navy personnel.'

The note went on to say that a repellent might help to quiet the fear of sharks. But it also said: 'However, it is considered that correct information relative to shark characteristics would be more universally operative in alleviating fear than any possible repellent.'

What the Navy took to be 'correct information' relative to shark characteristics emerged in March of 1944 in its manual *Shark Sense.* Illustrated with cartoons that depicted the shark as some sort of buffoon and written in a lighthearted style, *Shark Sense* was a hodge-podge of sound advice and misleading claptrap. Some examples of the latter:

'It becomes evident that few accurate facts are available regarding the habits of the shark. On the other hand, it is equally evident that the fear of sharks has originated because of wild and unfounded tales. . . .'

'Men who know most about sharks are the men who fear them the least. . . .

'Remember that the shark strikes with his mouth opened wide, and his vision blocked. If you can avoid his mouth by moving a foot or so out of his path, it is a miss for the shark. . . . If you can attach yourself to him by grabbing a fin, when he turns for another attack, you aren't there; you are riding with him, behind his mouth and out of danger from his teeth. Hold tight and hang on as long as you can without drowning yourself. In the meantime, after missing his target, the shark may lose his viciousness and become his usual cowardly self again.

'There is very little danger from sharks. . . .

'People suffer more from shark fright than from shark bite. . . .

'You can't win from a shark in a biting match, but you *can* win in a thinking match.'

There is no doubt that the Navy was sincere. But there is considerable doubt that *Shark Sense* went down well with survivors like Lieutenant (j.g.) A. G. Reading, a Navy pilot. Reading had to ditch his aircraft some 60 miles east of the Wallis Islands in the south-west Pacific. The impact knocked him unconscious, but his radio operator, E. H. Almond, pulled him free and got him into and inflated his life jacket. The Lieutenant's report—in it we have substituted the whole name Almond where Reading used only the initial A.—reads in part.

'After I came to, [Almond] told me the plane had sunk in 2 minutes and that he didn't have time to salvage the life raft. He pulled both our "dye markers" and had a parachute alongside of him. He did not have any pants on at all except for shorts. . . . We soon lost the chute and began drifting away from the dye. It was within a very short time (about $\frac{1}{2}$ hour) when sharks were quite apparent swimming around us. [Almond] and I were tied together by the dye marker cords . . . suddenly [Almond] said he felt something strike his right foot and that it hurt. I told him to get on my back and keep his right foot out of the water, but before he could, the sharks struck again and we were both jerked under the water for a second. I knew that we were in for it as there were more than five sharks around and blood all around us. He showed me his leg and not only did he have bites all over his right leg, but his left thigh was badly mauled. He wasn't in any particular pain except every time they struck I knew it and felt the jerk. I finally grabbed my binoculars and started swinging them at the passing sharks. It was a matter of seconds when they struck again. We both went under and this time I found myself separated from [Almond]. I was also the recipient of a wallop across the cheek bone by one of the flaying tails of a shark. From that moment on I watched [Almond] bob about from attacks. His head was under water and his body jerked as the sharks struck it. As I drifted away . . . sharks continually swam about and every now and then I could feel one with my foot. At midnight I sighted a YP boat and was rescued after calling for help.'

Despite its misgivings about the need for shark repellent the Navy, largely with morale in mind, asked that one be developed and work began on smooth dogfish, *Mustelus canis*, 18 to 30 inches long. 'High and low frequency sounds,' one scientist would later report, 'fish poisons such as rotenone, irritants such as chlorine, metallic poisons, chemical stenches, and a poison gas generator were tried on our group of experimental sharks with no success. A great many of our sharks were killed, but either the amount of material required to protect the food was excessive or the sharks ate or tried to eat the food before dying or while dying.'

The literature of science was of no help. There had never before been a scientific search for a shark repellent. Ultimately, however, it was found that one chemical, copper acetate, did seem to repel smooth dogfish. And after a series of promising field tests on larger shark species, the Navy in 1944—the same year it issued *Shark Sense*—also issued Shark Chaser, a water soluble $6\frac{1}{2}$-ounce cake of 80 per cent black nigrosine dye, to hide the castaways, and 20 per cent copper acetate to repel the sharks. The cake would be kept in a waterproof pouch until circumstances counselled otherwise and could then be made to last from two to four hours.

Shark Chaser did enhance morale, but it did not always repel sharks. Sometimes it did and sometimes it did not. Moreover, the post-war experiences of skin divers only added to the contradictory reports of its worth.

Conrad Limbaugh of the Scripps Institution of Oceanography in California was an accomplished diver and an ichthyologist with a particular interest in sharks. In October 1956, he visited Clipperton Island—an isolated atoll 600 miles south-west of Mexico—and his experiences and observations are valuable both for what they tell of Shark Chaser and for what they tell of a shark species' behaviour in a variety of contexts.

Limbaugh wrote of Clipperton: 'Sharks, particularly juvenile Galapagos sharks, *Carcharhinus galapagensis*, are extremely abundant and aggressive. . . . Dozens of sharks, primarily Galapagos and whitetip reef sharks, *Carcharhinus platyrynchus*, surrounded the ship on its arrival in 1956 . . . the Galapagos sharks followed the skiff and made frequent passes, occasionally hitting the oars as equipment was unloaded from the ship through the surf to the beach . . . some followed the boat into the surf almost onto the beach. Juvenile Galapagos sharks, ranging in size from 2½ to an estimated 6 feet, were frequently observed patrolling the shallow reef-flat area during the entire expedition stay. They often entered water so shallow that their backs were bare. . . . These sharks sometimes interfered with fish-collecting operations on the reef flat by taking the fish killed or stunned by rotenone . . . often they swam in the milky clouds of this fish toxin, apparently unaffected. The sharks were attracted to the fish wounded by spear-fishing within seconds during high tide, when the water over the reef flat was 2 to 3 feet deep.'

This, though, as Limbaugh went on to explain, was just the beginning of the party's travails with sharks. 'To SCUBA-dive [SCUBA being the acronym for self-contained underwater breathing apparatus] it was necessary to row the skiff until we found an area where sharks were less numerous. While one man rowed, another hung over the stern with his head in the water to watch the bottom, and a third man watched for sharks to keep the observer from being bitten. Once a diving spot was selected, we entered the water quietly and immediately descended to the cover of the coral bottom. Usually there were several small sharks in the area . . . schools of jacks swirled around us, and small, curious grouper and damselfish collected to watch. At first, the small sharks circled at a distance, but gradually they approached and became more aggressive. They swam faster and in tighter circles around us. They seemed to pay no attention to the clouds of Shark Chaser that surrounded us. They seemed particularly interested in the shiny regulator from which bubbles were expelled into the water. Generally they avoided the stream of rising bubbles, but occasionally one would pass directly through it.'

At this juncture the party resorted to diving lore. 'Various popular methods of repelling sharks proved unsuccessful. The sharks showed no indication of hearing [underwater] yells or screams. Quick movements of our hands attracted their attention, and they moved in closer. Sharks quite close to the diver could be startled with quick movements or a burst of air bubbles, but they circled back, bringing more sharks. One shark lightly wounded by a spear fled and then returned. As the other sharks crossed its path, they became excited. Even the wounded shark seemed excited as it crossed its own trail. We surfaced rapidly when the situation seemed to be getting out of hand. One diver with all equipment and specimens surfaced in the cover of the remaining divers' bubbles. He left a cloud of Shark Chaser around the skiff, and the last diver surfaced rapidly into the repellent. As the diver surfaced, we noticed that the sharks followed his fins.'

The sharks put a virtual stop to diving, but the collection of fish specimens continued albeit not smoothly. 'As we moved the boat from one area to the next,' Limbaugh related, 'we tried to frighten off the following sharks by splashing, but this only attracted more. . . . These sharks would strike at almost anything trailing. A fish tied to an open packet of repellent was taken almost as it was placed in the water. The same shark circled back and took the Shark Chaser. Shortly afterwards it spit it up. . . . The fish-collecting activities created feeding frenzies among sharks of all sizes. . . . Blasting with small charges of TNT seemed to bring the most immediate response. Sharks seemed to come from all directions. . . . If several were after the same food, they raced for it, with the largest shark usually winning and the smaller ones taking the pieces. A whitetip reef shark made a quick rush at a fish, bit it in three pieces, and left two pieces behind. During this frenzy, almost any floating or suspended object was attacked. Our marker buoys were bitten loose and the bottom of the skiff was struck. . . . We exploded additional charges of TNT during these frenzies. . . . The feeding activities ceased for only a few seconds and then were renewed with increased vigor. . . . During one of these frenzies, when the sharks seemed to be striking everything at the surface, they seemed to carefully avoid a large dead bird floating nearby.

The bird was too decayed to make an identification.'

By 1958 the United States Navy had decided that Shark Chaser might not be the best of repellents. So it sponsored, and the American Institute of Biological Sciences arranged, the first A.I.B.S. shark symposium to explore basic research approaches to the finding of repellents. The symposium was held for four April days in 1958 in New Orleans, Louisiana and 34 scientists participated. Among them was Limbaugh, who recounted his 1956 troubles at Clipperton Island, as well as Perry W. Gilbert, Stewart Springer and representatives from South Africa, Japan and Australia.

The *Shark Research Panel* was appointed, papers were read, and there was much discussion. But the consensus was that effective repellents would evolve only from a much greater insight into the biology of sharks.

Limbaugh, the following August returned to Clipperton Island and again made some absorbing observations. 'The larger Galapagos sharks were sometimes followed by schools of starry jacks or groups of rainbow runners [smallish bony fishes], which continually scratched themselves on the obviously irritated sharks. On one occasion, a large rainbow runner bumped a small shark, causing it to disgorge some food which the more agile runner promptly swallowed. These fish would often leave their host to take bits of food or to swirl around food too large for them to eat. This action seemed to attract the attention of the shark, which would move in and feed. Whitetip [reef] sharks were almost always accompanied by a cloud of rainbow runners. Sometimes it was impossible to see the shark hidden in the dense school surrounding it. Unlike the Galapagos shark, however, they seemed not to mind the scrapings.'

To learn something of food preferences, Limbaugh offered the Clipperton Island sharks a variety of baits and found that they were strongly repelled by decayed shark flesh. 'It seemed,' he noted, 'to drive them completely away from the area.'

He also tested Shark Chaser again although not during feeding frenzies. 'It obviously protected the baited hooks quite well', he reported. 'But it may prove to be ineffective against the blacktip shark [*Carcharhinus limbatus*], which took the protected bait without hesitation. Galapagos sharks, which did not take the protected bait in the experimental period, did take it on several occasions outside this period. . . . The present Navy Shark Chaser does have value.'

Limbaugh's finding about decayed shark flesh was not a new one. Actually, part of Shark Chaser's constituents stemmed from the fact that the repelling agent in decayed shark flesh was ammonium acetate which in water forms, to some extent, acetic acid. However, in 1961 after a stringent testing of Shark Chaser at the Lerner Marine Laboratory in the Bahamas, Perry Gilbert reported that not one of his subjects, six dangerous shark species, was in the least repelled by copper acetate. Nor was one repelled by extracts of decayed shark flesh and this matched the experience of other investigators in the Pacific. Yet Limbaugh and co-workers in two months time in 1958 had been unable to catch a shark with decayed shark flesh and when it was used offshore he observed that: '. . . the sharks wouldn't even come near our lines.'

Be that as it may, Gilbert also reported in 1961 that five of his six subject species were repelled by Shark Chaser's black dye. With opaque eye cups on they would swim into a cloud of dye. With eye cups off they would not, not even to get at fresh food. The exception was the nurse shark, *Ginglymostoma cirratum*, which according to Gilbert '. . . enters a dense cloud of nigrosine dye and feeds with no hesitation within it.'

Gilbert found, as had Limbaugh and others, that Shark Chaser was worthless when sharks were in a feeding frenzy. But he does not throw out the baby with the bath water. In 1963 in *Sharks and Survival* he writes: 'Substances should be tested on sharks which are actively feeding and, if possible, also on sharks in a "feeding frenzy". If, however, a substance does not work when sharks are in the latter condition, it does not mean that it is useless. A substance which will repel a curious or circling shark is of considerable value. Shark Chaser fulfills this function quite well. . . .'

The Navy, then, had a better repellent than it thought and Shark Chaser is still used by the United States military. But Shark Chaser still has limitations. Its life in the water is fairly short and it has not always turned aside sharks when it could have been reasonably expected to. So the search for yet better repellents continues and momentarily the Navy is quite hopeful about a bag.

The bag—called by the Navy the *Johnson Shark Screen* after C. Scott Johnson the scientist who designed it—is more or less what it says; a light, durable plastic bag which folds into a package small enough to be attached to life jackets. In the water, the castaway inflates three buoyancy rings at the top of the bag, fills the bag with water and climbs inside. Several purposes are thereby served. Sharks cannot see the castaway moving about and, unless it is so rough that water slops out over the buoyancy rings, they will not scent him or, if he is cut, his blood. Lastly, the bag will help to husband his body heat and perhaps give him the psychological comfort of being covered.

During 1966 many bags of many colours were subjected to weeks of testing with captive sharks in Hawaii and the Bahamas and with sharks in the wild at Eniwetok Atoll in the western Pacific. Eight shark species were involved and six of these were carcharhinids. Bags were tested in the daylight and the dark. They were tested empty and less often with someone in them. The results were encouraging. When the sharks were not aroused by food they tended to ignore or avoid the bag. Now and then, inadvertently or out of curiosity, a shark would nudge, bump or brush a bag. Inadvertent contacts were frequent when the sharks were fed close to a bag and became excited. No bag, though, was really attacked and the sharks had hundreds of opportunities. Three times in the Eniwetok tests a feeding shark bit at but did not damage the bag. Once in the Bahama tests a shark bit a small hole in a bag with no provocation except, possibly, the bag itself. However, the most important fact to issue from the tests was that none of the sharks nudged, bumped or brushed a black bag and they approached a black bag less often and kept a greater distance from it than a bag of any other colour. The colour is not in itself significant. Sharks are believed to be colour-blind. It is reflectivity that is significant and black is a colour of low reflectivity.

The deterrent qualities of the bag—repellent would be the wrong word—are some of them obvious and some of them not. Its screening of movement, its elimination or reduction of olfactory

Dr C. Scott Johnson at Bimini in the shark screen he developed. The shark with him is a large nurse shark, *Ginglymostoma cirratum*, and a dangerous one, but sharks in general tend to shun the screen.

stimuli and its low reflectivity are the obvious ones. The influence of size discrimination cannot at this point be assessed. As stated elsewhere, sharks are chary of things only a bit larger than they and none of the sharks involved in the testing of bags were substantially larger than the bags themselves. The largest were between 6 and 7 feet long, about as long as the bag though less bulky. The chances are that larger sharks will be bolder about approaching the bag, but this does not mean that its deterrent qualities will be invalidated. Conversely, the bag cannot always be expected to forestall attack. With the bag, however, and with Shark Chaser too, the lot of the castaway would seem to be a happier one. The Navy manual *Shark Sense*, incidentally, has been much revised. The text and the cartoons are still droll, but gone is the nonsense and in its stead is such advice as: 'Never count on a shark not attacking you. He may do it.'

Whatever the merits of the bag and of Shark Chaser, they do not meet every need. The commercial fisherman with no market for sharks needs a way to keep the creatures from thieving his catch and ruining his nets or lines. The diver needs something that is consistently effective beneath and at the surface. The bather needs a protected beach.

Research may satisfy the needs, but it has its frustrations. The chemical approach, for instance, which may yet yield a worthwhile shark repellent, has been as disappointing since World War II as it was in 1942. S. A. C. Watson reported in *The Australian Journal of Science* for July of 1961 that he had injected sharks with almost 30 poisons. 'Some substances tested', he wrote, 'including such powerful poisons as potassium cyanide and various forms of curare, were surprisingly ineffective. No irritant poisons tested gave a rapid result. Enough magnesium sulphate with chloral hydrate to bring down several large horses made no detectable difference to each of several small sharks, except to increase their swimming speed.'

Ultimately, Watson discovered that 30 seconds after an injection of strychnine nitrate the co-ordinated movements of one large shark ceased, that within two minutes the shark could be handled and within eight it died. He then suggested the development of a syringe which a diver could shoot at a shark and which would inject the shark on contact. The idea may have useful applications, but the thought occurs that for any shark bent on doing mischief, 30 seconds is quite time enough.

The protection of beaches is not the simple matter it might seem. A fixed barrier will keep sharks out, but sooner or later, in whole or in part, such a barrier succumbs to the force of the sea or to corrosion and the cost of maintaining its integrity may be prohibitive. Other and less costly contrivances have also been found wanting. Curtains of air bubbles have failed to restrain sharks and an electrical deterrent system has yet to prove itself though it may. There is left, then, at present, only one uncomplicated and very effective way of protecting a beach from sharks. Known as meshing, it involves the periodic setting of gill nets off a beach and the periodic taking in of the nets with the sharks they have caught.

Meshing originated in Australia in 1937. South Africa took it up in 1952. In the years since there have been virtually no shark attacks on bathers—we are aware of just two—at the meshed beaches of either country. Before, there had been, annually, as many as 10. Why the system works so well no one really knows. The nets do not constitute a barrier and they are not meant to. No effort is made to close the gap between net ends and shore and the gap is utilized. Sharks are often caught on the landward side of a net. Moreover, while meshing greatly reduces the number of sharks off a beach it does not altogether eliminate them. Meshing, nonetheless, is nearly an unqualified success and in the words of one scientist: '. . . its ultimate efficiency seems almost certainly to rest on purely behavioral grounds—of the sharks, not the bathers.'

Meshing is costly, but few resort areas are so pestered with sharks that they need to be meshed. Also, most resorts can suffer an occasional attack with no loss to profit and neither will they be meshed.

What must be borne in mind is that a shark attack along a beach is a true rarity. By the same token, however, imprudence can make the rarity more likely. It is not prudent to wear bright objects in the water. It is not prudent to swim in turbid water or in water where refuse has been jettisoned. It is not at all prudent to bother a shark no matter how indolent it might seem.

Should one be approached by a shark, one beats as calm and quiet a retreat—preferably under the water and facing the shark— as circumstances permit. Should the shark attack, one does what one can, but blows should be directed at the shark's nose, eyes and gills. Attacks have been aborted. One analysis of 126 attacks wherein the shark was about to bite or about to bite again, showed that 61·1 per cent of the sharks broke off the attack when hit or stabbed while the rest, some more aggressively, continued the attack. The analysis does not show the percentage of sharks that managed the first bite or the damage they did.

Another analysis—this and the foregoing both from the previously cited paper by Leonard P. Schultz—yields an inexplicable peculiarity about shark attack. In 144 attacks during which rescue was attempted, only 21 or 14·6 per cent of the rescuers were bitten and some were not bitten even though in several attacks the shark bit the swimmer time and time again brushing the rescuers aside to do so.

Possibly, the shark takes a sensory lock on its prey, but we may never know. Neither may we ever have a repellent or deterrent that is effective against all sharks in all situations. 'Both sharks and men,' the American scientist Willard Bascom has said, 'are complex biological organisms whose reaction to any specific set of circumstances is highly unpredictable. Therefore to devise any one solution to attack that will be effective under all conditions in which these two may be brought together may well be impossible.'

What, though, of the broad future of sharks? We have advanced the likelihood that shark populations will be hard pressed as a food resource. Some populations, indeed, are depleted already. Yet, at the present level of fisheries technology, fishing does not bespeak collective extinction. Unrestricted fishing can, to be sure, so deplete a population that further fishing becomes unprofitable. But the harvester then turns elsewhere, at which point enough of the population survives to sooner or later replenish itself. Thus, even if sharks prove to be otherwise commercially important, they still do not face extinction on that score.

Nor, we think, will sharks be eliminated because they are socially undesirable. Coasts may be swept barren of sharks, but there are always those far reaches of the sea where mankind seldom treads.

Sharks, it would seem, are destined to endure and surely there is justice in that. Through more than 400 million years they have survived environmental upheavals that spelled doom to less adaptable organisms. Through more than 2,000 years of written history they have, perhaps more than any creature, stirred the fear, admiration and curiosity of mankind. Of course, the future is thick with hazards known and unknown and predictions are only that. All things considered, however, the survival of sharks seems rather more likely than the survival of mankind itself.

A Key to the Families of Sharks

This key makes it possible to identify any shark as to its family. If more specific identification is wanted, reference should be made to those taxonomic works included in the Bibliography.

The key is formed of a series of couplets, each of which comprises two contrasting descriptions. To identify a shark, read each part of couplet 1 and determine which part best fits the shark in hand. Then, go to the next referred couplet and so on until the proper family is found.

Lastly, the anatomical characters used in the key are those included in the generalized figure of a shark below.

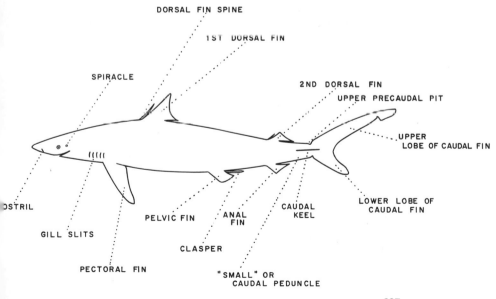

DORSAL FIN SPINE

1ST DORSAL FIN

SPIRACLE

2ND DORSAL FIN

UPPER PRECAUDAL PIT

UPPER LOBE OF CAUDAL FIN

LOWER LOBE OF CAUDAL FIN

NOSTRIL

CAUDAL KEEL

PELVIC FIN

ANAL FIN

GILL SLITS

CLASPER

PECTORAL FIN

"SMALL" OR CAUDAL PEDUNCLE

1. A. Anal fin present: go to couplet 2.
    B. Anal fin absent: go to couplet 17.

2. A. 6 or 7 gill slits: go to couplet 3.
    B. 5 gill openings: go to couplet 4.

3. A. Margins of first gill slits continuous across the throat like a frilled collar; upper and lower teeth similar in the centre of jaws: the *frilled shark* family CHLAMYDOSELACHIDAE.
    B. Margins of first gill slits not continuous across the throat like a frilled collar; upper and lower teeth dissimilar in the centre of the jaws: the *six- and seven-gilled sharks*, the family HEXANCHIDAE.

4. A. Dorsal fins preceded by stout spines: the *horned or bullhead sharks;* the family HETERODONTIDAE.
    B. Dorsal fins not preceded by stout spines: go to couplet 5.

5. A. Only one dorsal fin: the *cat sharks* (in part), the family SCYLIORHINIDAE.
    B. 2 dorsal fins: go to couplet 6.

6. A. At least half of the base of the first dorsal fin is behind the front of the pelvic fins: go to couplet 7.
    B. The base of the first dorsal fin terminates over or well forward of the front of the pelvic fins: go to couplet 9.

7. A. The caudal fin half-moon in shape; gill arches connected by spongy, sieve-like structures: the *whale shark*, the family RHINCODONTIDAE.
    B. The caudal fin not half-moon in shape; gill arches normal: go to couplet 8.

8. A. The nostril connected to the mouth by a deep groove with a barbel at the forward margin: the *carpet sharks,* the *wobbegongs;* the family ORECTOLOBIDAE.
    B. The nostril not connected to the mouth by a deep groove

but, if so, no barbel at the forward margin: the *cat sharks*, the family SCYLIORHINIDAE.

9. A. The head expanded to the sides and shaped like a hammer: the *hammerhead sharks*, the family SPHYRNIDAE.
    B. The head not expanded to the sides: go to couplet 10.

10. A. The caudal fin half-moon in shape: go to couplet 11.
    B. The caudal fin not half-moon in shape: go to couplet 12.

11. A. The teeth large and few in number: the *mako sharks*, the *porbeagle*, the *great white shark;* the family ISURIDAE.
    B. The teeth minute and numerous: the *basking shark*, the family CETORHINIDAE.

12. A. The first dorsal fin with a base longer than the caudal fin: the *false cat shark*, the family PSEUDOTRIAKIDAE.
    B. The first dorsal fin with a base much shorter than the caudal fin: go to couplet 13.

13. A. The caudal fin as long as the entire body: the *thresher sharks*, the family ALOPIIDAE.
    B. The caudal fin much shorter than the body: go to couplet 14.

14. A. Fifth gill slit well in front of the pectoral fin; eye without nictating membrane: go to couplet 15.
    B. Fifth gill slit over or behind the front of the pectoral fin; eye with nictating membrane: go to couplet 16.

15. A. The snout greatly elongated: the *goblin shark*, the family SCAPANORHYNCHIDAE.
    B. The snout normal: the *sand sharks*, the family ODONTAS-PIDAE.

16. A. Teeth low, rounded or with 3 or more cusps and usually in a mosaic arrangement: the *smooth dogfishes*, the

smooth hounds; the family TRIAKIDAE.

B. Teeth blade-like with only 1 cusp and not in a mosaic arrangement: the *typical sharks,* the family CARCHAR-HINIDAE.

17. A. The snout very long like a sword with sharp teeth on either edge and a long, fleshy barbel: the *sawsharks,* the family PRISTIOPHORIDAE.

B. The snout normal: go to couplet 18.

18. A. The body flattened; eyes on the top of the head; pectoral fins wing-like: the *angel sharks,* the family SQUATINIDAE.

B. The body cylindrical; eyes on the side of the head; pectoral fins do not overlap gill slits: go to couplet 19.

19. A. The number of upper teeth increases by one in each successive row to form a triangular patch; there is a prominent ridge on each side of the lower body: the family OXYNOTIDAE.

B. There are as many upper teeth in the first row as in successive rows, so that each row has about the same number of teeth; there are no ridges on the front of the body: the *spiny dogfish,* the *bramble sharks,* the *Greenland shark;* the family SQUALIDAE.

APPENDIX 2 | *Glossary*

The following is a glossary of the origins and meanings of shark scientific names including the word *shark* itself. The order, except for the word *shark*, is alphabetical as to family and species and all sharks mentioned in the species chapters of this book are listed. We have also, in the listing, given after each species the name of the author who described and named that species and the year in which he did so. It should be explained, however, that where the name of the author appears parenthetically it means the author originally assigned the species to a different genus. Such are the rules of zoological nomenclature. And, it should be explained that while the scientific names are usually descriptive of some family, generic or specific characteristic, the rules do not require them to be. Furthermore, few authors have explained the origins of or the reasons for their choice of names and the origins and meanings are therefore not in every instance clear. Lastly, as stated in the book, scientific names are compounded from latinized classical Greek, from Latin itself or from some other latinized tongue because Latin is by tradition the language of scholarship.

The family ALOPIIDAE, the thresher or fox sharks: from ἀλώπηξ (*alopex*) meaning *fox*; in reference to the long fox-like tail.

Alopias caudatus Phillips, 1932: *alopias*, as for the family; *caudatus* from *cauda* meaning *tail*.

A. greyi Whitley, 1937: *greyi* after the American author of western and angling tales, Zane Grey.

A. pelagicus Nakamura, 1935: *pelagicus* from πέλαγoʃ (*pelagos*) meaning *the high sea*.

A. profundus Nakamura, 1935: *profundus* meaning *of the deeps*.

A. superciliosus (Lowe), 1840: *superciliosus* from *supercilium* meaning *arrogance;* in reference to the expression lent this species by its enormous eyes.

A. vulpinus (Bonnaterre), 1788: *vulpinus* from *vulpes* meaning *fox.*

The family CARCHARHINIDAE, the typical sharks: from καρχαρός (*carcharos*) meaning *jagged* or *rough* and from ρίνη (*rhiny*) meaning a *shark* or a *file;* in reference to skin or teeth, or possibly both.

Carcharhinus altima Springer, 1950: *Carcharhinus*, as for the family *altima* from *altum* meaning *deep*.

C. galapagensis (Snodgrass and Heller), 1905: *galapagensis*, in reference to the Galapagos Islands, the type locality.

C. gangeticus (Müller and Henle), 1841: *gangeticus*, in reference to the Ganges River, the type locality.

C. leucus (Müller and Henle), 1841: *leucus* from λευχός (*leukos*) meaning *bright, white* or *pale;* in reference to the colour of the species although individuals living over dark bottom may be quite dark.

C. limbatus (Müller and Henle), 1841: *limbatus* meaning *tipped;* in reference to the black-tipped fins.

C. longimanus (Poey), 1861: *longimanus* meaning *long-handed* in reference to the long pectoral fins.

C. macrurus (Ramsay and Ogilby), 1887: *macrurus* from μακρός (*macros*) meaning *large.*

C. melanopterus (Quoy and Gaimard), 1824: *melanopterus* meaning *black on both sides;* in reference to the black-tipped fins.

232

C. milberti (Müller and Henle), 1841: *milberti* after Milbert, a French naturalist.

C. nicaraguensis (Gill and Bransford), 1877: *nicaraguensis*, in reference to Lake Nicaragua, the type locality.

C. obscurus Lesueur, 1818: *obscurus* meaning *dark* or *dusty;* in reference to the sooty-coloured topsides of the species.

C. platyrynchus (Gilbert), 1891: *platyrynchus* from πλατυσ (*platys*) meaning *broad* and from ρύγχος (*rhynchos*) meaning *beak* or *snout.*

C. zambezensis (Peters), 1852: *zambezensis*, in reference to the Zambezi River, the type locality.

Galeocerdo cuvieri (Lesueur), 1822: *Galeocerdo* from γαλέη (*galey*) meaning *weasel* or *shark* and from χερδός (*cherdos*) meaning *cunning;* *cuvieri*, after the great French naturalist and ichthyologist Baron Georges Léopold Chrétien Frédéric Dagobert Cuvier, (1769–1832).

Galeorhinus australis (MacLeay), 1881: *Galeo* as above, *rhinus* from ρίνη (*rhiny*) also meaning *shark; australis* after *Australia.*

G. galeus (Linnaeus), 1758.

G. zyopterus Jordan and Gilbert, 1883: *zyopterus* from ξυόν (*zyon*) meaning *soup* and from πτερόν (*pteron*) meaning *fin.*

Negaprion brevirostris (Poey), 1868: *Negaprion* from *nego* meaning *no* and from πρίων (*prion*) meaning *saw*, in reference to the smooth-edged teeth; *brevirostris* meaning *blunt-snouted.*

Prionace glauca (Linnaeus), 1758: *Prionace* from πρίων (*prion*) meaning *saw* and from ἀκνή (*acny*) meaning *edge*, in reference to the serrated teeth; *glauca* from γλαυχός (*glauchos*) meaning *blue-grey*, in reference to the colour of the species.

The family CETORHINIDAE, the basking shark, from κῆτος (*cetos*) meaning *whale* and from ρίνη (*rhiny*) meaning *shark.*

Cetorhinus maximus (Gunnerus), 1765: *Cetorhinus*, as for the family; *maximus* meaning *great.* *Note:* the family is thought to have just the one species.

The family CHLAMYDOSELACHIDAE, the frilled shark, from χλαμύς (*chlamys*) meaning *frill*, in reference to the frill-like gill slits, and from σέλαχος (*selachos*) meaning *shark*.

Chlamydoselachus anguineus Garman, 1884: *Chlamydoselachus*, as for the family; *anguineus* meaning *snaky* in reference to the body. *Note:* the family is thought to have just the one species.

The family HETERODONTIDAE, the horn sharks, from ἕτερος(*heteros*) meaning *different* and from ὀδούς (*odous*) meaning *tooth*, in reference to the fact that the front teeth are pointed for grasping and the back teeth are flattened for crushing.

> *Heterodontus portusjacksoni* (Meyer), 1793: *Heterodontus*, as for the family; *portusjacksoni* in reference to Port Jackson, Australia, the type locality.
>
> *H. francisci* (Girard), 1854: *francisci*, in reference to San Francisco, the type locality.

The family HEXANCHIDAE, the six and seven-gilled sharks, from ἕξ meaning *six* and from ἀγχός (*anchos*) meaning *bend* or *sinus;* in reference to the number of gill slits.

> *Heptranchias dakini* Whitley, 1931: *Heptranchias* from ἑπτά (*hepta*) meaning *seven* and ἀγχος (*anchos*) meaning *bend* or *sinus*, in reference to the number of gill slits; *dakini* after Professor W. J. Dakin of the University of Sydney.
>
> *H. perlo* (Bonnaterre), 1788: *perlo*, possibly from the French *perle* meaning *pearl grey*.
>
> *Hexanchus griseus* (Bonnaterre), 1780: *Hexanchus* (see the family HEXANCHIDAE); *griseus* meaning *grey*.
>
> *Notorynchus cepedianus* (Peron), 1807: *Notorynchus* from νῶτον (*noton*) meaning the *back* and from ρυγχός (*rhynchos*) meaning the *snout*, the reference being unclear; *cepedianus*, after Bernard Germain Etienne de la Ville sur Illon, Compte de la Cépède (1756–1825), known during the French Revolution as Citoyen La Cépède and who compiled his five volume *Histoire Naturelle des Poissons* (1798–1803) in the midst of revolutionary turmoil.
>
> *N. maculatus* Ayres, 1855: *maculatus* meaning *spotted*.

The family ISURIDAE, the mackerel sharks, from ἴσος (*isos*) meaning *equal* and from όυρά (*oura*) meaning *tail;* in reference to the fact that both lobes of the tail are of about the same length.

Carcharodon carcharias (Linnaeus), 1758: *Carcharodon* from καρχαρός (*carcharos*) meaning *jagged* or *rough* and from όδούς (*odous*) meaning *tooth; carcharias* also from καρχαρός (*carcharos*) the name being a redundancy in reference to the coarsely serrate teeth.

C. megalodon Agassiz, 1838: *megalodon* from μέγας (*megas*) meaning *huge* and from όδούς (*odous*) meaning *tooth.*

Isurus oxyrinchus Rafinesque, 1810: *Isurus* (see the family ISURIDAE); oxyrinchus from όξύ (*oxy*) meaning *sharp* and ρυγχος (*rhynchos*) meaning *snout.*

I. paucus Guitart Manday, 1966: *paucus* meaning *scarce* or *scant;* in reference to the small number of specimens.

Lamna ditropis Hubbs and Follett, 1947: *Lamna* from λάμνα (*lamna*) meaning a *large shark like a large boar; ditropis* from διτρόπις (*ditropis*) meaning *two keels;* in reference to the pair of keels on either side of the tail stem which are peculiar to the genus *Lamna.*

L. nasus (Bonnaterre), 1788: *nasus* meaning the *nose.*

L. philippi Perez Canto, 1886: *philippi* after Rudolf Amandus Philippi (1808–1904) a Chilean naturalist.

L. whitleyi Phillipps, 1935: *whitleyi* after Gilbert Percy Whitley of the Australian Museum.

The family ODONTASPIDAE, the sand sharks, from όδούς (*odous*) meaning *tooth* and from άσπίς (*aspis*) meaning *udder* or *snake;* in reference to the fang-like teeth.

Odontaspis taurus (Rafinesque), 1810: *Odontaspis*, as for the family; *taurus* from ταύρος (*tauros*) meaning *bull.*

O. arenarius (Ogilby), 1910: *arenarius* meaning *of the sand,* in reference to the habitat of the species.

The family ORECTOLOBIDAE, the nurse and carpet sharks, from όρεκτός (*orectos*) meaning *stretched out* and from λοβός (*lobos*) meaning *lobe;* in reference to the upper lobe of the tail.

Ginglymostoma brevicaudatum (Günther), 1866: *brevicaudatum* from *brevis* meaning *short* and *caudatus* meaning *tail*.

G. *cirratum* (Bonnaterre), 1788: *Ginglymostoma* from γύγλυμος (*gynglymos*) meaning *hinge* and from στόμα (*stoma*) meaning *mouth; cirratum* meaning *bearing cirri* or *barbels*.

G. *ferrugineum* Lesson, 1830: *ferrugineum* from *ferrugineus* meaning *rust-coloured*.

The family OXYNOTIDAE, no generally accepted common name, from ὀξύ (*oxy*) meaning *sharp-pointed* and from νῶτον (*noton*) meaning *back;* in reference to the dorsal spines.

Oxynotus bruniensis (Ogilby), 1893: *Oxynotus*, as for the family; *bruniensis*, in reference to Bruny Island, Tasmania, Australia, the type locality.

O. *caribbaeus* Cervignon, 1961: *caribbaeus* meaning *of the Caribbean Sea*.

O. *centrina* (Linnaeus), 1758: *centrina* from κεντρόν (*centron*) meaning *sting* or *prick* in reference to the dorsal spines.

O. *paradoxus* Frade, 1929: *paradoxus* from παράδοξος (*paradoxos*) meaning *unexpected* or *strange*.

The family PRISTIOPHORIDAE, the saw sharks, from πρίστις (*pristis*) meaning *saw* and from φορέω (*phoreo*) meaning *to carry;* in reference to the elongated family snout and its laterally-set teeth.

Pliotrema warreni Regan, 1906: *Pliotrema* from πλέος (*pleos*) meaning *well provided* (with) and from τρῆμα (*trema*) meaning *aperture(s)*; in reference to the fact that the genus *Pliotrema* has six gill slits. The other family genus, *Pristiophorus*, has five; *warreni* after Dr E. Warren of the Natal Museum, South Africa.

Pristiophorus cirratus (Latham), 1794: *Pristiophorus*, see the family PRISTIOPHORIDAE; *cirratus* meaning *bearing* a *cirrus* or *barbel;* in reference to the barbel on the underside of the saw which is typical of the family.

P. *japonicus* Günther, 1870: *Japonicus* meaning *Japan*.

P. *nudipinnis* Günther, 1870: *nudi* from *nudus* meaning *bare* and from *pinnis* meaning *feather* or *wing;* in reference to the fact that the greater part of the dorsal fins and the topsides of the pectorals are naked of scales.

P. owenii Günther, 1870: *owenii*, after the British ichthyologist Sir Richard Owen (1810–1890).

P. schroederi Springer and Bullis, 1960: *schroederi*, after William C. Schroeder, the American ichthyologist and elasmobranch specialist.

The family PSEUDOTRIAKIDAE, the false cat sharks, from ψευδό (*pseudo*) meaning *false*, from τρέιʃ (*treis*) meaning *three* and ἄκιϛ (*akis*) meaning *point;* the latter two words in reference to the *three-cusped teeth.*

    Pseudotriakis acrages Jordan and Snyder, 1904: *Pseudotriakis*, as for the family; *acrages* from ἀκράγής (*acrages*) meaning *speechless* or *dumb.* This species was described and named from Japan where it is called *Oshizame* or *the dumb shark.*

    P. microdon Brito Capello, 1867: *microdon* from μῑκρός (*micros*) meaning *small* and from ὀδούϛ (*odous*) meaning *tooth.*

The family RHINCODONTIDAE, the whale shark, from ῥίνη (*rhiny*) meaning *rasp* and ὀδούϛ meaning *tooth.*

    Rhincodon typus Smith 1829: *Rhincodon*, as for the family; *typus* meaning *typically. Note:* the family is thought to have just the one species.

The family SCAPANORHYNCHIDAE, the goblin sharks, from σκάφιον (*scaphion*) meaning *shovel* and from ῥύγχος (*rhynchos*) meaning *beak* or *snout.*

    Scapanorhynchus jordani Hussakof, 1909: *Scapanorhynchus*, as for the family; *jordani*, after David Starr Jordan (1851–1931), the American educator, first president of Stanford University, and ichthyologist.

    S. owstoni (Jordan) 1898: *owstoni* after Alan Owston of Yokohama who collected Japanese fish specimens.

The family SCYLIORHINIDAE, the cat sharks, from σκύλλιον (*scyllion*) meaning *a small shark* which derives from σκύλλω (*scyllo*) meaning *to rend* or *mangle* and from ῥίνη (*rhiny*) meaning *shark;* in reference to family members' size and feeding habits.

Cephaloscyllium uter (Jordan and Evermann), 1896: *Cephaloscyllium* from κεφαλή (*cephaly*) meaning *head* and from σκύλλω (*scyllo*) as in the family name; *uter* meaning *an inflated bag or bottle;* in reference to the ability of the species, as a defence mechanism, to inflate itself with air.

Scyliorhinus caniculus (Linnaeus) 1758: *Scyliorhinus*, as for the family: *caniculus* from *canis* meaning *dog or hound.*

S. retifer (Garman), 1881: *retifer* from *rete* meaning *a net* and *fero* meaning *to bear;* in reference to the pattern of body markings.

S. stellaris (Linnaeus), 1758: *stellaris* from *stella* meaning *star*; in reference to the species' spots.

The family SPHYRNIDAE, the hammerhead sharks, from σφῦρα (*sphyra*) meaning *hammer.*

Sphyrna blochii Cuvier, 1817: *Sphyrna*, as for the family; *blochii* after Marc Elieser Bloch (1723–1799) the German ichthyologist.

S. corona Springer, 1940: *corona* meaning *crown.*

S. couardi Cadenat, 1951: *couardi*, after M. Couard, then Director of the shark fishery at Joal, Senegal.

S. diplana Springer, 1941: *diplana* from *diplanus* meaning *two planes;* another reference to head shape.

S. lewini (Griffith and Smith), 1834: *lewini*, after Cape Leeuwin, Australia; in reference to the type locality.

S. media Springer, 1940: *media* from *medius* meaning *middle* or *medium.*

S. mokarran Rüppell, 1835: *mokarran* we are unable to find; the species was described from the Red Sea and the name is perhaps a local one.

S. tiburo (Linnaeus), 1758: *tiburo* or *tiburon*, Spanish for *shark.*

S. tiburo tiburo (Linnaeus), 1758: as above.

S. tiburo vespertina Springer, 1940: *vespertina* from *vespertinus* meaning *of the evening.*

S. tudes (Valenciennes), 1822: *tudes* meaning *hammer.*

S. zygaena (Linnaeus), 1758: *zygaena* from ζυγόν (*zygon*) meaning *yoke*.

The family SQUALIDAE, the spiny dogfish, the bramble sharks, the Greenland sharks and others, from γάλη (*galy*) or *squalus* meaning *shark*.

Centroscymnus coelolepis Bocage and Capello, 1864: *Centroscymnus* from κέντρον (*centron*) meaning *spine* and from σκύμνος (*scymnos*) another word for *shark*, in reference to the dorsal spines; *coelolepis* from κōιλοɒ (*coilos*) meaning *hollow* and λεπίς (*lepis*) meaning *scale;* in reference to striated scales or denticles on nape and head.

Echinorhinus brucus (Bonnaterre), 1788: *Echinorhinus* from ἐχίνος (*echinos*) meaning *hedgehog* or *sea urchin* and from ρίνη (*rhiny*) meaning *shark*, in reference to the thorny hide; *brucus* from βρύχω (*brucho*) meaning *to gnash the teeth*, in reference to the temperament of the species.

Isistius brasiliensis (Quoy and Gaimard), 1824: *Isistius*, after *Isis* the goddess of light, in reference to the fact that the species is bioluminescent; *brasiliensis* meaning *Brazil*, in reference to the type locality.

I. plutodus Garrick and Springer, 1964: *plutodus* from πλοῦτος (*plutos*) meaning a *wealth* and from ὀδούς (*odous*) meaning *tooth*.

Somniosus antarcticus Whitley, 1939: *Somniosus* from *somnus* meaning *sleepy;* in reference to the lethargy of the genus.

S, longus (Tanaka), 1912: *longus* meaning *long.*

S. microcephalus (Bloch and Schneider), 1801: *microcephalus* from μικρός (*micros*) meaning *small* and from κεφαλή (*cephaly* meaning *head*.

S. pacificus Bigelow and Schroeder, 1944.

S. rostratis (Risso), 1826: *rostratis* meaning *beaked.*

Squaliolus laticaudus Smith and Radcliffe, 1912: *Squaliolus* from γάλυ (*galy*) or *squalus* meaning *shark* and from ὀλίγο ς (*oligos*) meaning *least;* in reference to the size of this smallest of known shark genera; *laticaudus* from *latus* meaning *broad* or *wide* and from *caudus* meaning *tail.*

S. sarmenti Noronha, 1926: *sarmenti* after Alberto Arthur Sarmento, a Madeiran (Portugal) naturalist.
Squalus acanthias Linnaeus, 1758: *acanthias* from ἄκανθα (*acantha*) meaning *spine;* in reference to the dorsal spines.

The family SQUATINIDAE, the angel sharks or monkfish, from *squatina* an ancient name for sharks.
Squatina australis Regan, 1906: *Squatina,* as for the family.
S. africana, Regan, 1908.
S. californica Ayres, 1859.
S. dumeril Lesueur, 1818: *dumeril,* after the French ichthyologist Auguste Henri Andre Dumeril (1812–1870).
S. tergocellata McCulloch, 1914: *tergocellata* from *tergus* meaning *bask* and from *celo* meaning *hidden.*

The family TRIAKIDAE, the smooth dogfish, from τρεῖς (*treis*) meaning *three* and from ἄκις (*akis*) meaning *point(ed);* in reference to the teeth.
Mustelus antarcticus Günther, 1870: *Mustelus* meaning *weasel.*
M. canis (Mitchell), 1815: *canis* meaning *dog.*
M. mustelus (Linnaeus), 1758.
M. punctulatus Risso, 1826: *punctulatus* from *punctum* meaning *spot(s)* and from *latus* meaning *bearing.*
Triaenodon obesus (Rüppell), 1835: *Triaenodon* from τρίαινα (*triana*) meaning *trident* and from [ὀδούς] (*odous*) meaning *tooth; obesus* meaning *fat, plump* or *swollen.*
Triakis semifasciata Garman, 1913: *Triakis,* see the family TRIAKIDAE; *semifasciata* from *semifasciatus* meaning *half-banded;* in reference to the body markings.

THE WORD 'SHARK'

Scholars are reasonably certain that before the middle of the sixteenth century the words *shark, shirk* and *sherk* were synonymous and applied to human lowlife. The root word may have been Dutch,

French or Italian but opinion—including that of the *Oxford English Dictionary* which devotes more than a page of very small print to *shark* and its variants—favours the German *schurk* or *schurke*. It meant originally *a sharper* or *greedy parasite*; later a *sharper, rook, rake, rogue* or *shark*; today a *rascal, scoundrel* or *villain*. But, whatever, its antecedents, the word *shark* first appeared in written English in 1569 after the display, in London, of a creature in which seamen must have seen the worst of humankind. 'Ther is,' an observer made note, 'no proper name for it (a marvcilous straunge Fishe) that I knowe, but that sertayne men of Captayne Hawkinses doth call it a sharke.'

APPENDIX 3 | *Bibliography*

For the reasons stated in our *Preface* this bibliography is in no way comprehensive. Rather, it is a brief listing of regional and general works in English which are for the most part scientific, and which will help the reader to set the course of his choosing through shark literature. Many of the works have already been cited in the body of this book, though without bibliographic detail. All are illustrated. Lastly, where we thought comment useful we have made it. Where, for example, a work is mainly descriptive, which means that the information given is mainly for the purpose of identifying various species, we have said so.

WESTERN NORTH ATLANTIC

Bigelow, Henry B. and Schroeder, William C.
1948
Sharks. In: *Fishes of the Western North Atlantic.* Memoir of the Sears Foundation for Marine Research, Yale University, No. 1, Part 1, p. 59–576.

This is still the standard work on sharks. Little of it has been invalidated and it was reissued in 1967. It deals at length with the characteristics and life history of each shark species and its value is by no means limited to the Western North Atlantic (which is all of the Western Atlantic north of the equator). The references are exhaustive and global in scope. With the references, furthermore, is a synonymy which gives for each shark species the scientific names which that species has borne since 1758, the year marking the advent of the binomial system of nomenclature.

Böhlke, James E. and Chaplin, Charles C. G.
1968
Fishes of the Bahamas and adjacent tropical waters. Livingston, Wynnewood, Pennsylvania, for the Academy of Natural Sciences of Philadelphia, 771 pp.

EASTERN NORTH PACIFIC

Clemens, W. A. and Wilby, G. V.
1961
Fishes of the Pacific Coast of Canada. Second Edition. Fisheries Research Board of Canada, Bulletin No. 68, 443 pp.

Roedel, Phil M. and Ripley, Wm. Ellis
1950
California sharks and rays. California Department of Fish and Game, Fish Bulletin No. 75, 88 pp.

BRITISH ISLES AND ADJACENT WATERS

Day, Francis.
1880–1884
The fishes of Great Britain and Ireland. Williams and Norgate, London, Edinburgh, Vol. II, 388 pp., 85 pls.
Still a worthwhile source of field observation and natural history.

Jenkins, J. Travis
1942
The fishes of the British Isles, both fresh water and salt. Second Edition, Frederick Warne & Co. Ltd., London, New York, 408 pp.
A third edition was in press at the time of this writing.

Wheeler, A., illustrated by Heaume, V. de
1969
The fishes of the British Isles and North-West Europe. Macmillan
& Co. Ltd., 672 pp., 16 pls., 417 text fig.

Brief descriptive and natural history treatment of each fish with
keys and distributional maps. The most useful work since Day.

WEST AFRICA

Fowler, Henry W.
1936
*The marine fishes of West Africa, based on the collection of the
American Museum Congo Expedition,* 1909–1915. Bulletin of the
American Museum of Natural History, Vol. 70, Part 1, 609 pages.

Mainly descriptive; some natural history.

SOUTH AFRICA

D'Aubrey, Jeannette D.
1964
*Preliminary guide to the sharks found off the East Coast of South
Africa.* Oceanographic Research Institute, Durban, Investigational
Report No. 8, 95 pp.

Davies, David H.
1964
About sharks and shark attack. Shuter and Shooter, Pietermaritz-
burg, South Africa, 237 pp. In 1966: Hobbs, Dorman & Co. Inc.,
New York.

Smith, J. L. B.
1961
The sea fishes of southern Africa. Fourth Edition. Central News
Agency, Ltd., Cape Town, South Africa, 550 pp.

AFRO-ASIA

Fowler, Henry W.
1956
Fishes of the Red Sea and southern Arabia. The Weizmann Science Press of Israel, Jerusalem, Vol. 1, 240 pp.

Mainly descriptive; some natural history.

INDIAN OCEAN

Day, Francis.
1875–1878
The fishes of India, being a natural history of the fishes known to inhabit the seas and fresh waters of India, Burma and Ceylon. Facsimile Edition, 1958, William Dawson & Sons Ltd., London, Vol. 1, Text, 778 pp. Vol. II, 195 pls.

Also a still worthwhile source.

Munro, Ian Sr
1955
The marine and fresh water fishes of Ceylon. Department of External Affairs, Canberra, Australia, 351 pp., 19 text fig., 56 pls.

Mainly descriptive; some natural history and local vernacular names are given.

Smith, J. L. B. and Smith, Margaret Mary
1963
The fishes of Seychelles. The Department of Ichthyology, Rhodes University, Grahamstown, South Africa, 215 pp.

Mainly descriptive; some natural history and local vernacular names are given.

JAPAN

Okada, Yaichiro
1955
Fishes of Japan, illustrations and descriptions of fishes of Japan.
Maruzen Co., Ltd., Tokyo, Japan, 434 pp.

SOUTH SEAS

Fowler, Henry W.
1928
The fishes of Oceania. Memoirs of the Bernice P. Bishop Museum,
Honolulu, Hawaii, Vol. 10, p. 1–540.

_____

1931
The fishes of Oceania. Supplement 1. *ibid.,* Vol. 11, No. 5, p. 311–
381.

_____

1934
The fishes of Oceania. Supplement 2. *ibid,* Vol. 11, No. 6, p. 383–
466.

_____

1949
The fishes of Oceania. Supplement 3. *ibid,* Vol. 12, No. 2, p. 35–186.

Mainly descriptive; some natural history.

Gosline, William A. and Brock, Vernon E.
1960
Handbook of Hawaiian fishes. University of Hawaii Press, Honolulu, Hawaii, 372 pp.

AUSTRALIA AND ADJACENT WATERS

Marshall, Tom C.
1964
Fishes of the Great Barrier Reef and coastal waters of Queensland.
Angus & Robertson, Sydney, Melbourne, London, 566 pp.

Mainly descriptive; some natural history.

Scott, Trevor D.
1962
The marine and fresh water fishes of South Australia. Government
Printer, Adelaide, Australia, 338 pp.

Mainly descriptive; some natural history.

Whitley, Gilbert Percy
1940
*The fishes of Australia, part 1, the sharks, rays, devil-fish and other
primitive fishes of Australia and New Zealand.* Royal Zoological
Society of New South Wales, Sydney, Australia, 280 pp.

A delightful and informative mélange of fable, anecdote and science
itself. There are also 303 photographs and drawings.

GENERAL

Gilbert, Perry W., ed.
1963
Sharks and survival. D. C. Heath & Co., Boston, 578 pp.

An informative compilation of papers resulting from a symposium.
The papers, 22 in number, range from field observation to physiology and most have extensive bibliographies.

Gilbert, Perry W., et al., ed.
1967
Sharks, skates and rays. The Johns Hopkins Press, Baltimore, Maryland, 624 pp.

Like the foregoing, a compilation of papers. In this case there are 39 and the heavy emphasis is on physiology.

Maxwell, Gavin
1952
Harpoon venture. Viking Press, New York, 304 pp.

_____

1952
Harpoon at a venture. Rupert Hart-Davis, London.

The same work. The account, with considerable natural history, of the author's attempt to commercially fish the basking shark, *Cetorhinus maximus*, in British waters.

Norman, J. R. and Fraser, F. C.
1949
Field book of giant fishes. G. P. Putnam's Sons, New York, 375 pp.

Includes brief natural histories of the larger sharks, skates and rays and is what the title suggests; a conveniently-sized field guide.

Thomson, D'Arcy Wentworth.
1910
Historia animalium. The works of Aristotle translated into English, Vol. IV, Oxford Press, entries 486a to 633b.

ANATOMY

Daniel, J. Frank
1934
The elasmobranch fishes. Third, Revised, Edition. University of California Press, Berkeley, California, 332 pp.

Still the standard work.

Gans, Carl and Parsons, Thomas S.
1964
A photographic atlas of shark anatomy. The gross morphology of SQUALUS ACANTHIAS. Academic Press, New York, London, 106 pp., 40 pls.

EVOLUTION

Romer, Alfred Sherwood
1966
Vertebrate paleontology. Third Edition. The University of Chicago Press, Chicago and London, 468 pp.

Index

Abe, Tokiharu: 157–58
Agassiz, Louis: 180
AIBS: *see* American Institute of Biological
  Sciences
Allen, W. E.: 138
Alopias caudatus (thresher): 140
Alopias greyi (thresher): 140
Alopias pelagicus (thresher): 140
Alopias profundus (thresher): 140
Alopias superciliosus (big-eyed thresher): 140,
  159
Alopias vulpinus (common thresher): 136–42;
  angling for, 141; colour, 137; common
  names, 139–40; in folklore, 141–42; food,
  138; range, 140–41; reproduction, 141, 186;
  size, 137, 140; use of tail, 137–39
Alopiidae (alopiids): 136–42, 186
American Institute of Biological Sciences
  (AIBS): 48, 85, 92, 220
American Museum of Natural History: 50,
  51, 206
angel shark: see *Squatina* spp. and
  Squatinidae
Aphanopus carbo (black swordfish): 159
Aristotle: 31–2, 139, 177, 180–82
Aronson, L. R. & F. R.: 206–7
Atwood, Nathaniel E.: 100

barracuda (*Sphyraena barracuda*): 51–3
Bascom, Willard: 226
basking shark: see *Cetorhinus maximus*
Batoidei (skates and rays): compared with
  sharks, 174–75, 176; eaten by killer whale,
  38; food of hammerheads, 89–91; pilot fish
  and rays, 40; relationship with sharks, 20;
  sawfish a ray, 174; subject of electro-
  reception experiment, 204
Beaumaris shark: 95
Beebe, William: 50

Belon, Pierre: 139
Bennett, Frederick D.: 159–60
Berland, Bjørn: 165–66
Bigelow, Henry B. & William C. Schroeder:
  72–4, 76, 77, 114, 133, 142, 152–54
big-eyed thresher (*Alopias superciliosus*):
  140, 159
binomial system of zoological nomenclature:
  56–7
blacktip shark (*Carcharhinus limbatus*): 68,
  220
black whaler (*Carcharhinus macrurus*): 66
Blake-Knox, Harry: 136–37
bluefish (*Pomatomus saltatrix*): 134
blue pointer: 57, 102, 114
blue porpoise shark: 102
blue shark: see *Prionace glauca*
blue whaler: see *Prionace glauca*
Bøje, Ove: 164
bonito, oceanic (*Katsuwonus pelamis*): 207
bonito shark: 102
Bonnell, B.: 42
bonnethead: see *Sphyrna tiburo*
bony fishes (Teleostei) compared with sharks:
  19–24, 86–7
Borlase, William: 95
bramble shark (*Echinorhinus brucus*): 163
Breder, Charles M. Jr.: 138
briar shark (*Echinorhinus brucus*): 163
British Museum: 38, 51, 62, 171, 176
Budker, Paul: 81
bullhead shark: 170
Bullis, Harvey R.: 60
bull shark: see *Carcharhinus leucas*
Burrough, Stephen: 142, 143

Caius, John: 95, 139
California Academy of Sciences: 183
Campbell, G. D.: 81

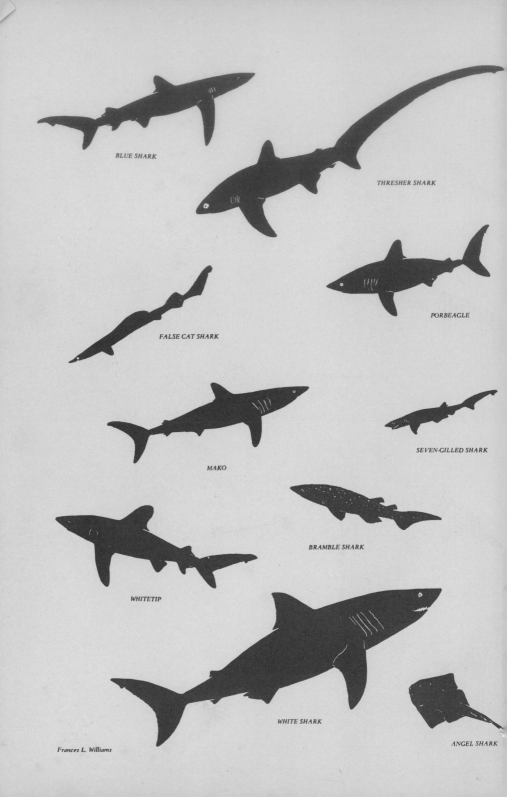

BLUE SHARK

THRESHER SHARK

PORBEAGLE

FALSE CAT SHARK

MAKO

SEVEN-GILLED SHARK

BRAMBLE SHARK

WHITETIP

WHITE SHARK

ANGEL SHARK

Frances L. Williams